DATE DUE

JUL 27 1993			
JUN 07 1995			
JUL 11 1995			
SEP 16 1998			
MAY 11 2000			
MAR 20 03			

DEMCO 38-297

Mother-Infant Bonding

Mother-Infant Bonding

A SCIENTIFIC FICTION

DIANE E. EYER

Yale University Press   New Haven & London

Designed by Sonia L. Scanlon.

Set in Berkeley type by DEKR Corporation, Woburn, Mass.

Printed in the United States of America by Vail-Ballou Press, Binghamton, N.Y.

Library of Congress Cataloging-in-Publication Data

Eyer, Diane E., 1944–

    Mother-infant bonding : a scientific fiction / Diane E. Eyer.

        p.   cm.

    Includes bibliographical references and index.

    ISBN 0-300-05682-6 (alk. paper)

    1. Mother and infant.   2. Attachment behavior.   3. Maternal deprivation in infants.   4. Feminist psychology.   I. Title.

  BF720.M68E84   1992

  155.42′28—dc20   92-17292

                                        CIP

A catalogue record for this book is available from the British Library.

The paper in this book meets the guidelines for permanence and durability of the Committee on Production Guidelines for Book Longevity of the Council on Library Resources.

10 9 8 7 6 5 4 3 2

For all the new mothers and those who would help them.

Contents

Acknowledgments   ix

CHAPTER ONE
Introduction   1

CHAPTER TWO
The Bonding Research: A Weak Foundation   15

CHAPTER THREE
Maternal Deprivation and Attachment   47

CHAPTER FOUR
Models and Reasoning in the Scientific Community   71

CHAPTER FIVE
Constructing Motherhood and Infancy   99

CHAPTER SIX
Medicine Frames Motherhood and Infancy   129

CHAPTER SEVEN
The Reform Movement   163

Conclusion   197

Notes   201

References   209

Index   229

Acknowledgments

I wish to express my gratitude to the many individuals who assisted and supported this work. Jack Byer, my husband and fellow scholar, has been a mainstay of intellectual and personal support. His enthusiasm and care have helped to make the writing of this book a pleasure. I am also grateful to Jennifer Spratt for her meticulous reading of several sections of the manuscript and Jean-J. Steichen for his insights into the world of the neonatologist and the helpful reading of several chapters. Special thanks also to Michelle Fine, Brian Sutton-Smith, and Dan Wagner, my mentors at the University of Pennsylvania, who inspired intellectual independence and critical thinking. Bob Echenberg, my parents Charles and Elizabeth Eyer, Ben Harris, Margaret Honey, Lynne and Bill Headley, Michael Lamb, Louisa Lance, P. H. Leiderman, Jacqueline Litt, Jill Morowski, Beverly Seckinger, and Dorothy Wertz in their various ways have contributed to the fruition of this book.

Dr. John Kennell and Dr. Marshall Klaus were also helpful during several interviews I requested, although they preferred not to be quoted directly. Their research on bonding represents a small portion of the work they continue to pursue in their efforts to humanize birth practices.

Finally, I am most grateful to Yale University Press for their excellence and enthusiasm. Senior editor Gladys Topkis provided exceptional insight and wisdom throughout the editorial process, and Lorraine Alexson was meticulous and affirming in the final stage of editing.

Introduction

This book is about the transformations that scientific research sometimes undergoes as it becomes unleashed from its empirical moorings and is pulled into the maelstrom of popular beliefs and the institutional goals that inspire science. In fact, it raises a critical question regarding the power of science: To what extent is science a product of social influence, and to what extent can we expect to find a valid empirical base of information that we can use? The book is an analysis of how one particular scientific idea, mother-infant bonding (although poorly constructed) was readily embraced as an appealing solution to some rather complex problems of hospital childbirth and postnatal care. Finally, it is an analysis of how research and ideology become entangled.

The research on bonding was inspired by the popular belief that women, one and all, are inherently suited for motherhood. This belief coincided with a number of institutional goals, including the needs of the psychological and medical professions, especially obstetrics, to secure women and infants as patients and to find pathology in this clientele, which they could then treat. New mothers, whether feminist or traditional, also embraced the ideology of motherhood at a time when their sex role was being challenged. Bonding promised insurance against the psychological damage that might be caused by women's increasing involvement in work outside the home.

Bonding is, in fact, as much an extension of ideology as it is a scientific discovery. More specifically, it is part of an ideology in which mothers are seen as the prime architects of their children's lives and are blamed for whatever problems befall them, not only in childhood but throughout their adult lives. Yet the bonding research, which purports to show that there is a biological need for mothers to be physically close to their infants immediately after birth, also served to reform hospital childbirth. Bonding appeared to give women more control over their birth experience, and it supported their wish to have their newborn infants and other family members with them in what had previously been a lonely and often demeaning experience. Unfortunately, most of those who sought to reform hospital birthing practices (doctors and nurses as well as parents) failed to see the trap: Because bonding was a construction of medicine, it would ultimately serve to protect the interests of that institution. The promised revolution in childbirth became a product of the politics of science.

The saga of bonding began in 1972 when two pediatricians, John Kennell and Marshall Klaus, published a study in the *New England Journal of Medicine* purporting to show that mothers having sixteen extra hours of contact with their infants right after birth showed better mothering skills and their infants did better on developmental tests than mothers and infants who did not have the extra contact. These dramatic effects were said to be the result of a sensitive period in women following birth during which they are hormonally primed to accept or reject their infants. The authors were inspired by research with animals, rats and goats in particular, which showed that maternal hormones were especially powerful determinants of behavior in the period during and after birth. Female goats, for example, if separated from their offspring for as little as five minutes after birth, will reject the infants upon being reunited with them. By analogy, it was thought that if human mothers were separated from their infants during this time, they too might have trouble accepting the infants later. In fact, Kennell and Klaus postulated that the high rates of abuse involving infants kept in neonatal intensive care units might actually be a result of extended postpartum separation from their mothers.

The notion of a sensitive period for bonding quickly became institutionalized in the 1970s. Kennell and Klaus toured hospitals around the country in the early part of the decade, giving workshops on bonding, and in 1976 they published an influential book, *Maternal Infant Bonding*. The notion of bonding seemed to strike a chord in groups as diverse as fundamentalist religious organizations and feminists, all of whom seemed eager to embrace at least one aspect or another of the bonding discovery. Organizations promoting natural childbirth and the mass media popularized the idea. Hospitals provided special rooms for bonding, and medical staff claimed responsibility for ensuring that bonding would be accomplished during the hospital stay. The imperative to bond, however, distressed many parents who had not been able to be with their babies during the crucial period, either because the babies were adopted or premature or, more often, because the mothers or babies had been ill during the postpartum period. As a result, these parents were overwhelmed with regret and guilt. In response, Kennell and Klaus in 1982 published *Parent-Infant Bonding,* essentially a revision of their 1976 book, in which they attempted to reassure parents: "Obviously, in spite of a lack of early contact . . . almost all . . . parents became bonded to their babies." Unable to give up their original idea, however, they continued to assert that the immediate postpartum period is an especially sensitive time with consequences for infant development and that mothers are hormonally primed for bonding during that period. "We believe . . . there is strong evidence that at least thirty to sixty minutes of early contact in privacy should be provided for every parent and infant to enhance the bonding experience" (Klaus and Kennell 1982, 55–56).

By the early 1980s, research on the bonding of mothers and their newborns had been dismissed by much of the scientific community as having been poorly conceived and executed. Yet many pediatricians and social workers still see postpartum maternal bonding as a way of preventing child abuse. While the emphasis on bonding immediately after childbirth seems to have subsided, the concept has continued to flourish ideologically; women's proximity to their infants (whether they desire it or not) is still seen as a formula for preventing later problems of the child. For example, a *New York Times* editorial on a center for teenage mothers quotes a representative of the agency that runs the residence: "During their first 30 days at the residence mother and child are inseparable, whether the former likes it or not. We want to make sure that the bonding process takes place" (20 February 1989, A18). Many parents continue to believe that if mothers leave their infants in order to work outside the home, an important bonding time will be missed and their infants will be deprived of a crucial experience. In fact, in a public television series called "The World of Ideas" (1988), journalist Bill Moyers and pediatrician T. Berry Brazelton discussed whether women should stay home from work to rear their infants during the bonding period, which Brazelton describes as lasting a year: "Does the first year really make a difference?" asks Moyers. "It does," replies Dr. Brazelton, "the child gets a sense of being important . . . if he doesn't have that through infancy, it's hard to put it in later . . . and these kids that never get it . . . will become difficult in school, they'll never succeed in school; they'll make everybody angry; they'll become delinquents later and eventually they'll become terrorists." Moyers asks, "And you think that goes back . . . to this bonding period?" "Yes."[1] Fantastic as these claims may be, Dr. Brazelton, a professor of pediatrics at Harvard University Medical School and the author of many books and television programs addressed to parents, is regarded as the premier child-rearing expert in the country, the "Dr. Spock of the 1980s," according to Moyers.

In spite of their claims to the contrary, it appears that Doctors Kennell and Klaus agree with Dr. Brazelton about the critical importance of early bonding, although for Kennell and Klaus the immediate postpartum period is crucial, whereas for Brazelton bonding is essential throughout the first year of life.[2] According to Dr. Klaus, "If all women throughout the country experienced extended contact with their infants in the first few days after birth, it might well reduce child abuse" (personal interview, June 1990).[3] According to Dr. Kennell, researchers will eventually return to the question, and the existence of a biologically based sensitive period in women in the few days after birth will be confirmed (personal interview, June 1990).

Unfortunately, claims regarding the presumed biological bases for human behavior have often been interpreted along the most reactionary lines. In fact, bonding is part of a long-standing tradition in which both scientists and laypeople use research to affirm conservative values. Either they extend biological research beyond the data to construct universal principles of human behavior by selective analogy, or they distort and even fabricate their own data to suit their own intuitive notions of reality. For example, the social Darwinists used Darwin's biological theories as a rationale for their advocacy of laissez faire government rather than policies to help the poor, who were "obviously" the least "fit to survive" in the supposed evolutionary struggle for existence. In the studies of craniometry (the relation of head size to intelligence) and IQ, data were fabricated to illustrate the researcher's commonsense notions regarding the inherent inferiority of minority groups such as blacks and Indians, and women. More recently, some interpretations of sociobiology suggest that men force women to have sex (rape them) as a means by which to enter the gene pool and make their evolutionary mark (Barash 1979). The current flurry of research that finds sex differences in everything from brain functions to empathic ability comes at a time when most of the old ideology delineating inherent sex differences is obsolete and can also be seen as a means of reifying the old power relations based on sex. (See, e.g., Tavris 1992.)

Bonding is another example of this scientific fictionalizing. Although bonding researchers did not fabricate data, their studies were profoundly influenced by their unquestioned assumptions about women and about the adequacy of research traditions from which they drew. By selecting the behavior of a few species of animals that coincided with popular notions about women's maternal "instinct," bonding research reduced women to automatons who behave the way they do, not because of their capacity to reason, their complex psychology, or their economic or social circumstances, but rather because of their inherent and inevitable inferiority. This inferiority then requires the full services of science and medicine to guide it. Curiously, those who conducted and adopted the bonding research saw themselves as enlightened reformers, freeing women of institutional constraints and saving children from abuse and neglect. Where and how did these noble intentions go wrong?

To understand the process, this book explores both the scientific construction of the bonding research and the politics of its social construction. In chapter 2 I demonstrate the rather astonishing poverty of science in the bonding research, which was published in some of the most esteemed medical and social science journals. Analysis shows that the 1972 Kennell and Klaus study—the model for dozens of other bonding studies—fails to conform to some of the basic rules of research design. Moreover, the fundamental premise on which the research was based—the role of instinct in human behavior—is a highly questionable biological premise. For a decade, however, dozens of studies were produced using this model. Then suddenly, in the 1980s, the research was heavily attacked on the ground that there was little evidence to suggest any but the most fleeting effects of bonding. Those who had conducted the research, however, continued to defend it.

Chapter 3 explores the paradigmatic foundations of bonding in the research on maternal deprivation and attachment. Freudian psychology made the claim that the roots of a child's personality are established by its emotional relationship with its mother. Research conducted by psychoanalyst René Spitz and others in the 1940s and 1950s found that infants kept in nurseries suffered depression and attendant physical illness, even death, because of *maternal deprivation*. On the basis of this research and his own study of war orphans, British psychiatrist John Bowlby concluded that infants and children during the first few years of life must have one devoted caretaker. In the 1960s Bowlby claimed that this need for attachment had an instinctual basis, analogous to the imprinting behavior necessary to the survival of some species of birds. For example, on the critical third day of a gosling's life—not before or after—it will learn to follow its mother (or a substitute) and will thereafter follow only that "mother"; it will be imprinted or attached.

Reassessment of the maternal-deprivation research reveals that research claims were exaggerated in the service of reform—in fact, some of Spitz's data appear to have been fabricated. Moreover, the severe deprivation experienced by institutionalized infants was to a large extent the result of their having had as many as fifty different caretakers and very little attention. Research on attachment is also undergoing reassessment. The tremendous variability in animal behavior, not just among species but also in the same species in differing environments; the evidence that even abused animals continue to "attach" to their abusers; the emotional adjustment of young children to day care—all suggest that the interpretation of attachment behaviors as requiring the sensitive attention of one continuously present caretaker, has been biased. (The existence of infant behaviors that promote proximity to the caretaker, however, appears to be established by the research.)

Because the idea of maternal deprivation had been established by several decades of research (criticism notwithstanding), bonding broke little new ground. It was an extension of an accepted science and for that reason was more readily accepted. Bonding was an extension of the attachment paradigm.

In chapter 4 I explore the question of how research that is demonstrably unsound can be accepted in a scientific community and under what circumstances criticism will emerge and be influential. The answer lies in part in the way paradigms function in science. The bonding research was determined not so much by a process of empirical discovery and verification as by the conduct of "normal science," a concept developed by Thomas Kuhn that suggests there are long periods in which a community of scientists works within a particular paradigm or model for doing research without questioning its basic premises. The response to bonding research was also based on the traditions of two differing scientific subcommunities: pediatricians, who generally accepted bonding, and developmental psychologists, who were more skeptical. Pediatricians, on the one hand, generally have little formal training in research. When they do receive training, it is primarily to conduct biomedical research. Moreover, pediatricians generally conduct clinical studies in which the goal is to treat patients—to find out what works—rather than to establish what will happen to every subject under controlled conditions. The goal of much psychological research, on the other hand, is to establish what typically constitutes the behavior of a particular group, not just to treat patients.

Another reason some professionals embraced bonding was its promise to solve a new clinical problem created by the burgeoning neonatal intensive-care unit; growing numbers of doctors needed guidance in dealing with the special problems of the parents of premature and sick infants. These parents sometimes lost interest in their infants and often found them difficult to care for. But bonding quickly found wider appreciation in the powerful movement to reform hospital childbirth practices, for it was a rationale to change without challenging the fundamental sources of medical authority.

Another powerful factor in the acceptance of bonding concerns the semantic properties of the bonding analogy. Observations of the postpartum behavior of goats revealed that they reject their offspring, butting them away and failing to feed them if they are separated after birth for as little as five minutes (Klopfer, Adams, and Klopfer 1964). The authors of the mother-infant bonding research postulated that something similar occurs with human mothers. The analogy with abused and neglected infants was simple and vivid. Moreover, it brought to mind a chemical bonding process like that seen in the action of glue. Both analogies were vivid, succinct, and easily understood by anyone who had heard of instinct or glued two things together. The analogs suggested something automatic and instantaneous—an appealing notion in a culture where most social problems require highly complicated solutions. Hence, the properties of mother-infant relations were readily confused with the less complex phenomena to which they were being compared.

The zeal with which bonding was accepted, however, cannot be explained adequately by either the power of analogy, the tradition of maternal deprivation and attachment, the problems of professional organization and reasoning in science, or the need to reform hospital practices. Perhaps the most profound influence of all on the construction and acceptance of bonding was a deeply embedded ideology regarding the proper role of women. The feminist challenge of the 1970s and the continuing movement of women into the labor market altered social relations and threatened to undermine longstanding ideals about motherhood. In chapter 5 I look at the social construction of motherhood and infancy, which has swayed the interpretation of both the attachment research and the bonding research toward widely held cultural assumptions. Motherhood and infancy have had different meanings in different eras in western history. Ideas of femininity have been tied to the shifting currents of socioeconomic and cultural conflicts within the society and have influenced the periodically redefined tenets of motherhood.

The notion that woman's proper sex role requires her to stay at home had its origins in the industrial revolution, a time when many women might have been tempted to leave the home for the wage labor force. In response to the conflict this choice produced, the *cult of true womanhood* emerged, in which women's femininity was said to be tied to the preservation of Puritan values. To protect these values against the growing (sinful) commercialization of the industrializing world, woman was to become the virtuous "guardian angel" of the hearth. A woman's place was in the home, and her charge was to raise the virtuous child. In the post–World War II period, another time when there was a need to regulate women's labor and redefine social values, the *hearth angel* concept reemerged, with the support of Freudian psychology, to become the "feminine mystique." It was in this period that the idea of maternal deprivation gathered force as a means of persuading women to stay out of the wage labor force and devote all of their energies to their children.

The meanings given to infancy also shift according to economic issues in the adult world and to the zeitgeist. Empirically based research on infancy is often used symbolically to address the conflicts of adult life. In the twentieth century, concepts of infancy seem to change with almost every decade. The infant of the 1920s and 1930s was known to be in need of discipline. He should not be picked up every time he cried or he would become spoiled and would not learn the important habits of living according to a strict and efficient schedule. Such advice reflected the great respect adults had for the efficiency of science and industry, although there was little research evidence to corroborate this belief. In the 1940s and 1950s the infant was known to be in need of constant gratification. He should be picked up every time he cried or he would become frustrated and develop a neurotic personality. Such advice reflected the influence of Freudian psychology, which was also in the service of promoting the nuclear family as a consumption unit.

In the 1970s, this idealized dyad was threatened with dissolution. The women's movement exposed the restriction of women's role to homemaking as a myth. And women in increasingly significant numbers were working outside the home. Divorce rates, moreover, were skyrocketing and families were coming apart. Bonding was a kind of social medication for these problems at the same time that it seemed a means to humanize birth. It was eagerly purchased by parent consumers who wished to preserve at least some remnant of the power of the early maternal relationship as a kind of insurance against the unknown. As a product of medical research, however, bonding helped to preserve the authority of medicine and the version of motherhood it had helped to construct.

One of the primary forces contributing to the most conservative fictions regarding mothers and infants has been medicine. I examine in chapter 6 how the profession of medicine redefined mothers and infants to enhance its own power. In its constant battle to retain the lion's share of the childbirth market in the face of midwives, general practitioners, and the home-birth movement, obstetrics has consistently created an atmosphere of fear around childbirth by defining it as a pathological process. Pediatricians have also claimed authority to dictate the behavior of mothers and infants in a struggle to legitimate their profession. They originally had to compete with general practitioners for patients, and once the prevailing childhood diseases were largely conquered in the 1930s, they were in search of a new sphere of influence. They allied themselves with developmental psychology and offered advice about "normal" (and abnormal) child behavior and parenting practices. The current medical definition of motherhood and infancy authorizes doctors to monitor every aspect of family life, from treating childhood diseases to diagnosing and providing services for drug abuse, child abuse, and marital problems. Using the epidemiological risk model of perinatal medicine in which women are either high or low risks for problems of mothering (there is no category of no risk), doctors now collect information on every aspect of a woman's life. Combining these extensive data with the increasing use of complex technology, they exert greater control over women and children than at any time previously. A woman may now be sued by her doctor for jeopardizing her fetus if she fails to follow the doctor's orders. It is not surprising that the concept of bonding ultimately enhanced the power of medicine to control women by redefining their postpartum behavior as potentially pathological.

In the 1970s, the constraints of "medicalized" childbearing precipitated a move to reform childbirth practices. The role of bonding in the reform of hospital childbirth is explored in chapter 7. The natural childbirth movement, which began after World War II, gathered force in the 1970s as it coalesced with the women's movement and the counterculture. The media and America's favorite child rearing experts also publicized the need for reform. Bonding appeared to resolve certain growing contradictions in the way childbirth should be conducted. Hospital practice, presumably rooted in scientific research, demanded that infants be separated from their mothers right after birth and sequestered in the nursery to protect them from infection. Husbands and families were viewed primarily as potential sources of infection, not as rightful participants in the birth. Parental wishes (and the wishes of many reformers) conflicted with this medical regime. Women wanted their husbands with them during birth, and they wanted their babies with them in the hospital. They wanted more control over their own birth process. As a result, they began to seek alternatives to the hospital in home births and birth centers run by midwives. Bonding became a scientific rationale by which women and their families could be with their infants after birth in the traditional hospital and doctors could maintain their authority by claiming to know how to regulate this new scientific discovery. The discovery, however, was a conservative fiction, rooted in medicine and in myths about the true nature of motherhood.

Not surprisingly, women experiencing hospital childbirth are subject to more control than ever before, in part because of the complex technology that enhances the doctor's power and the atmosphere of fear and danger surrounding birth. In fact, one in four mothers now experiences a surgical birth—a cesarean section (Wertz and Wertz 1989, 234). The majority are hooked up to (inaccurate) fetal monitors (Wertz and Wertz 1989, 258; MacDonald et al. 1985), inhibiting their ability to move about during labor and contributing to the high cesarean rate, and they are required to give birth during a standardized (and increasingly narrow) laboring time. Bonding may have ushered the family into the hospital, but it contributed little to a more natural birth controlled by women.

The investigation of bonding was distorted by the overwhelming need to reform childbirth and by the overpowering assumptions people have about instincts, the proper role of women, and the infinite malleability of infants. This distortion does not mean that the concept of bonding should be dismissed entirely, although it is doubtful that the extensive claims made for the role of instinct in women's behavior will be supported. It is important to know whether a few hours or days of postpartum contact will in fact enhance a child's development or a parent's love. If bonding does have such effects, are they based in any way on the release of maternal hormones? What kind of learning is involved? According to Confucius, "A misunderstanding of the truth is responsible for all the miseries of the world." It would certainly seem that the mother-infant bonding imperative is one such misunderstanding of the truth.

Perhaps it could be argued that it is a harmless misunderstanding: The bonding imperative did contribute to some much-needed reforms regarding the hospital organization of childbirth. If doctors are actually enhancing family closeness by encouraging bonding, does it really matter if it is the bonding time or other factors, such as learning or socioeconomic circumstances or psychological characteristics, that determine what intrafamilial relations will be like? By providing an organizational formula for closing certain growing loopholes in the social fabric, such as the increasing atomization and alienation of individuals from each other, bonding presents people with a ceremonial means of addressing these threatening issues in a ritual that serves as a reminder of potential hazards.

There are, however, serious negative consequences to this mythologizing. At a time when obstetricians pay the second-highest premiums for insurance against lawsuits, and when some have actually sued women on behalf of the fetus, the level of mistrust and the struggle for power between doctor and patient are notable. Overstated imperatives that prove to be groundless cannot enhance trust. Moreover, the history of child rearing expertise is full of fads and formulas of varying utility that simply confuse parents who increasingly wonder what to believe. The requirement to give active love to their babies right after birth is a standard many women find impossible to meet. Locking women into such practices and then blaming them for failing to conform constitute an emotional drain not only on women but on the entire family. Counselors and social workers who are being taught that bonding can help to prevent child abuse may overemphasize bonding at the cost of dealing with the complex social and emotional problems of family members.

For researchers in the social sciences it is a matter of self-defense to understand how seemingly carefully constructed research findings can be distorted and why. For clinicians it is important to understand the implications of basing practice on research findings. And for parents and potential parents, it is important to sort out what is fact and what is fiction in the advice they receive on childbirth and child rearing.

Interestingly, although the bonding research and even the bonding craze have subsided, the term itself has migrated even farther from its original basis, illustrating the profound social need for the concept. Bonding is no longer seen as something that is *like* what happens in chemistry, ethology, and anthropology, but rather it is used as a term to describe a simplistic social process in which human relations are reduced to something mechanical, instinctual, and automatic. In fact, bonding may be the Velcro of new terms, apparently able to attach itself to the description of almost any form of social connection. A human resources newsletter tells management how to bond employees to new ideas. A television character tells his sister not to worry about the likelihood that a school chum will let him down: "We're real bonded." An article in a geriatric journal refers to "pair bonding" among the elderly. In the psychological journals, articles on "pet bonding" now abound. A businessman overheard on an airplane tells his colleague, "We bonded them real good."

How was bonding transformed from an instinctual phenomenon triggered by female hormones to a kind of magical social glue, a way of describing all social connections while illuminating nothing about them? The answer lies in the fact that science is socially constructed. Researchers have their own professional agendas and unquestioned assumptions that distort the interpretation of data; consumers of research also twist data in the direction of their own needs. People have a tendency to believe what fits the zeitgeist, regardless of the facts. In the case of bonding, the widespread social need for people to be connected, to maintain a continuity of relations in the face of high divorce rates, lawsuits, frequent geographic moves, sudden changes in social status, interactions with anonymous institutions, have all contributed to the necessity of bonding—a social epoxy for constantly breaking social relations. As so often happens in avoiding a complex, cultural problem, it is projected onto women, who are then required by the tenets of their sex role to perform a symbolic redress. The ritual of mothers bonding to their infants is a symbolic act of inoculation—these bonded infants will be protected from the current anomie of the adult world. The feeling that it would be good for all if mothers and infants bonded is a social myth that has done little to help mothers or their infants but has created a new and much needed magic word.

The Bonding Research: A Weak Foundation

The research on bonding lasted but a decade. During this time hundreds of articles on the subject were published in dozens of prestigious journals, including the *New England Journal of Medicine, Pediatrics, Child Development,* the *Journal of Maternal Child Nursing,* and *Social Work.* Largely on the basis of these studies, hospitals changed their policies regarding the sequestering of infants in nurseries in the hope of preventing later child abuse and other ills. Now parents could cuddle their newborns immediately after birth; in fact, it was required. The research on bonding extended to social work and child psychiatry, where early bonding came to be viewed as a means of preventing child psychopathology, abuse, and neglect. The studies of bonding, however, were clearly full of conceptual and methodological errors; *good* or successful bonding was never consistently defined, and the very meaning of bonding shifted from study to study. Yet for a decade the poorly conceived and conducted bonding research met little objection from any quarter.

Kennell and Klaus

The first study that claimed to find a biologically based sensitive period in human mothers right after birth, "Maternal attachment: Importance of the first postpartum days," was published in the *New England Journal of Medicine* in 1972 (Klaus et al.). The authors began their report by explaining the rationale for researching a biologically based sensitive period in human mothers. They believed that women's behavior may be like the instinctive behavior of some species of animals:

> In certain animals such as the goat, cow, and sheep, separation of the mother and infant immediately after birth for a period as short as one to four hours often results in distinctly aberrant mothering behavior such as failure of the mother to care for the young, butting her own offspring away and feeding her own and other infants indiscriminately. In contrast, if they are together for the first four days and are then separated on the fifth day for an equal period, the mother resumes the protective and mothering behavior characteristic for her species when the pair is reunited
> . . .
>
> In recent years several investigators have studied whether a similar phenomenon occurs in mothers of premature infants. . . . Early results from these studies suggest that the long period of physical separation common in most nurseries may adversely affect maternal performance of some women.

The important concept of a sensitive or critical period refers to the idea that there are times in the development of an organism when certain things must happen for the subsequent development of the organism to be normal. If they do not, the damage is irreversible, as when pregnant women took the drug thalidomide at the critical period when the fetus's arms were developing. The result was a human being with stunted appendages, from which damage the organism could never recover.[1]

John Kennell and Marshall Klaus, who followed their subjects over five years (see Kennell et al. 1974; Klaus et al. 1972; Ringler et al.

1975; Ringler et al. 1978), claimed to have found a sensitive period in human mothers that affects the ongoing bonding of the mother to the child. The use of "sensitive period" in this context necessarily differs from the standard use of the term because there can be several sensitive periods in the life of a woman or a nonhuman animal mother, although just once for each mother-infant pair.

To investigate these phenomena, Kennell and Klaus studied the bonding of twenty-eight low-income unmarried primiparae (first-time mothers) of normal-birthweight babies. Fourteen of these mothers experienced one hour of skin-to-skin contact with their newborns during the first three hours after delivery, plus an additional five hours of contact on each of the next three days. The fourteen mothers in the control group, matched to the experimental mothers in age, social class, marital status, race, medication, and infant's birthweight, went through the regular hospital routine, feeding their babies every four hours until discharge.

One month after giving birth, the mothers returned to the hospital for interviews and observations. One of the interview questions related to an assessment of their caretaking was: "When the baby cries and has been fed, and the diapers are dry, what do you do?" On a scale of 0 to 3, a score of 0 was given for letting the baby cry it out and 3 for picking it up every time. Another interview question was: "Have you been out since the baby was born, and who sat?" A score of 0 was given if the mother had been out, felt good about it, and did not think about the infant while she was out, and a score of 3 was given if she did not leave the baby or if she did go out but thought constantly about the baby. The extended-contact mothers more often reported picking the baby up more when it cried and being reluctant to leave it. The researchers interpreted these findings as evidence of stronger mother-infant bonding in the group that held their babies for sixteen extra hours.

Mothers' behavior during the pediatric examination at this time was also observed. The authors also noted whether or not the mother attempted to soothe the baby when it cried. If she did not interact with the baby, she was given a score of 0; if she was consistently soothing, she was given a score of 3. Of fifty behavioral measures taken by a team of trained observers during the examination, three significant group differences were noted. The mothers who had had early and extended contact with their babies were more attentive (stood near the examining table and watched), exhibited more soothing behavior, and engaged in more fondling than mothers in the control group. These behaviors were also interpreted as evidence of better maternal bonding.

The mothers were also videotaped while feeding their infants and scored for twenty-five specific activities ranging from caretaking skills (such as the positioning of the bottle) to maternal interest and affection, such as "*en face* looking" (the mother's face directly opposite the baby's), whether the mother's body was touching the infant's trunk, and whether she fondled the infant. Experimental mothers spent more time in the en face position and more time fondling, though they spent no more time holding the infants close or looking at them. Again the group differences were interpreted to mean that the mothers who had the extra contact showed evidence of a stronger mother-infant bond. (The experimenters do not mention whether the observers were blind to group membership.) These mothers and infants were examined again a year later. The authors continued to find evidence of better mothering and infant development in the extra-contact group.[2] At two years and five years, with only nineteen mother-infant pairs remaining in the study, they still reported evidence of better bonding in the extra-contact mothers.[3]

Problems with the Research Design

These studies provided the model for other bonding studies.[4] Yet even the first study is clearly flawed by poor conceptualization and methodology. To understand the problems with these studies we must look at some fundamental concepts of research design and analysis that are generally shared in the sciences and medicine. Experimental research involves the "treatment" of an experimental group. In this study one group of mothers was given extra contact with their babies; in medicine subjects might be treated with a drug. The effects of the extra contact are called dependent variables (or outcome measures) because they depend on the treatment. In the bonding study the dependent variables would be measures of better caretaking, better child health, or better child development. The authors of the study used over seventy such measures, including the mother's picking up the baby when it cried and holding the baby en face.

An important, and troublesome, feature of the experiment is validity, the question of whether what is being measured is an accurate representation of what is being investigated. In the case of bonding, are the maternal behaviors being measured a valid indication that hormonal changes or biological factors are at work? Do the behaviors that are designated dependent variables, such as holding the infant en face, actually represent better mothering?

Validity may also be affected by confounding variables, factors that were not considered to be potential influences on the outcome when the research was designed. For instance, if researchers suggest that the extended postpartum separation of mothers from their infants causes later child abuse and base this claim on a study of infants separated by virtue of being in neonatal intensive care units (NICU's), it is possible that the abuse was at least partially the result of such confounding variables as the mother's poverty, lack of social support, mental state, the difficult behavior of the baby, or some other characteristic that is then confounded with the effects of separation. Researchers try to anticipate these factors. One precaution Klaus and Kennell took was to match the subjects in each group for potential confounding factors such as age, social class, marital status, race, and so forth. Another type of confounding variable might be the by-products of the treatment. People behave differently simply by virtue of being observed, by having attention focused on them. In the first bonding study, women who were given extra contact with their infants were also necessarily receiving extra attention from the medical staff, who were bringing the infants to them; the effects of this extra attention may have become confounded with the effect of extra contact with their babies.

The other troublesome matter is reliability. If the same experiment is conducted again, will it yield the same results? One way to protect against the confounding effect of the treatment and to promote reliability is to conduct a double blind experiment, in which both the subjects and the researchers are blind to the purpose of the experiment and to experimental or control-group membership.

Finally, of course, there is the use of statistics to determine whether an experimental manipulation worked. Statistics allow us to compare one group to another. Suppose there are twenty-eight mothers and just one outcome measure—cuddling. In our experimental group we observe a total of seven cuddles; the control group exhibits only five. We want to know if the difference is significant—that is, really a product of the extra contact or a random or chance occurrence. To say that the difference is statistically significant at an .05 level means that there is only a 5 percent possibility that it happened by chance and not as a result of the treatment. Note that each time an outcome measure is added, the likelihood that something happened by chance also increases. If, on the one hand, one mother is being tested on seventy-five variables, it is quite possible that some behaviors were not the result of the treatment. On the other hand, the more subjects and the fewer variables, the greater the likelihood of establishing an effect. If we observe 2,800 for the single factor cuddling and find 700 vs. 500 cuddles, we can be far more certain that the group differences were the result of our treatment.[5] In any case, statistical tests can be used to determine the mathematical probability whether group differences were the result of our treatment by taking into account group size, the number of variables, and the relative probability of chance occurrences.

Given these rules of evidence, serious problems with the bonding study are evident. First, there is the question of the extent to which many of the dependent variables—letting the baby cry it out, not going out without thinking about the baby—are actually valid measures of caretaking. A woman who cannot leave her baby might be overanxious or might not have anyone reliable to leave the baby with. A woman who is able to forget about the baby when she goes out might have a trusted babysitter or might be self-assured and highly competent. Standing near the examining table during the pediatric exam could be an indication of anxiety, attitudes toward medical authority, or overprotectiveness. It could could also result from the different treatment of the experimental group; mothers might be less shy with doctors and nurses who had witnessed them holding their babies during the extra-contact treatment. Moreover, the study does not take account of preexisting group differences in pertinent maternal characteristics and attitudes toward the newborns (such as whether the baby was wanted or whether social support was available to the mother) or for differing characteristics of the infants (for example, some infants are temperamentally agreeable, others difficult). Also, the study suggests that the researchers used the test data selectively, recording a host of dependent variables and then selecting those that appeared to confirm the hypothesis. Of seventy-five measures in the first study, it appears that there were no group differences in the majority of measures. Finally, what actually constitutes bonding is not clear. Must contact be right after the birth? Skin-to-skin? For how long and how often?

Another fundamental problem with this research is that evidence of a biological basis for maternal behavior rather than for a process of learning was never established. The women were not breastfeeding their infants, so that a fundamental, *natural* biological process was not operating. The authors did not analyze maternal hormone levels to see if there were differences between those who experienced extra contact with their infants and those who experienced the standard hospital routine. Curiously, the authors conclude that although there is a striking parallel in nonhuman animal behavior (for example, if a goat's kids are removed for only a few minutes after birth, a biologically based instinctual process is interrupted and mother goats will reject the kids when they are reunited), "it is possible that the early presentation of a baby shortly after birth is taken by a mother as a special privilege . . . that in itself may have altered her behavior." The authors nevertheless continue to refer to bonding as a biologically based phenomenon.

The Problem of Instinct

The significance of the assumption of instinctual parallels between women and other animals benefits from an examination of the term *instinct.* Charles Darwin's view (in *The Origin of Species,* 1859; *The Descent of Man,* 1871) was that the differences between the behavior of man and that of other animals are matters of degree, not of kind; thus he gave the study of animal behavior a new relevance to the understanding of man (Boakes 1984, 6–7). Darwin claimed that humans evolved from lower-order animals whose unlearned or instinctual behavior had programmed them for survival in a process of natural selection. As environments change, the group of animals best adapted to an environment are naturally selected to survive. For instance, in the nineteenth century a particular species of moth was common in Sussex, England. Ninety-five percent were white, the rest were dark. Over the course of fifty years, coal mining, factories, and railroads had sent a continual stream of soot into a misty sky permanently darkened by the debris. In this changed environment, the white moths were easily picked off by birds, and the dark ones, now better adapted, survived. They lived on to reproduce so that after fifty years the dark-colored population of the species reached 95 percent. These moths were naturally selected.

In addition to such protective physical features, some innate behaviors—mating, nesting, giving birth, and feeding, for instance—are especially important to promoting survival and exist across many species. Darwin's theory suggested to some, especially so-called social Darwinists, that defining and understanding adaptive behaviors in humans could help to advance our own future evolution; we might even guide ourselves into becoming a more evolved species.

Speculation about evolutionary parallels between animal and human society in the late nineteenth century tended to justify aristocratic and conservative values. British philosopher Herbert Spencer, who coined the phrase *survival of the fittest,* claimed that those on the bottom of the socioeconomic structure were there because they were the least fit to survive. He repudiated state interference with the "natural," unimpeded growth of society, including all state aid to the poor. "The whole effort of nature," he said, "is to get rid of such, to clear the world of them, and make room for the better" (quoted in Hofstadter 1959, 41). According to William Graham Sumner, a Yale University professor and Puritan preacher who popularized Spencer's ideas in America, the huge fortunes of the captains of industry were legitimate rewards for their special organizing talent. Millionaires were the "bloom of a competitive civilization." Other popularizers of Darwin suggested that certain industrialists had an instinct for success; Negroes had an instinct for savagery and so forth.

When science took up the question of instinct in the early part of the twentieth century, the focus was on defining its properties in animal and human behavior. An instinct, it was said, was behavior that was innate and automatic. A typical study of nonhuman animal instinct at that time illustrates the concept. The female wasp, without any opportunity to learn the behavior, would dig a hole, place some caterpillars in it, paralyze them by stinging, lay eggs on them, then fill up the hole and go off to die. This required a good deal of searching behavior that appeared to go beyond mere reflex, although there was automaticity in the sequence in that if the activity was interrupted in some phase of the cycle, the wasp might abandon the project and start over (Peckham and Peckham 1905).

The greatest problems arose when the concept of instinct was applied to man. Although more instincts were generally assigned to lower-order animals than to man because man controlled more of his behavior through intelligence, the proportion varied greatly according to the theorist. Psychologist William James, at the turn of the century, decided that man had more instincts than any other animal. Others were quick to find an instinctual rationale for every sort of behavior. For instance, one scientist explained that a man jumped off a cliff because he had a suicidal instinct; another claimed that wolves behave as they do because they possess the lupine form of the herd instinct (Boakes 1984, 216). By the 1920s the concept of instinct had come under attack, particularly by sociologists, who had begun to turn their backs on the earlier, social Darwinism (Hilgard 1987, chaps. 10–11). One review of the instinct concept showed that in the first twenty years of the century, some four hundred books or articles had proposed nearly six thousand classes of instinct encompassing over fourteen thousand individual cases (Bernard 1924). Among the examples this survey discovered were the aesthetic instinct of girls to pat and arrange their hair and the antisocial instinct of upper-class Mexicans. Dozens of papers were soon published claiming that instinct was a catchall for vague and indefinite ideas about the causes of human actions.

As the concept of instinct became more controversial, some psychologists in the second quarter of the century substituted the concept of drive, an impulse based on some physiological need, focusing on the motivational aspect of instinct. Much of this research was conducted in the laboratory, inspired by biological and comparative animal research, but it was also influenced by the theories of psychoanalysis (Hilgard 1987, chap. 10). Sigmund Freud developed an elaborate theory of drive or instinct in man that explains human behavior in terms of the pursuit of instinctual gratification (especially of sexual and aggressive urges) and the conflicts encountered in the course of that pursuit. How we resolve these conflicts determines the shape of our personality. Freud defined instinct as a stimulus to the mind that arises from within the organism, appears as a constant rather than a momentary force (like a reflex), and cannot be escaped (Fletcher 1968, 173).

In 1910 Freud proposed that all instincts could be divided into two great classes: instincts for the preservation of life (located in the ego) and instincts directed toward the attainment of pleasure, called libido and located in the id. In 1920 he published a profoundly revised theory of instinct in which libido, Eros, was contrasted with the newly discerned death instinct, Thanatos. The pleasure principle was now replaced as the fundamental rule by the even more basic compulsion to repeat. Freud suggested that the individual often repeated unpleasurable events despite their painful quality in the hope that they could ultimately be mastered. He further asserted that the instincts, when viewed from the perspective of the nervous system's ultimate goal of tension reduction, seemed to function to repeat the past—to return to the excitation-free state prior to stimulation. In its most fundamental form, the compulsion to repeat is the ultimate conservative trend: the urge to gain complete freedom from stimulation and need—in short, death.

In the 1930s another group of scientists, led by Konrad Lorenz of

Austria and Germany and Nicholas Tinbergen of the Netherlands, began to study instinct in nonhuman animals, especially fish and birds, and in natural habitats, not the laboratory. English translations of their work appeared in the early 1950s. Some American naturalists objected to these ethologists' use of the term instinct because of its vagueness and its political history, and for a time the ethologists substituted *species-specific*. As Beach (1960) has pointed out, though, speech and language are species-specific behaviors but cannot be termed instinctive. By the early 1960s these terms had been abandoned because of their imprecision. Searching for something as clearly definable and recognizable as the bones and teeth used by morphologists, the ethologists began to identify sequences of behavior that could be observed and compared across species—so-called microbehavioral systems. The terms *fixed action pattern* and *specific action potential* served to describe some of the behavior patterns that once might have been described as instinct (Lea 1984, 34).

In the 1970s another field of inquiry related to the idea of instinct emerged: behavioral endocrinology (see Beach 1975, 1981). This research looked at correlations between behavior and chemical changes associated with menstruation, fertility, pregnancy, parturition and lactation, sexual development, sexual experience, brain extirpation, and the administration of hormones (Hilgard 1987, chap. 11). For example, J. S. Rosenblatt transferred blood from newly delivered rats to mature virgin rats and found that the virgin rats then exhibited maternal behaviors (Terkel and Rosenblatt 1972). In fact, the studies of hormonally altered maternal behavior in rats by Rosenblatt and his colleagues were seen by Kennell and Klaus as support for their postulate of human maternal postpartum bonding.

What makes this history central to understanding bonding is that the validity of the research rests on this vague notion of instinct. The term used by Kennell and Klaus is species-specific, a theoretical construct that requires considerable caution on the part of the researcher. Yet it was an integral and unexamined cornerstone of bonding studies. In spite of the serious problems evident in the first study, subsequent research followed this basic model, with considerable variation in the backgrounds of the mothers and also in the measures of bonding. During the mid-1970s and early 1980s, over two hundred articles on bonding were published in some of the most prestigious pediatric, child psychology, allied health sciences, and social work journals—an indication of how strongly the idea had become an established framework for investigating a hypothesis. For ten years, no major objections to these fundamental empirical matters were raised.[6]

The Problem of Parent-Infant Management

The research on bonding really began in the 1960s as a response to problems created by the neonatal intensive care unit, which necessitated the separation of infants from their mothers for weeks and even months following birth while trained professionals managed the complex high-tech care of these babies. The parents sometimes felt disengaged from and reluctant to care for the infants, and often found them difficult to care for. This situation presented a heartbreaking problem for doctors and nurses who had used heroic measures to keep the infants alive and to treat their critical medical problems. Sometimes the babies would later return to the hospital, having been battered by their parents.

The rationale for keeping infants in central nurseries was that only there could proper precautions be taken to prevent the spread of infection. Parents and other family members were thought of as potential sources of infection, but as early as the late 1950s, studies began to show that most neonatal infections are hospital-acquired and that in fact breast milk provides infants with substances that enhance immunity (see Young 1982, 239–42). In 1964, at Stanford University's Premature Research Center Nursery, four researchers, including Marshall Klaus, conducted a pilot study to determine whether mothers could be admitted to the premature nursery without increasing the babies' risk of infection or disrupting the organization of care (Barnett et al. 1970). The authors say they were prompted by studies of maternal behavior in nonhuman mammals that suggested that the level of interaction permitted between mother and infant in the postpartum period would influence later maternal attachment (the term used at the time instead of "bonding") and infant development.[7] Therefore, they attempted to look at "commitment, feelings of competence and behavior" in two groups of mothers (a total of twenty-nine)—those admitted and those not admitted to the NICU—and to relate the differences found to the motor and mental development of the infants. They found that there were no increases in the rate of infection among infants whose mothers were admitted, nor was the organization of care disrupted. These authors did conclude, however, that owing to the large number of variables affecting the mother and the small number of subjects used, "no rigorous statement of outcome regarding differing maternal behaviors could be expected."

In a subsequent study (Leifer et al. 1972), the authors did not find observable behavioral differences between the separated mothers and those who had had early contact with their infants (a total of about forty mothers). They claim, however, that the fact that two mothers in the separated group chose to relinquish custody of their infants and that five divorces occurred in this group (vs. one in the extra-contact group) indicated "severe disturbance of normal maternal and marital behavior" and suggested "that early separation of mother and infant may seriously disrupt normal maternal behavior."[8]

Klaus continued his research on early parent-infant contact with Kennell at the Department of Pediatrics of Case Western Reserve University School of Medicine.[9] In their concern with the problems of parental and patient management in the relatively new pediatric discipline of neonatology, Kennell and Klaus were already guided by the belief that maternal behavior could be understood in terms of instinct. In 1970 they studied the sequence of initial touching behaviors typically engaged in by mothers as they first get to know their infants. They usually start by touching the infant's outer extremities with a fingertip and end with palm contact with the infant's trunk. Kennell and Klaus referred to this as "human maternal behavior at the first contact with her young" (Klaus et al. 1970) and concluded that it was "species-specific behavior in human mothers"—that is, biologically based. They claim as evidence for a biological basis the existence of related behaviors in nonhuman mammals, such as "nesting, retrieving, grooming, and exploring"; the "evidence" is by analogy. The authors claim that this "species-specific behavior requires a re-evaluation of the present hospital policies regulating care of the mother and infant." The same behaviors had previously been described by Reva Rubin (1963), a maternity nurse, who included them, without postulating an instinctual basis, in nursing assessments that also addressed the mother's psychological and socioeconomic background, the behavior of the infant, and many other pertinent factors.

Expansion of the Bonding Idea

In 1976 Doctors Kennell and Klaus consolidated their concept of bonding in a book for both professional and popular consumption: *Maternal Infant Bonding: The Impact of Early Separation or Loss on Family Development*. The book includes critical commentary by such authorities as Brazelton and J. S. Rosenblatt. Throughout the book the term bonding is used primarily to refer to the idea that instinctual behavior in nonhumans is paralleled by instincts that motivate human behavior. The concept of maternal infant bonding they describe, however, is a broad one, encompassing not just postpartum separation but also loss—that is, the death of an infant and its impact on the development of the entire family.

The authors explain that their research was prompted by mothers of premature and sick infants who found it difficult to care for their babies and to believe that the babies were their own and would survive through maternal care. Kennell and Klaus were also influenced by the burgeoning research on the capacities of infants to take in their environments and by new knowledge about the reciprocal biological and social interactions between mothers and infants.[10] Also important was the home-birth movement, which threatened to take more and more births out of the hospital. Especially compelling were the startlingly high rates of battering and failure-to-thrive, a syndrome in which the child fails to gain weight with little or no evidence of organic cause, found among premature and sick infants.

The authors state seven principles they believe to be "crucial components in the process of attachment":

1. There is a sensitive period in the first minutes and hours of life during which it is necessary that the mother and father have close contact with the neonate for later development to be optimal.

2. There appear to be species-specific responses to the infant in the human mother and father that are exhibited when they are first given their infant.

3. The process of the attachment is structured so that the father and mother will become attached optimally to only one infant at a time. Bowlby (1958) earlier stated this principle of the attachment process in the other direction and termed it *monotropy*.

4. During the process of the mother's attachment to her infant, it is necessary that the infant respond to the mother by some signal such as body or eye movements. We have sometimes described this as as "You can't love a dishrag."

5. People who witness the birth process become strongly attached to the infant.

6. For some adults it is difficult simultaneously to go through the processes of attachment and detachment—that is, to develop an attachment to one person while mourning the loss or threatened loss of the same or another person.

7. Some early events have long-lasting effects. First-day anxieties about the well-being of a baby with a temporary disorder in the first day may result in long-lasting concerns that may adversely shape the development of the child. (Kennell and Rolnick 1960, 14)

The model on which Doctors Kennell and Klaus believe human "parental attachment" is based is stated directly in a chapter called "Maternal Behavior in Mammals": "Just as the neonatologist who is interested in the respiratory changes occurring at birth has used the models of the fetal lamb and monkey, . . . the study of human parental attachment has been partly aided by observation of animal mothers. This is done not to explain human behavior but rather to

view human beings within the context of evolutionary development"
(1976, 16).

This evolutionary premise also derives directly from the attachment
theory of Bowlby, which argues the need for mothers and infants to
be near one another and in harmony during the first three years of
the infant's life. In fact the word *attachment* is used so much throughout the Kennell and Klaus book that one wonders whether bonding
was not an afterthought, a later choice of book title that was subsequently worked into the text. However, according to Kennell and
Klaus, "maternal-infant attachment" refers to the *infant's* instinctual
proximity-promoting behaviors; bonding is "a kind of attachment in
the opposite direction, from parent to infant," precipitated by hormonal changes in the *mother*.

The term bonding can be used, however, in a number of ways.
Kennell and Klaus use it in the anthropological sense, to refer to the
social connections among people based on kinship, social roles, and
group survival functions—that is, as rooted in some mutually beneficial social function. "Most of the richness and beauty of life is
derived from the close relationship that each individual has with a
small number of other human beings—mother, father, sister,
brother, husband, wife, son, daughter, and a small cadre of close
friends. With each person in this small group, the individual has a
uniquely close attachment or bond. This book deals with one of
these special attachments, the bond a mother or father forms with
his or her newborn infant" (p. 1). So bonding is presumably a subset
in a class of close human *affectional* relations and is a type of
attachment.

Eventually, Kennell and Klaus move toward their unique use of
the word: "Immediately after the birth the parents enter a unique
period during which events may have lasting effects on the family.
This period, which lasts a short time, and during which the parents'
attachment to their infant blossoms, we have named the *maternal
sensitive period*. Because we believe this concept is crucial to the
understanding of the *bonding* process, we will examine in detail the
evidence supporting its existence" (pp. 50–51). The meaning of
bonding is stretched even further by the continual emendation of

"mother" to read "parent" even when the actual referent is based on research regarding the relationships of human and nonhuman *females* with their offspring. No mention of animal research on paternal behavior is ever made.

The Burgeoning of Bonding Research

A number of bonding studies were conducted by other groups of researchers, in Europe as well as in the United States and Canada, throughout the decade. All were patterned after the Kennell and Klaus model, but definitions of bonding varied from study to study, as did the phenomena that were considered outcome measures. Some of the subjects were middle class; many were poor.

In the research that finds support for the bonding period, a series of studies conducted in Sweden by pediatrician Peter de Chateau and his colleagues (de Chateau 1976, 1980, 1981; de Chateau and Wiberg 1977) is often cited.[11] The researchers studied twenty-two middle-class mothers who experienced fifteen to twenty minutes of skin-to-skin contact beginning ten minutes after delivery and claimed to have found significant effects of bonding on three out of thirty-five behavioral measures at thirty-six hours after birth. The extra-contact mothers held their babies more than the twenty control group mothers during a twenty-five-minute observation. Two other differences are reported, but their significance is unclear: The experimental group mothers sat up more, and the control group mothers leaned on an elbow more. These effects were found only for the mothers of boys. The authors claim they found positive effects of bonding. When the children were one year old the differences seemed even more pronounced. The experimental group mothers reported a longer duration of breast feeding (for boys but not girls), a lower incidence of returning to outside employment, a higher incidence of putting the baby in its own room for sleeping, a lower incidence of early bladder training, and fathers who were less active in helping to care for the infant. Their infants showed superior performance on the Gesell Developmental Test (although the differences are small—a week to two weeks). De Chateau interprets all of these differences as indicating a superior mother-infant relationship for the experimental group.

At three years a great many variables were measured by means of observation of mother-child play with a doll house, observation of the child, an interview with the mother and father, and the Denver Development Screening Test. Three differences were found: the experimental group mothers were more satisfied with the time they had spent with their babies postdelivery, had more subsequent children, and said their children had achieved two-word utterances sooner than control children. Again, these are interpreted as positive effects for the experimental group. Other studies of middle-class mothers reported similar findings. (See Kontos 1978; Grossman, Thane, and Grossman 1981.)[12]

The claim that failure to form an appropriate mother-infant bond in the first few hours or days after birth is the root cause of child abuse or neglect has also prompted a host of studies. Most studies of the link between bonding and child abuse were small and retrospective and found higher abuse for the NICU population.[13] Where we do have data from a prospective, relatively large-scale investigation, the hypothesized relation between neonate bonding and maltreatment either is not supported or constitutes only one factor among many that predict abuse and neglect. For instance, a study of 240 mothers drawn from known abuse, neglect, and normal control populations found that six of twelve variables discriminated among these groups of mothers at a high level of significance. Infant risk, determined on the basis of neonatal complications requiring hospitalization and separation, was not a successful discriminator (Gaines et al. 1978).

In another prospective study (sometimes cited as evidence for the importance of postpartum bonding), Susan O'Connor and her colleagues (1978) randomly assigned 301 low-income mothers to either rooming-in or routine hospital care. In a follow-up at twenty-one months, the authors found only one case of child abuse in the rooming-in group but nine cases of failure-to-thrive, battering, or foster care among the control group. This finding suggested that extra early contact had an effect. The researchers cautioned, however, that besides the extended contact with the infant, mothers in the rooming-in group were allowed almost unlimited visits by the baby's father, thus solidifying the family unit; this confounding variable might account for the treatment effect (O'Connor et al. 1980).

In another study of 321 low-income women, Earl Seigel and his colleagues (1980) examined the effects of two interventions—extra postpartum contact and home visits by health care professionals—on maternal attachment and child abuse and neglect. They found that the home visits were not significant and that the extra contact had a very small effect (2.5 percent of the difference on some variables at four months and 3.2 percent of the difference of one variable at twelve months). The interventions were unrelated to later child abuse. (They were related to attachment.) The authors concluded that the maternal background variables of race, marital status, parity, education, age, and verbal test scores were the most important factors in predicting abuse. (Also see Collingwood and Alberman 1979; Helfer and Kempe 1976; Hunter et al. 1978; Williams and Money 1980.)

In addition to child abuse, it has been suggested that the problems of maternal bonding are responsible for failure-to-thrive. Again, early studies investigating this problem were generally retrospective. The behavior of mothers of children who were failing to thrive was scrutinized, pathology was found, and the mothers were blamed for causing the problem. (In fact, a disturbed relationship might well be the *result* of a child's failure-to-thrive.) The validity of such studies was difficult to assess as they often relied on distorted or inadequate parental reports and clinical records. Prospective studies were less likely to find disturbed maternal bonding or attachment as a significant factor. For example, a 1980 longitudinal study of 1,400 women allowed researchers to examine precursors of failure-to-thrive (Vietze). The authors found no significant differences between mothers whose infants remained normal and those whose infants were later diagnosed as nonorganic failure-to-thrive. Since the infants had not been identified at the time the data were collected, the mothers were not subject to the search for pathology that might have taken place after the diagnosis of growth failure was made. A significant number of the failure-to-thrive infants were, however, premature or low-birthweight babies. The authors do not use this finding to invoke a bonding failure explanation. Instead, they postulate that there is a complex chain of events, including certain characteristics of the infants, that results in the syndrome. (Also see Dunn and Richards 1977.) Evidence for the role of postpartum separation in causing later abuse or pathology is negligible. Increasingly, attempts to understand these problems focus on factors related to poverty and social isolation. There is considerable debate about whether such problems can be predicted from infancy (see Montgomery 1982; Parker, Greer, and Zuckerman 1988).

Evidence from several studies investigating bonding failed to find any support for the bonding hypothesis. Marilyn Svejda, Joseph Campos, and Robert Emde (1980) attempted to replicate the original Klaus and Kennell study (1972), avoiding some of its methodological errors. For instance, in order to eliminate a feeling of specialness in extra-contact mothers, they gave the mothers' roommates the same treatment, even though they were not part of the study group. The observers were blind to group membership. No differences in behavior were found between the special contact group of thirty primiparous lower-middle-class mothers with healthy full-term babies and the control group. (Also see Minde et al. 1978; Egeland and Vaughn 1981; Taylor et al. 1979.)

In sum, the accumulation of evidence during the 1970s did not show clear support for the existence of a postpartum sensitive period for bonding, nor did it clearly indicate that such a period does not exist. It did appear that extra postpartum contact was likely to produce more effects in women who were poor and had relatively few social and economic supports, suggesting that important learning may have been taking place. These effects appeared to be of short duration. But, as there were so many conceptual and methodological problems in these studies, even these trends are of questionable verity. (See Montgomery 1982.)

If there were problems with the research itself, there were other problems with the doctrine that evolved as hospital staff began to apply bonding religiously as a prophylactic against child abuse and family failure and as parents who had not had the postpartum bonding experience began to feel a sense of loss and guilt. In the preface to their 1982 book *Parent-Infant Bonding,* therefore, Kennell and Klaus stated that they were distressed when bonding came to be "confused with a simple, speedy, adhesive property rather than the beginning of a complex human psychobiological process" (xiii). In this revision of their 1976 book, the chapter on maternal behavior in mammals is relegated to chapter 4. The emphasis in *Parent-Infant Bonding* is on the involvement of fathers and siblings in childbirth.

In chapter 2, "Labor, Birth, and Bonding," the authors review seventeen studies which they claim focused on whether additional time for close contact between the mother and full-term infant in the first minutes, hours, and days of life alters the quality of the maternal-infant bond. (Several of these studies examine the effects of varied contact on breast feeding.) By reinterpreting the data from some of these studies, the authors conclude that "no matter at what point the early contact was experienced, later differences were observed in the behavior of the experimental group of mothers when compared with the behavior of the control group" (p. 53). They end their review by stating, "We believe that there is strong evidence that at least thirty to sixty minutes of early contact in privacy should be provided for every parent and infant to enhance the bonding experience" (p. 56). They also note that "in spite of a lack of early contact experienced by parents in hospital births in the past twenty to thirty years, almost all these parents became bonded to their babies. The human is highly adaptable. Sadly, some parents who missed the bonding experience have felt that all was lost for their future relationship. This was (and is) completely incorrect" (p. 55).

Criticism of the Bonding Research

In the early 1980s the bonding research met with an avalanche of criticism. The most influential critic was developmental psychologist Michael Lamb. In *Psychology Today* (April 1982), Lamb claimed that a review of the research (conducted with Carl-Phillip Hwang, a Swedish researcher) "found only weak evidence of temporary effects of early contact and no evidence whatsoever of any lasting effects." In response to a critical editorial by Lamb in the October 1982 *Journal of Pediatrics,* Barbara Korsch suggested that critics of bonding research were reacting as much to "the exaggerated practices triggered by the teaching of Kennell and Klaus as to the ideas presented originally" (Korsch 1983). In defense of Kennell and Klaus, she points out that they qualified their claims in their 1982 book, "which it would appear Lamb did not consider in his review." Lamb, in a November 1982 *Pediatrics* article, reviewed the research on bonding, citing many of the above-mentioned methodological problems. Referring to the 1972 Kennell and Klaus study, Lamb asserted:

> [The] findings provide very little support for claims regarding the beneficial effects of early contact for several reasons. First, only a small proportion of the measures (five out of at least 75) revealed significant differences. . . . Second, early contact was confounded with extended contact. Third, the nursing and medical staff members (including the physician who conducted the pediatric examination) were aware that the mothers in the early contact group were special, and they are likely to have been treated differently as a result.

Lamb concludes:

> The preponderance of the evidence thus suggests that extended contact has no clear effects on maternal behavior. By contrast, some researchers seem to have shown that early contact has positive short-term effects. This conclusion appears premature, however, as serious methodologic problems compromise the research. First, there is the problem of nonreplication. Even though many studies report positive consequences, they usually fail to find effects on similar measures, even when the same subjects are followed over time. Otherwise comparable studies often fail to demonstrate similar effects.
>
> . . . Many of the researchers have employed multiple measures and observed statistically significant differences on a small proportion of these: generally, the number of significant group dif-

ferences usually hovers around the number that would be expected to occur by chance.

   . . . It is not clear that any effects observed are accounted for by early contact rather than differences in treatment by medical and nursing staff who know that the study group subjects are special.

   In sum, claims regarding the effects of early contact on maternal-infant bonding are not well supported by the empirical evidence. Early contact has no enduring effects on maternal attachment, but may sometimes have modest short-term effects on some mothers in some circumstances.

In the October 1983 issue of *Pediatrics,* Elizabeth Anisfeld, Mary Ann Curry, Deborah Hales, Kennell, Klaus, Evelyn Lipper, O'Connor, Seigel, and Robert Sosa (1983) (those whose studies were critiqued by Lamb) contributed a joint rebuttal: "Inaccuracies in Lamb's recent review of studies of maternal-infant bonding have resulted in considerable confusion and misunderstanding among those not well-acquainted with the field." Curiously, Kennell and Klaus have little to say about Lamb's specific criticisms of their own studies. They only mention, "In Klaus [Klaus et al. 1972] there were positive results in 5/25 comparisons, not in 5/75 as noted by Lamb." The only other reference to Kennell and Klaus's research in the rebuttal is the following:

Many of Lamb's criticisms would not have been written had he reviewed *Parent-Infant Bonding* [1982] in which these [being reviewed by Lamb] and other studies are described in detail. In summary, we say again, we agree that it is necessary to evaluate critically the evidence for the effect of early and extended contact on maternal behavior, but we suggest that a more thorough, careful, and objective approach to such an evaluation is necessary.

In a joint reply to the joint rebuttal published in the same issue of *Pediatrics,* Lamb, joined by Campos, Hwang, P. Herbert Leiderman, Abraham Sagi, and Svejda, reiterates: "The preponderance of the evidence now available . . . suggests that early skin-to-skin contact has no clear, universal, and enduring effects on maternal behavior. This was the central conclusion of the review and it is not challenged in the rebuttal."

They add that although the humanization of birthing practices that Kennell and Klaus helped bring about is laudable, "the authors appear to have a weak understanding of some of the more thorny aspects of research design and analysis."

In 1981 Leiderman, with whom Klaus had conducted the first protobonding study, published a review and criticism of bonding research, summarizing his own earlier investigations. (See also Reed and Leiderman 1983.) He states that even after a two- to three-month separation from their premature infants, mothers establish social bonds that cannot be differentiated from the bonds established by mothers who were not initially separated from their infants. He concludes that early contact does not necessarily facilitate social bonding; the data suggest only that this possibility exists for some individuals. Leiderman stated in a personal interview in May 1990 that while he feels there is no "biological basis for bonding" he still feels that bonding is especially important for poor mothers and mothers with few social supports.

In 1982 three British researchers, Martin Herbert, Wladyslaw Sluckin, and Alice Sluckin, published an extensive critique in the *Journal of Child Psychology and Psychiatry* that was published a year later as a book. Their analysis went beyond that of other critiques, claiming flatly that there is *no* support for human bonding. In addition to describing the methodological problems of the research, the authors cite evidence from animal research that contradicts the idea of a biologically based critical maternal period. They point out that the adoption of strange lambs and kids and even cross-species adoptions can be established and that these adoptions remain stable. Moreover, with ungulates (hooved animals), the acceptability of kids is actually a matter of olfactory labeling—identifying offspring in the herd by smell. The authors also suggest that mothers and babies are often so vulnerable and exhausted in the postpartum period that it might be more adaptive for nature to make this a time that is buffered against emotional difficulties.

Another facet of the criticism focuses on the consequences for women of the ideology of bonding. In "The 'Blame the Mother' Ideology," Stella Chess and Alexander Thomas (1982) point out that bonding appears to be another oversimplification of complex phenomena in which mothers are unjustly blamed for their children's problems. (See also Chess 1982, 1983.)

In the final engagement of opposing research camps, Barbara Myers, in *Developmental Review* (1984a), describes the same methodological and theoretical problems cited in the previous critiques. She concludes: "Reviewing the evidence presented thus far, it is difficult to find support that the postpartum period is a critical period for human mother-infant affectional bonding. There are too many weaknesses in the 'positive' studies and too many negative findings in the remaining studies to suggest that maternal-infant contact just after birth is central to the mother's affection for her infant."

In their reply to Dr. Myers in the same issue of *Developmental Review*, Kennell and Klaus presented their "current" concepts and provided additional details about their original study reported in 1972.

We were particularly careful to avoid generalizing findings from other species to human relationships and to assess that studying maternal behavior in animals "is done not to explain human behavior but rather to view human beings within the context of evolutionary development" (Klaus and Kennell 1982, 130).

The major area of disagreement concerning studies of parent-infant bonding has revolved around whether or not for a small number of mothers there are any *lasting* effects of early maternal-infant contact on the mother's behavior toward her baby and on their subsequent relationship. We have speculated that there might be a sensitive period of several hours or days after birth during which contact with the baby might enhance a mother's relationship and bond with her baby. We have never suggested that early contact for additional hours or days after birth is the sole determining factor that will produce a certain maternal behavior or change in child development at some point far off in the future, independently of anything that might happen in between.

. . . In answer to Myers' questions about the methods used for our patients and researchers in our original 1972 study, neither group of mothers knew of this study in advance or to our knowledge was aware of the arrangements made for the other. The women in both groups had agreed to participate in a study of how mothers get started with their newborn infants. We never place[d] the experimental and control mothers together, and we were meticulous about providing equal amounts of nursing time and investigator time with the mothers in both groups . . .

. . . We let the mother interact with her infant as she wanted. The mothers said they planned to bottle feed so all the mothers were gowned during the early and extended contact and there was no skin-to-skin contact. In this and all our extra contact studies the outcome observers were blind to the group status of the mother being observed.

. . . In the 1972 report of our first study and in our recent books we emphasized that the results were not consistent with imprinting or a critical period. We said our data suggest that this may be a special attachment period for an adult woman—special in the sense that what happens during this time may alter the later behavior of the adult toward a young infant for at least as long as one month after delivery. It would be useful to have a special term for this period, such as "maternal sensitive period."

Unfortunately, some misinterpretations of studies of parent-to-infant attachment may have resulted from a too literal acceptance of the word *bonding,* suggesting that the speed of this reaction resembles that of epoxy glue.

Finally, in the same issue of *Developmental Review,* Myers reiterates that the evidence does not support a sensitive period for mother-infant contact for the establishment of a maternal bond. Kennell and Klaus, she claimed, not only exaggerated their own findings but distorted the findings of other studies in favor of the sensitive period. The bonding studies, she went on, were not consistent in what they looked for, and when they did look for the same thing, they did not replicate each other's findings. Myers does, however, commend Kennell and Klaus for their role in bringing about more humane practices in hospital childbirths.

Possibly the last word on this controversy to appear in the pediatric journals is a three-page review by K. Minde published in 1986 in *Developmental Medicine and Child Neurology*. Minde concludes that the research evidence continues to confirm the existence and importance of attachment but finds no evidence to support the existence of bonding.

Nursing Applications of Bonding

Although the pediatric literature illustrates the rise and demise of bonding research, the allied health science literature reveals the readiness with which bonding was accepted and worked into the structure of hospital childbirth and nursing care. Most of the early articles on bonding in the allied health sciences journals discussed the rewards of increased maternal-infant contact. The first articles on bonding introduce the idea in the context of admitting parents to the NICU. In 1974, in *JOGN Nursing,* Sandra Eckes, an NICU nurse, claims that the "open door policy" allowing parents into the previously off-limits NICU of her hospital has dramatically reduced mothers' fears about being able to care for their infants. She cites a Stanford study (Barnett et al. 1970) and the early Kennell and Klaus studies as evidence that infection rates do not increase when mothers are admitted to the NICU and also refers to recent studies of "mammalian mothers" indicating that separation may violate a biologically based sensitive period for attachment.

Nurses also used bonding in assessing maternal care. Nursing checklists had originally been designed in the 1940s and 1950s to assess breastfeeding and other maternal caretaking skills that were later referred to as matters of attachment. For example, Ann Clark, in the *American Journal of Maternal Child Nursing* (March/April 1976), models her intervention on Reva Rubin's checklists, which assess the mother's perception of herself and her infant, the infant's behavior, and the mother-infant interaction. Clark refers to Kennell and Klaus's research as an indication that early assessment is important because the postpartum period may be a "sensitive period." Eventually, many of the assessments were reduced to just a few maternal behaviors that were thought to index bonding as a potentially pathological process leading to child abuse if it were not adequately conducted (see Jenkins and Westhus 1981).

It appears that the institution of bonding in nursing care quickly became a simplistic and rigid dictum in some hospitals. Herbert Barrie's 1976 commentary, *Of Human Bondage,* indicates the lengths to which this process was sometimes taken:

> Frankly, I am sick and tired of all the talk about bonding. Mothers and babies have to be bonded like sticking two bits of wood together we are told. The carpenters of mother-child-attachment—doctors, midwives, health visitors, and social workers—are not competent until they have been instructed in the bonding art by self-professed experts. Mothers who have or have not bonded are the topic of interminable discussions. Converts to the faith have a real feast day when someone who has got unstuck can be singled out for special treatment. According to the Gospel, bonding failure is the root of all evil. Battered babies are unbonded babies and separation the cause of deprivation stretching into generations. "At risk" scores of bonding failure are catching on. (p. 182)

If one wonders how bonding became gospel, an article published in 1978 illustrates one likely source. Hugh Jolly, a British pediatrician, explains why the consequences of separation for even a short period can be "far more disastrous than infection."

> [A mother's love for her baby right after birth] is particularly vulnerable to interference from outside influences of which the greatest is separation of mother and infant. . . . A normal baby should be delivered straight into his mother's arms. . . . The infant should lie nude and unwashed in contact with his mother's breasts for some time, using an overhead heating pad if necessary.

The parents and the new baby should then be left alone for the
first hour. . . . Animal studies of the effects of short periods of
separation of mother and offspring have shown *disastrous consequences—rejection and even killing of the baby.* (19–21; emphasis
added)

As bonding replaced attachment as a rationale for nursing interventions, the designers of assessments became less concerned with
the self-concept of the mother, the responsiveness of the infant, or
the interactional dyad. Assessment was soon reduced to a minimum
of maternal-attitude factors said to index bonding. In 1980, Margaret
Rhone provided a bonding inventory consisting of only seven assessment categories. Women received a score of 0 if they were found
to exhibit any of the following behaviors: "Verbalizes concern for
self. Seeks support for self. No questions about baby. Does not speak
to baby. Expresses anger or dissatisfaction at outcome of labor.
Refuses to hold baby. Does not touch or look toward baby." In this
system an exhausted, irritated, or suffering mother would be at risk
for child abuse. According to Rhone, mother-infant bonding is an
unfolding relationship beginning with the first fetal movement, at
which the mother "falls in love" with her baby; yet none of this
ongoing development is reflected in Rhone's assessment tools. In
fact, the focus is on pathology. Bonding is "a fragile and protracted
process; while it is taking place it can be disturbed or even broken
and it may take weeks, months or even years for the union to
solidify" (p. 40). As evidence for the importance of bonding, Rhone
cites studies (not specified) indicating that better attachment occurs
when parents experience rooming-in (p. 38). Jenkins claims that
"systematic assessment of the touching process [alone] can identify
the quality of parent-infant bonding," as certain species-specific
touching sequences are a universal index of bonding (Jenkins and
Westhus 1981, 114–18).

In over forty articles introducing nurses to bonding—a process
that they would presumably assess and teach—there is no common
definition of the concept. The words attachment and bonding are
used interchangeably, and it becomes crucial for nurses to rate and

to teach specific bonding behaviors as defined by Kennell and Klaus, such as skin-to-skin postpartum contact, en face looking, and a certain sequence of touching behaviors. The rationale for doing so is never fully explained, however, nor do the behaviors assessed remain consistent from one study to another. Responding in part to criticisms by Chess (1983) and Lamb (1983), Mitchell and Mills (1983) and Elliott (1983) simply expand the concept, concluding that nursing interventions can probably be useful at any time since people are more adaptable than the sensitive-period hypothesis would suggest. Throughout the 1980s, nursing articles continued to refer to the assessment of bonding and attachment (for example, Davis 1987; Fortier 1988).

Bonding in Social Work

In the social work and child psychiatry literature, bonding is incorporated into the prevention and early diagnosis of childhood psychopathology, child abuse, and child neglect. As in the nursing literature, a range of views about the nature and formation of bonds is presented. Some writers regard bonding as an imprinting-like phenomenon emerging during a critical period of the first few hours and days after birth; others take the view that mother-child relations can be facilitated during a foundational period in the first few days after birth, which is optimal for the formation of bonds, but that mothers can form bonds after this period. Regardless of the definition of bonding, failures or deficiencies of the maternal bond are said to be related etiologically to the quantity and quality of the postpartum contact between the mother and infant and are blamed for later incidents of child rejection and cruelty. Researchers and practitioners differ in how much they see bonding failure as a cause of abuse. At one extreme: "Evidence for the absence, weakness, or distortion of the usual affectional bond between parent and child can be found in virtually every case of child abuse" (Argles 1980). According to ten Bensel and Paxson (1977), as few as twelve hours of postpartum bonding could reduce the prospect of child abuse. (Also see Valman 1980.)

As in the nursing literature, a variety of assertions are made about bonding without specific documentation and with varied terminology and definitions of bonding:

The mother is pleased when the infant looks at her. She tends to caress the child gently. All of this exploring is part of the claiming process. During this process the mother is consciously and unconsciously looking for ways to tell her child from others. Studies based on videotapes of mother and child interactions made during deliveries and postpartum hospital stays indicate that when the mother doesn't take an active part in this claiming process the family is at high risk for severe parent-child difficulties in future years. (Fahlberg 1981; also see Brimblecombe et al. 1978; Floyd 1981.)

No citations are provided for the studies this author describes, but it is suggested that there is a disproportionate number of child abuse incidents affecting premature and sick infants as compared with the normal population.

Although social workers held out considerable hope for both the remedial and diagnostic uses of bonding, a growing body of evidence militated against optimism. In 1982 Stuart Montgomery criticized the notion that abuse could be predicted on the basis of the early behavior of the mother toward her infant. He claimed that because pediatric medicine was responsible for discovering child abuse in the 1960s and mobilizing concern for it, the problem had been framed in the medical model—a conceptualization that focuses on diagnosis and treatment by medical practitioners. The idea that abuse could be accurately predicted had great appeal for social workers, he felt, but a closer look at the research that seems to support such claims should lead social workers to be cautious about accepting them. Montgomery challenged the claims by Ray Helfer and Henry Kempe (1976), who were most instrumental in bringing child abuse to public attention in the early 1970s, that the best predictor of child abuse is maternal behavior during the perinatal period. In an interesting parallel to the criticism of the bonding studies, the author criticizes the studies of Helfer, Kempe, and their associates for both "haphazard" research methodology and "eclecticism" in choosing data to fit their hypothesis.

Discussion

This review of bonding research raises some major questions. To what degree is bonding a legitimate idea that should continue to be researched? Perhaps, as Kennell and Klaus maintain, criticism of bonding research interrupted the pursuit of an important idea. The research on bonding became the basis for a doctrine by which medicine was practiced, birth conducted, and parenting evaluated. Why was bonding research published and applied for an entire decade without criticism when the scientific basis for it was so questionable? And how could there be such extensive disagreement among researchers regarding what constitutes sound research?

The disparity between the legitimacy of research evidence and its widespread acceptance can be explained only by probing more deeply into the unquestioned assumptions with which the scientific community was operating. Philosophers of science in recent years have made it amply clear that science, far from being a purely objective process that uncovers truths, is in fact a process in which knowledge is also socially constructed.[14] The paradigms that declare what questions are to be asked and what methods of investigation are to be used involve agreement among members of a scientific community. Moreover, paradigms gain their status because they are more successful than their competitors in solving problems that the group of practitioners has come to recognize as acute. This raises the critical question—to what degree is science a product of social influence, and to what degree is there a reliable and valid empirical base of information that we can use?

That, of course, is the real question of this book. The answer to the puzzle begins with the matter of maternal deprivation and attachment. Bonding was accepted in part as an extension of this idea.

Maternal Deprivation and Attachment

The ready acceptance of bonding was due in no small measure to a body of research that emerged in England and America in the 1940s. This research rested on the Freudian theory that personality is shaped primarily by the emotional relationship we have with our parents, especially our mothers. A number of studies purported to show that separation from their mothers in the early part of their lives caused the devastating pathology of institutionalized infants and was also the prime source of juvenile delinquency. In the following decades, studies with animals as well as children enumerated the damage caused both by inadequate mothering and by separation from mothers.

The Freudian rationale espoused by Spitz and later by Bowlby and others at the Tavistock clinic in London was bolstered by an instinctual rationale. In the 1950s, Bowlby began to postulate that infant behavior that promotes proximity to the mother is an adaptive behavior, rooted in the survival of the species, similar to imprinting in birds. By the 1970s it was but a small step from blaming maternal absence or inadequacy in the first few years of life, as Bowlby had done, to indicting the relationship between mothers and infants right after birth as the cause of everything from retarded development to child battering.

In addition to sharing a common assumption about the cause of a child's emotional and social problems, the maternal deprivation and bonding paradigms share a strikingly parallel history. Both paradigms sprang from problems caused by the practices of institutions and were used as rationales to redress those problems. Moreover, both paradigms were based on research that was later found to be of questionable methodological soundness. Both ideas were generalized far beyond the original institutional and clinical situations they were intended to address in order to act as moral guidelines for maternal behavior. Although these ideas were criticized by various professional subcommunities, they were also made into doctrines by practitioners who used them as a source of authority in administering their services and aggrandizing their own professional positions.

John Bowlby and the Idea of Maternal Deprivation

The idea of maternal deprivation was first brought to widespread international attention in 1951 by John Bowlby with the publication of his *Maternal Care and Mental Health,* commissioned by the World Health Organization. This was a report on the condition of children in Europe and the United States who had been orphaned or separated from their families. Bowlby found these children to be generally retarded in their development and to have a variety of emotional problems as well, which he and most child guidance workers agreed stemmed from maternal deprivation.

In support of this assessment, Bowlby reviewed a body of pediatric research on infants published in the 1930s and 1940s, which indicated that the development of infants in institutions was almost always inferior. Studies by Rheingold (1943), Levy (1947), and Goldfarb (1943–49) found mental and emotional deficits in children institutionalized in the first three years of life (as cited in Bowlby 1951, 15–20). This research originated in studies conducted during the first decade of this century, which uncovered the phenomenon

of *hospitalism,* a term coined by Arthur Schlossman, a German pediatrician. In 1907, Dr. Schlossman discovered that 72 percent of
the previously healthy but motherless infants entrusted to his institution had died while there from conditions in the hospital itself.
He published a paper in 1920 describing the phenomenon as the
vitiated condition of the body resulting from long confinement in
the hospital. Schlossman found that simple cleanliness, seeing that
infants were properly fed, and attending to other rudimentary matters of physical care caused the mortality rate to drop to 17 percent.
Once the physiological problems of institutionalized infants were
attended to, the importance of the psychological aspects of care
became more evident (van den Berg 1972, 13–15).[1] Bowlby also
reviewed retrospective studies of juvenile delinquents and patients
suffering from "affectionless psychopathy" (lack of ability to form
enduring relationships), which revealed that these children, too, had
experienced disruption of their maternal relationships in infancy.
Bowlby was the first to pull these studies together into one coherent
argument—a case for the profound effects of maternal care on mental
health.

Bowlby's argument went beyond the data on institutionalized infants and troubled children, however. Maternal deprivation, he
claimed, could even take place in a seemingly normal home: "a child
is deprived even though living at home if his mother (or permanent
mother substitute) is unable to give him the loving care small children need." Moreover, "partial deprivation" could also occur at
home, as a result of "(a) an unconsciously rejecting attitude underlying a loving one, (b) an excessive demand for love and reassurance
on the part of a parent and (c) a parent obtaining unconscious and
vicarious satisfaction from the child's behavior, despite conscious
condemnation of it" (Bowlby 1951, 11, 12).

Bowlby claimed, however, that even bad parental care was pref-
erable to the care of institutions. He advised child-guidance counselors to search out cases of partial deprivation and give as much
time to the therapy of the parents as to that of the children. Arguing
that "Deprived children, whether in their own homes or out of them,
are a source of social infection as real or serious as are the carriers

of diphtheria and typhoid" (p. 157), he called for a public health campaign to detect causes of deprivation on a mass scale.

The report had tremendous impact and aroused world-wide attention regarding the unfavorable effects of separating children from their parents.[2] The World Health Organization set up a European study group to specify institutional remedies and sponsored further research (Buckle 1968, 3–8). The report also became a best-seller in England. A simplified version was published in 1953 as *Child Care and the Growth of Love,* emphasizing the young child's need for his mother as an ever-present companion. This book ran into many editions and is largely responsible for defining what some historians and critics have referred to as *Bowlbyism*—the emphasis on keeping mothers in the home.[3] Bowlby's work was institutionalized by its absorption into social work theory in the 1950s (Riley 1983, 103). According to Bowlby, "the social workers took to it with enthusiasm; the psychoanalysts treated it with caution . . . pediatricians were initially hostile but subsequently, many became very supporting . . . of course the academic psychologists were bitterly hostile. . . . Insofar as my views were influential, it was because the social workers took them up and implemented them." In America, he notes, reception of his ideas was "spotty. . . . The idea seemed to be more identified with the work of Spitz" (Senn 1977, 19–21).

Bowlby's report on maternal deprivation prompted practical changes in the hospitalization of children, a great deal of theory and research regarding the child's ties with his mother, and experiments with nonhuman animals; it influenced public policy regarding child welfare and early care. Because Bowlby had claimed that "full-time employment of [a] mother" is on a par with the "death of a parent, imprisonment of a parent, war, famine," and so forth, as "reasons for family failure" (1951, 73), research on maternal deprivation was often used in the ensuing decades to discourage mothers from working or even using day-care centers (Rose 1985, chap. 7). In fact, Bowlby's claims regarding the importance of mother love in infancy and early childhood led some people to place an almost mystical importance on the role of the mother.

René Spitz: Anaclitic Depression

Bowlby's report had focused on research in two areas of children's experience. The first was that of institutionalized infants. The studies of René Spitz were particularly dramatic because they were systematic and illustrated a direct link between emotional deprivation and physical suffering, even death. In 1945, Spitz published a study of two groups of babies. The infants in the first group were confined to a nursery in a penal institution for delinquent girls and had frequent contact with their mothers; those in the second group were in a foundling home, where one nurse had the care of at least a half dozen infants. The difference was striking. When the infants had been confined longer than six weeks, the foundling home children showed symptoms of severe hospitalism, whereas the nursery children appeared to have suffered only slightly. The more severe condition of the foundling home babies is attributed in part to the practices of the institution but primarily to the loss of the mother. Spitz interprets his findings to have far-reaching implications.

> This study will offer the possibility of how to compensate for unavoidable changes in the environment of children orphaned at an early age. It will also shed some light on the social consequences of the progressive disruption of home life caused by the increase of female labor and by the demands of war; we might state that we foresee in the course of events a corresponding increase in asociality, in the number of problem and delinquent children, of mental defectives, and of psychotics. (Spitz 1945, 72)

A follow-up study published in 1946 and a series of films made even more vivid the consequences of separating infants from their mothers. Spitz described in detail the emotional condition of infants who had been separated from their mothers between the sixth and ninth months of age for at least three months. Infants who had appeared normal, happy, and outgoing during the first six months of life developed weepy behavior in the second six months. After a time, the weepiness gave way to complete withdrawal. During this period, if the infants were insistently approached, they would weep and even scream until they could withdraw again. The children lost weight, suffered from insomnia, and showed greater susceptibility to illness. In the foundling home, "notwithstanding the satisfactory hygiene and asepsis," thirty-four of the ninety-one infants studied died in the course of two years. Spitz termed their condition *anaclitic depression*—a depression resulting from the loss of the mother or a mother figure. The deaths of a third of the infants in the foundling home were attributed in most cases to their greater susceptibility to disease, but there were also cases of cachexia—a wasting away directly due to depression.

These reports helped to precipitate a revolution in the thinking about the care of infants (Kanner 1972). As a result, adoption procedures were changed around the world. Until that time babies awaiting adoption were generally placed in an institution for a prolonged period. It was thought that this would provide for the developmental unfolding of the baby's intellect and personality and thus facilitate an appropriate match with adoptive parents. That a great many of these infants never met the standards for intellect and sociability was considered a reflection of the morally inferior nature of women who conceived out of wedlock. In fact, many of these women and their paramours were suspected of being "psychopathic constitutional inferiors." This diagnostic label, used in the 1930s, crystallized the prevailing attitude that the misery of these people was to a large extent constitutional. Spitz's observations, however, produced a counterview: It was the experience of the institutionalized infants, he claimed, not their constitution, that had led to their developmental retardation and depression. Moreover, Spitz extended the consequences of hospitalism to the realm of adult abnormal behavior by suggesting that this early experience could produce "delinquent children, mental deficiency, and psychosis."

These assertions created widespread concern in 1945 because they were spoken at the end of World War II when millions of women had been in the paid labor force, their children often in the care of others. During the war, more than seven hundred thousand children in England alone had been separated from their parents. Foster families and institutions reported countless difficulties. Children could not concentrate, they wet their beds, and many even suffered from a moderate form of hospitalism (van den Berg 1972, 13–15). The maternal deprivation theory offered an explanation for these problems that was both simple and intuitively appealing.

Juvenile Delinquency and the Child Guidance Movement

The study of juvenile delinquency added another support for the maternal-deprivation idea. In 1927, Bowlby had become interested in the effect of the loss of a mother figure when he worked in a home for emotionally disturbed boys, and it was this experience that led him to become a child psychiatrist.[4] In 1936, he began work at the London Child Guidance Clinic, where he conducted the famous study later published as "Forty-Four Juvenile Thieves" (1944, see also Senn 1977, 6). Bowlby found that many of these delinquent boys, aged five to sixteen, had suffered early maternal separations, and he concluded that these separations had been the primary cause of their delinquency and "affectionless psychopathy." Bowlby proposed that the sudden loss of a parent or sibling or of care in a succession of foster homes might cause such a depression. His explanation was psychoanalytic: During infancy and early childhood, the ego and superego are not fully operating, and consequently the child is dependent on the mother to perform ego-functions for her or him. She permits the satisfaction of some impulses and restricts others. She is the child's ego and superego. Only when these primary relationships are continuous and satisfactory can the ego and superego develop.

Bowlby's work at the clinic had been made possible by a major shift in thinking about the problems of children, especially juvenile delinquents. Before the establishment of the guidance clinics, the mental hygiene movement had dealt with children's mental health problems primarily through education. Juvenile delinquency, thought to be the product of constitutional weakness, faulty training, and various environmental conditions such as poverty, was handled by the juvenile courts.[5]

In America, the psychotherapeutic approach to delinquency was launched by William Healy, whose report on his five years of research, published in 1915, was one of the first studies to explain juvenile delinquency as a result of psychological factors (Sears 1975, 15–18). In 1922, the Commonwealth Fund established the first child guidance clinics, with a mandate to prevent mental illness and treat maladjusted children. At first, the American clinics were characterized by both psychodynamic theories and the theories of the mental hygiene movement. By 1930, however, the influence of the mental hygiene movement had subsided, and understanding and changing intrapsychic factors became the primary goal of intervention, in part because of the increasing impact of Freudian ideas on the psychiatric profession.

The East London Child Guidance Clinic, the first of its kind in England, opened in 1927. Like the American clinics, it was run by a team of psychiatrists, psychologists, and social workers. It was the assumption in these clinics that neuroses, maladjustment, and juvenile delinquency were caused by the unsuccessful direction of emotion within the child. An influential British psychologist, Cyril Burt, published *The Young Delinquent* in 1925, providing support for this approach. Burt asserted that the problem of delinquency was caused by overly energized instincts that combined with defense mechanisms when the child met with conflict. Something unpleasant blotted from consciousness might return through other channels of discharge such as stealing, violence, running away. Burt claimed that he had found traces of such repressed complexes in 57 percent of his cases. Psychoanalysis, for Burt, was a kind of reeducation of the psyche to free repressed energy and rechannel it along socially acceptable lines.[6] Although psychodynamic theory was now dominant in treating children's problems, both the English and the American clinics were so uncomfortable with the psychosexual basis of Freudian theory that they revised it (Rose 1985, chaps. 4, 8).

Freudian Underpinnings

An understanding of Freudian psychology is crucial to understanding not only maternal deprivation but the deeper underpinnings of bonding. Freud's theory of personality begins with the unconscious, the area of our experience that is not normally accessible to us because its contents are in some way threatening and so have been pushed from our awareness. This repressed material can cause neurosis because it is out of conscious awareness and therefore cannot be rationally managed. The ability to manage this material is determined by our personality structure, which is formed in early childhood. Personality begins with a construct Freud called *id*. This is the original personality system from which the ego and superego develop. As life unfolds, the id continues to represent the inner world of subjective reality. It is entirely unconscious and is in close touch with bodily processes. It operates on the pleasure principle: it tries to obtain pleasure and avoid pain. The id is powered by a kind of psychic energy called instinct—a psychological representation of a bodily need. The hunger instinct, for instance, derives from a nutritional deficit in body tissues and is represented mentally as a wish for food. The id, which seeks only pleasure, finds tension painful and therefore is constantly seeking its reduction. The ego is a mediator between the internal needs of the id and the demands of reality. At first it has no energy of its own but gradually acquires more of the id's energy because it is successful in identifying reality, regulating the id, and therefore reducing tensions by satisfying the organism's needs. Freud proposed two general categories of instinct: the life instincts and the death instincts. The life instincts—hunger, thirst, and sex—are in the service of survival and reproduction. The energy of the life instincts is called libido. Freud also described death or destructive instincts connected with aggression and the unconscious wish to die.

Many therapists in the child guidance clinics were uncomfortable with this theory, especially the attribution of sexual impulses to young children, so they revised it. In England, the so-called new psychology originated at the Tavistock clinic, largely through the work of therapist Ian Suttie.[7] In *The Origins of Love and Hate* (1935), Suttie emphasized the need for love and companionship as an autonomous force in development, at least equal in importance to the sexual instinct and probably innately present in infants because of its evolutionary adaptiveness. He considered the need for love to be the basis for anxiety and *psychogenic mental disorder*." He claimed the neurotic was suffering from separation anxiety and argued that separation anxiety or loss gives rise in certain circumstances to hate, in others to grief, and in still others to psychosomatic illness.

The Children's Department of the Tavistock clinic was the model for other child guidance clinics in England that practiced the new psychology.[8] There was also an increasing focus on *object relations* and *ego psychology*. For Freud, gratification of instinctual drives was the primary motivating force in human behavior. For the object relations theorists, it was the love *object* or person with whom those drives were bound up that was important. Object relations theorists focused on the formation of the self in infancy through specific emotional relations with family members, especially the mother. They widened the horizons of psychoanalytic theory by proposing that gratifying and nurturing interactions with adults, as well as frustrating and depriving ones, could affect the child and its future style of interacting with people.

The early ego psychologists were led by Anna Freud, who worked with children and adolescents and focused on helping them to develop normal social responsiveness. Many of these early child therapists blamed a child's ego deficiencies on inadequate mothering, either the cool mechanical handling of the child or guilt-motivated overprotectiveness was deemed the primary cause of ego failure and psychosis.

The Clinics and Reform

The child guidance clinics in both England and America attributed disturbance in a child to disturbed family relations. The objective of intervention now was to preserve the family, to enhance its emotional vitality by acting on the inner feelings of family members. Social workers attached to the child guidance clinics would go into the homes and talk to the parents, looking for unconscious beliefs and wishes, feelings of guilt and disappointment, that might affect the child. Increasingly, in part because it was the mother with whom they had contact, it was her fantasies, desires, and conflicts they engaged in the therapeutic relationship. Thus maternal disturbances increasingly came to be seen as the root of the child's problems (Rose 1985, chap. 7). For example, psychiatrist David Levy (1931), a notable figure in the child guidance movement, conducted research that focused on problematic maternal attitudes of overprotection and rejection. (See also Levy 1933, 886–89; 1944.) The emphasis was on the rehabilitation of the child's ego that had been damaged by the conscious and unconscious feelings of the parents (especially the mother) in childrearing.[9]

After World War II, scrutiny of the mother-child dyad became even more intense. In England, Bowlby, who had been a psychiatrist for the army during the war, became director of the Children's Department of the Tavistock clinic, where he established a special research unit to examine young children's responses to separation from the mother (Bretherton and Waters 1985). The new social psychiatry and social research, as well as an increasing emphasis on psychoanalysis, marked the postwar department. The "Tavi" was especially concerned with problems of widespread family resettlement, the changing status of women and mothers, and the significance of child development (Dicks 1970, 143, 158).

At that time, parents of hospitalized children were allowed only very limited visits; there was concern that the children would become too dependent on adults as a result of being spoiled—and often their negative reactions to separation were seen in this light. James Robertson, a social worker trained as a psychoanalyst, worked with Bowlby in systematically studying the effects on young children of temporary separation from their mothers. According to Bowlby, "pediatricians were threatened by Robertson's claim [that such separations were truly devastating to the children] because it meant that their practices were harmful (they often liked to boast 'there is no crying on my ward'" (Senn 1977, 24). Robertson therefore acquired a movie camera and produced a series of films, the first of which was entitled "A Two-Year-Old Goes to Hospital," to demonstrate the problem. In the film, a little girl who has to go to the hospital for minor surgery for eight days is prepared by her parents and is received by hospital personnel with understanding. Yet the moment the child loses sight of her parents she becomes quiet, absentminded, less expressive, and occasionally rebellious. When she returns home, she is for a considerable time distant from her parents (Dicks 1970, 191). Robertson's studies showed the real despair children experienced as a result of separations. They were influential in changing the policies of hospitals, opening them up to parents and preparing children and parents for the experience.

By the time Bowlby had become director of the Children's Department, the new psychology had largely been replaced by a revised psychoanalysis that took as its central concern not so much the emotional relations among family members as the specific relationship between the mother and child, or rather the child's need to be mothered and the woman's desire to be a mother. According to this emphasis, the proper sex role for women rested on the desire to be a wife and mother. Any wavering from this goal was seen as penis envy, a serious form of gender maladjustment (Rose 1985, 190). Children who experienced faulty mothering and children who experienced separation from their mothers were found to be deprived.

Harlow's Monkeys

The study of maternal deprivation continued in another arena as well. In the animal laboratory at the University of Wisconsin in the 1950s, psychologist Harry Harlow's experiments with rhesus monkeys provided shocking evidence for the effects of maternal deprivation (Harlow 1958, 673–85; Vander Zanden 1978, 292–97). Harlow was an experimental psychologist who in the mid-1940s had accidentally discovered that infant monkeys—which he had isolated to keep them disease-free for experiments in learning—had become socially abnormal as a result. Harlow found that after six months of isolation in an environment that was sensorily stimulating but that lacked a monkey caretaker, the monkeys emerged frightened, maladjusted, and unable to mate. He pursued this line of research to establish the parameters of a critical period in infancy and found that the time limit beyond which there seemed to be no hope for recovery was a year of isolation. Monkeys that had been deprived for the first year of life could never play or copulate normally, did not know how to interact safely with other monkeys, and, if they happened to reproduce, were abusive to their offspring. Harlow concluded from these studies that mothering is central to normal development in all primates.

Apparently, the effects of maternal deprivation in infancy could be staggering. Harlow also explored the Freudian concept of drive reduction with these animal infants using surrogate or mechanical mothers. According to Freudian drive reduction theory, because mothers gratified their infants' hunger drive, the infants came to associate them with this gratification and therefore came to "love" them. Harlow developed a wire mesh dummy that provided milk and a cloth one that did not provide milk but offered merely tactile comfort. He found that when the monkey infant was obliged to choose, it selected the cloth dummy even though this could have meant starvation. Next Harlow attempted to find out how infants would react to these surrogate "mothers" when frightened; so he scared them with a wind-up toy. They sought refuge in the cloth dummy if they had been "raised" by it; those raised by the wire object clutched themselves, rocked back and forth, and threw themselves on the floor. This behavior was later said to illustrate the infant's need for an attachment figure (Vander Zanden 1978, 292–97).

Critiques of Maternal-Deprivation Research

By the mid-1950s, research on maternal deprivation had led to the reform of hospital practices, discouraged the placement of young children in institutions, and encouraged adoption or stable foster care. It was partly responsible for a shift in pediatrics from a sole concern with the child's physical well-being to include a concern for emotional well-being. The reader may now begin to wonder at the variety of phenomena the term maternal deprivation came to include. The fact is that the term actually covered a range of discrete phenomena, including the effects of institutionalization, stimulus deprivation, neglect, separation from a mother, multiple and discontinuous caretakers, and distortions in the qualities of caretaking—rejection, overprotection, ambivalence, and complete social isolation.

Indeed, in the ensuing decade, serious criticisms of the research began to emerge to address both methodological and conceptual problems. In 1955, Pinneau leveled a devastating criticism of Spitz and Wolf's (Spitz 1945; Spitz and Wolf 1946) studies of anaclitic depression, questioning everything from the validity of the measures used to assess the development of the infant, to preexisting group differences, to the allegation that infants appeared to have been added to the sample and studied for widely varying periods. It also appears that a large but undisclosed number of children who died in the foundling home may have been victims of a measles epidemic (Pinneau 1955a, 429–52). The major thrust of Pinneau's criticism concerned Spitz's inadequate descriptions of the social background of the infants, the exact location of the studies, as well as his observational methods. Subsequent studies, however, have provided evidence that Spitz's inferences regarding the links between maternal separation and depression were essentially correct (Emde 1983, 84–85).

A series of replies and counterreplies by Spitz and Pinneau in the *Psychological Bulletin* (Spitz 1955, 452–59; Pinneau 1955b, 459–562) is reminiscent of the exchanges between Kennell and Klaus and some of their critics. Spitz asserts that he used his experimental and statistical data merely as supportive evidence to illustrate his clinical findings, which would be sufficient evidence in themselves. Pinneau, however, finds even the clinical evidence contradictory. In a familiar postscript, he adds, "It may well be that the burden of blame for the uncritical acceptance of his work does not rest with Spitz, who has published his results as he sees them, but rather with those who have acclaimed his work and whose research training should enable them to make a critical evaluation of such reports."

Once again the parallels with bonding research are striking. The research of Spitz, like that of Kennell and Klaus, was used as a rationale for reforming hospital practices. It was accepted uncritically because it was politically useful. Prior to these studies, hospitals and nurseries tried to prevent infants from becoming too attached to any one caretaker in order to minimize the emotional trauma caused by the inevitable separation when the infant left the institution. Finally, the criticisms of both paradigms emerged from psychologists trained to do research. Spitz, like Kennell and Klaus, was primarily a clinician; Pinneau was trained in experimental psychology.

In 1961, Leon Yarrow, another experimental psychologist, called for a reconceptualization of the maternal deprivation concept, recognizing that the term incorporated several disparate phenomena, that *separation* and *deprivation* were not equivalent terms, and that the results of deprivation were not always as severe as the early studies implied. Bowlby's 1951 report was described as "a book that has become something of a bible for social workers." Yarrow emphasized the need for research to distinguish between perceptual, social, biological, and psychological types of deprivation, even though these types often tended to accompany one another. Mary Ainsworth (1962), a developmental psychologist and researcher on attachment, also voiced concern about seeing maternal deprivation as a specific syndrome with unitary causation.

Bowlby's Attachment Theory

In spite of criticism, Bowlby continued to focus on the importance of the mother-infant tie, and in the 1950s he began to develop a theory of attachment. *Attachment,* according to Bowlby, was a warm, continuous relationship with a loving mother or mother substitute. This bond, formed in infancy, would be the foundation on which all other relationships would be formed. Ainsworth applied some of Bowlby's ideas to her study of infancy in Uganda in 1955. Indeed, she was able to identify consistent types of signals in infants (and their mothers' responses) that could be said to constitute attachment. Using sixteen proposed measures, such as the child's crying when the mother left the room and delight upon her return, she found that most infants were attached by six months and began to fear strangers at about nine months. She also found three types of attachment: secure, insecure, and unattached (later changed to avoidant), which she saw as related to the level of sensitivity and responsiveness in the mother (Dicks 1970, 243; Ainsworth 1967). Although the psychoanalytic basis for attachment was difficult to prove empirically, Bowlby's colleagues, Ainsworth, Schaffer, and Emerson, began to document the course of attachment behaviors in early childhood, specifying the components and observing them under varying conditions. For instance, Schaffer and Emerson (1964) studied infants in Scotland and found consistent age-related attachment behaviors. Up to three months of age, infants seek arousal equally from human and nonhuman aspects of the environment; between three and seven months they become most responsive to humans; around seven months they prefer one person—the mother in 65 percent of the cases, the father in 5 percent, simultaneously the mother and someone else in 30 percent of the cases. At eighteen months only 13 percent displayed attachment to only one person.

In the meantime, Bowlby was formulating his attachment theory (Bowlby 1958, 350–72). It posed a *primary social bond*—the instinctual attachment of infant to mother—as the entire basis on which social relations are constructed. This attachment instinct was so fundamental that its influence could be noted throughout the animal kingdom. According to Bowlby, separations from the mother are disastrous developmentally because they thwart an instinctual need. Bowlby proceeded to define a series of developmental stages. During the first year the child displays a complete range of *attachment behaviors:* protesting his mother's departure, greeting her return, clinging when frightened, following when able. Such actions, he claimed, are instinctual and rooted in the fact that nearness to the mother is essential to survival.

In the 1950s and 1960s, Bowlby explored the ethological basis for attachment, which he found to be comparable to the process of imprinting in birds. Konrad Lorenz and others had observed that there is a critical period in some birds during the first few days of life when they attach themselves to their mother, responding to species-specific cues (Lorenz 1950, 1952). Once they have responded to this attachment figure, they will thereafter follow it and only it; they are *imprinted*. Moreover, this early imprinting has implications for later adult behavior. A jackdaw that had attached to

Lorenz in infancy later courted him in adulthood, dropping worms on his hat and trying to put them in his mouth and ears in a courting gesture. This adult bird behavior was taken as evidence that infant attachment had far-reaching implications for human adult emotional development (Bowlby 1969).

Bowlby postulated that there is an evolutionary basis for this attachment behavior, rooted in the survival instincts of the animal, that should not be disturbed. In humans, proximity-promoting behaviors such as crying, gazing, cooing, and gesturing were essential to the infant's survival as well as to later emotional development. Attachment develops when parents respond to these instinctual cues, and in parents, too, these responses are adaptive. Bowlby's use of the ethological paradigm gave his psychoanalytically oriented research on the effects of separation a far more empirical cast. This new, more acceptable theoretical base was found to account for the seemingly regular and universal patterns of maternal-child closeness that are evident in the first few years of life. Indeed, the accumulating body of observations with humans suggested that children go through regular stages of attachment during the first three years of life (see Bowlby 1969).

The Freudian Response

The response of psychoanalysts to this theory was predictably hostile, for it reduced complex human behavior to a simplistic formula and then linked it to psychoanalysis. Even Spitz charged Bowlby with having gone too far. In 1957, Bowlby presented "The Nature of the Child's Tie to the Mother" to the London Psychoanalytic Society, the first in a series of papers in which he applied his ethological principles to infant behavior. Anna Freud, the architect of child psychoanalysis, was not at the meeting but later said that she felt Bowlby's paper had sacrificed all the gains of psychoanalysis—namely, the principles of mental functioning and ego psychology—and offered little in exchange (Grosskurth 1986, 403–7). Both Anna Freud and Melanie Klein, another important theorist of child psychoanalysis, charged Bowlby with gross oversimplification in asserting that all pathology results from disturbances of the infant-mother tie. They pointed out that a variety of other early traumas could be equally at fault. Moreover, the infant might also develop a negative concept of his mother simply because, for example, she is unable to relieve his suffering. Other critics charged Bowlby with being too mechanistic. Even D. W. Winnicott, a popular psychoanalytically oriented pediatrician who saw childhood separation as a central problem, was apparently disturbed by the direction of Bowlby's thinking: He "ignores love and anguish, the real stuff of human life" (Grosskurth 1986, 403–7).

The Freudian theories of child development at this time were far more complex than the account Bowlby was proposing. Anna Freud adapted her father's theories to the treatment of children. She studied nursery school children as well as children who were in psychoanalytic treatment at her Hampstead clinic. Thus, her writings reflect theory and practice that evolved from work with and observation of both normal and disturbed children. Her writings had an enormous impact on child psychoanalytic treatment and on theories of child-drearing. She proposed that each child should be evaluated along several developmental lines, or dimensions of functioning, from dependence and self-orientation to self-mastery and healthy relations with others. Anna Freud also built on her father's original conception of the defense mechanisms by which the ego is defended from unacceptable unconscious material. She expanded the number of defenses and related them to developmental level, suggesting that some of these were adaptive and useful to the child's adjustment to the world (Dyer 1983).

In 1938, Anna Freud had emigrated to England with her parents to escape the Nazis. She and her friend Dorothy Burlingham established the Hampstead Wartime Nursery, later the Hampstead Child Therapy Clinic, for children who had to be separated from their parents or who were orphaned. Their nursery aimed to provide as much continuity in the children's lives as possible in a familylike atmosphere. The children were organized into groups of four or five, each with a staff "mother." Anna Freud argued that it was not simply the separation from their mothers that traumatized nursery children, but the manner of their separations. Wherever possible, she tried to make the separations gradual and encouraged the mothers to visit as often as possible. When the children could finally return to their families, Freud tried to maintain some continuity by staying in touch through letters and visits. In 1944, Freud and Burlingham published a book on the experience, *Infants without Families: The Case for and against Residential Nurseries*. They concluded that spending the first two years of life in a nursery is advantageous for "all those spheres of life which are independent of the emotional side of his nature; [it puts the child] at a disadvantage wherever the emotional tie to the mother or to the family is the mainspring of development" (p. 558).

Melanie Klein was another important figure in the British psycho-analytic community. A Vienna-born analyst, Klein espoused a version of Freudian theory that focused on the terrible impulses of the infant, such as guilt and aggression, as innate and inevitable. Emotional separation from the mother was also an inevitable and central infantile conflict, and mourning the central theme of emotional development (Riley 1983, chap. 3). Bowlby's concern, however, had not been with this inevitable emotional separating but with the preventable harm of actual separation from the mother. Klein and her camp were constantly at odds with the Anna Freudians of the American school, who continued to see psychosexual conflicts as forming the central problem of early development (Young-Bruehl 1988, 250). Both camps were at odds with what they viewed as Bowlby's reductionist account.

Attachment Research

Research on mother-infant attachment continued and in the early 1970s accelerated. At Johns Hopkins and later at the University of Virginia, Ainsworth and her associates worked with a large group of graduate and undergraduate students, including Michael Lamb. Ainsworth, in a study of twenty-six middle-class mother-infant pairs in Baltimore (1963–67), had developed a laboratory procedure called the *strange situation* to evaluate the attachment of one-year-olds. The strange situation test consists of a standard series of eight episodes during which the child's attachment to the mother is assessed. Some children show secure attachment: In the mother's presence they play comfortably, happily exploring their new environment; when she leaves, they are distressed; when she returns, they seek contact with her. Other infants show insecure attachment: They are less likely to explore their surroundings and may even cling to the mother; when she leaves, they cry loudly; when she returns, they may be indifferent or even hostile toward her (see Ainsworth et al. 1978, for an overview). Ainsworth, on the basis of her earlier observations of these maternal-infant pairs in the home, concluded that sensitive, responsive mothers who responded appropriately to their infants had infants who developed secure attachments. Insensitive, unresponsive mothers, mothers who attended to their babies when they felt like it but ignored them at other times, tended to have infants who became insecurely attached. Ongoing attachment research also finds consistent characteristics of children that correspond to the type of attachment they have formed. Alan Stroufe and his colleagues have found, for instance, that two-year-olds assessed as securely attached were enthusiastic and persistent in solving easy tasks and were effective in using maternal assistance when the tasks became more difficult. In contrast, their anxiously attached counterparts tended to be frustrated and whining (Karen 1990, 49). Ainsworth's strange situation test is the foundation of a multitude of studies that infer the type of parenting a child has experienced. It has been used by many other developmental psychologists to measure and compare attachment, as, for instance, in groups of children in day care versus home-reared children.

Although Bowlby's ethologically based attachment theory continued to flourish in a host of studies conducted primarily by American developmental psychologists, the concept of maternal deprivation described by Spitz and Harlow was dissected and found lacking. By the late 1970s, the findings of maternal deprivation research had been exposed as having been a product of iatrogenic conditions created by the practices of institutions and of overstated experimental examples. Michael Rutter, in a series of reviews, questioned a number of the research conclusions, pointing out once again that a variety of disparate phenomena—separation and deprivation, for instance—are often seen separately (Rutter 1972, 1974, 1979, 1981). Rutter asserted that antisocial disorders in children are usually due to the discord in families that leads to separation rather than to the separation itself. He emphasized the extreme deprivation often experienced in institutions and concluded that separations are not the most crucial factor in most varieties of deprivation.

Rutter asserted that most of the effects attributed to maternal deprivation were due to dysfunctional practices of the institutions, not merely to the lack of a primary caretaker or to a poorly functioning caretaker. The infants studied in institutions had often had as many as fifteen, even fifty, caretakers in the first two years of life. Moreover, these infants were stimulus-deprived. In the foundling home described by Spitz, for instance, the children lived in cubicles enclosed on three sides so that they were rarely able to see what was going on in the ward. About the only objects the infants had to play with were their own hands and feet, and they were left alone for most of the day. Moreover, it appears that many of the infants who died in Spitz's foundling home may have been victims of a measles epidemic. Regarding the effects of animal deprivation, Rutter points out that Harlow's infant monkeys were deprived of *all* animal contact, not just the nurturance of a mother.[10]

Another aspect of the maternal-deprivation concept that came into question in the 1970s was the whole idea of sensitive periods in development. There was growing evidence that organisms could recover from early trauma, and much of the research on behaviors related to these sensitive periods did not extend far enough into the subject's future to confirm the existence of later effects. Contrary to expectation, research also showed that the attachment of human infants did not seem to be harmed by the child's enrollment in an infant day-care center (see, for example, Kagan, Kearsley, and Zelazo 1978).

An analysis of attachment phenomena published by Lamb and his colleagues in 1978 (Rajecki and Lamb) pointed out that attachment theory was unable to account for such critical phenomena as the abuse of both animal young and infants, which does not appear to interfere with the formation and persistence of social bonds. Also, it was found that animal young and infants appear to form attachments to inanimate objects (styrofoam objects, cloth surrogates, and blankets), which do not of course respond. The attachment theory of Bowlby and Ainsworth, by contrast, claims that infants form secure attachments to individuals who emit appropriate and sensitive responses to their signals—that is, who are better mothers. Lamb also criticized Ainsworth's Baltimore study on methodological grounds.

Another study bringing into question the claims made for the importance of attachment was conducted by Reed and Leiderman (1983). Their study of twenty-eight Gusii infants in Kenya reared polymatrically suggested that attachment is a plastic phenomenon, not tied to a sensitive period or to a consistent primary attachment figure.

Finally, developmental psychologist Jerome Kagan has cast doubt on the way in which Ainsworth's strange situation test has been interpreted and is now applied. According to Kagan, the strange situation is not a reliable measure and thus much attachment research is flawed. The sample on which Ainsworth based this test was small and narrow. Moreover, the interest in attachment is mainly a sign of contemporary mores. Kagan claims that in the 1940s and 1950s the children now called "securely attached" were called "overprotected." He also argues that some children Ainsworth would label securely attached become upset when left alone in a strange situation because they have been trained for dependency. Kagan adds that many other differences seen in the attachment research may be partly the product of differing inborn temperaments. He cites studies indicating that children assessed as irritable shortly after birth are likely to be classified as anxious a year later. Children labeled avoidant may be simply constitutionally less fearful and therefore in less need of proximity to their mothers. Such interpretations challenge the core of attachment theory, that consistent parental availability and warmth result in autonomous children.

Regardless of the critical reassessments, attachment is still one of the major contemporary propositions about human development. In the past twenty years, mothers and infants have been observed as never before, with some researchers using videotapes and frame-by-frame analysis. Such work has tended to bolster and spread attachment ideas partly because it has demonstrated a level of attunement and communication between mother and infant that was not perceived before. During the 1960s and 1970s, however, research showed great variability in attachment and several attachment phenomena that were not consistent with the presumed importance of good mothering or good parenting. Mothers were not necessarily the primary attachment figures, and the bonds to abusing parents remained strong. Research showed, moreover, children whose mothers work do not experience attachment problems as a result of being in day care. Today the attachment concept has broadened almost enough to describe the successful development of babies being raised by multiple caretakers—a situation originally thought to cause maternal deprivation.

Maternal Deprivation, Attachment, and Bonding

The "discovery" of mother-infant bonding was but one branch of a convoluted network of theories urging the reform of institutions together with the reform of motherhood by suggesting that infants and mothers need to be near one another. Research conducted by individuals concerned with the plight of troubled children successfully altered institutional practices; it also helped to extend the authority of pediatricians over the emotional lives of children and their families. The precedent set by the child guidance clinics and by Anna Freud's attention to the importance of the family in treatment provided a rationale for extending pediatric care. In America, one of the first pediatric departments to develop a family-centered curriculum and clinic inspired by Anna Freud was at (Case) Western Reserve University in the early 1950s (personal interview with Kennell, June 1990). It was here that Doctors Kennell and Klaus (in the company of Dr. Benjamin Spock) developed their theories of parent management and childrearing.

There is no question that maternal deprivation and attachment theory made the bonding research possible. It established a set of assumptions about the primacy of the maternal-infant relationship and its profound effects on development and on the adult personality. It enhanced the legitimacy of claiming that research on non-human animal behavior can be analogized to human behavior. By now, however, the reader must be concerned that research that sets guidelines for parent-child behavior and for institutional policy is not to be trusted. How can we know what research is likely to stand or to be discarded? An understanding of the way paradigms function in science may be of some help. The story of the bonding paradigm is not unlike that of the maternal deprivation and attachment model.

Models and Reasoning in the Scientific Community

I n recent decades, philosophers of science have been discovering the extent to which science—long thought to be a purely objective process proceeding by strict rules of evidence, achieving an ever more objective account of nature—is actually socially constructed. Philosopher Thomas Kuhn, in *The Structure of Scientific Revolutions* (1962), maintained that the sciences develop through *normal periods* and periods of crisis or *revolutions*. This course of evolution is determined not only by rational factors, a course of proof and disproof, but also by group pressure, group competition, and prevailing cultural assumptions unwittingly shared by researchers. Kuhn does not deny the possibility of empirical progress, but he is interested in how paradigms shift: revolutions occur as a result of changes in the commitments of the researchers, not just in response to new or disconfirming evidence (Kuhn 1962). Of course, paradigm shifts are influenced by new empirical discoveries, and in fact one characteristic of the changes seems to be that a new empirically based explanation is entirely substituted for another. For example, in the mid–nineteenth century, tuberculosis was regarded primarily as a socially transmitted disease. In the 1880s, Robert Koch discovered the tubercle bacillus and its role in the disease. The causal attribution then switched to the bacillus and a new paradigm, the germ theory, came to govern a notion of causality that attributed specific diseases to specific agents (Susser 1988). It is also often the case that empirical evidence that would challenge the tenets of a paradigm—normal science—is ignored by researchers who are comfortable working within the paradigm. In the normal scientific period, problem solving is a bit like solving a jigsaw puzzle. The inspiring picture or model has already been drawn; the pieces, the empirical studies, merely need to be put into place, and the picture will be filled in.

For the bonding research, the inspiring models were maternal deprivation and attachment, which establish that mothers and infants have a biological need for each other and that interruption of this connection will cause harm to the young child. Far from being a revolutionary scientific idea, as its authors claimed, the bonding theory was simply the product of normal science within the maternal deprivation paradigm (see Kennell 1980). According to Kuhn, as research proceeds, anomalies begin to build and new theories are required. But researchers generally resist seeing the anomalies because they are comfortable with the normal science; they understand it, accept it, have reputations based on it, and so forth. In the case of maternal deprivation, attachment, and bonding, the claim could be made that the anomalies were abundant from the start. How can we account for the resistance to perceiving them?

Paradigms and Conservative Values

Both scientists and the public are likely to accept models that converge with their own view of the world. Scientific conclusions have a symbolic function above their actual scientific content, which affects the substance and conclusions of research. These social dimensions of research also have a political cast that has often favored the more powerful members of society. Bonding was ultimately used conservatively, despite the progressive intentions of bonding researchers to enhance women's birth experience and the early parental care of infants. The importance of women's intelligence, complex psychology, social and economic circumstances, not to mention the array of nonmaternal factors influencing a child's life, were lost to concerns about the presumed threat of women's instinctual power to shape their children. Research involving inherited characteristics and biological bases for behavior has contributed to some of the most conservative interpretations of human behavior because they can so readily be thought to show that the inferior status of certain groups is due to some inherent characteristic. For instance, the aspects of Darwin's theory of evolution that suggested that those creatures who were best adapted to the environment survived and therefore directed the evolution of the species were interpreted as favoring the abandonment and even the intentional elimination of the poor and minorities.

It seems that science plays an especially important role as a source of authority at critical moments in history when a system of exploitation is forced onto the public stage for analysis. At such times, elaborate justifications become popular and scientific evidence is stretched beyond the limits of empiricism. In the late 1960s and 1970s, in the wake of the civil rights movement, for instance, the issue of race, IQ, and the heredity of intelligence once again became the subject of a raging scientific controversy (Bleier 1984, chap. 2). The work of Arthur Jensen, purporting to show that blacks have, on the average, a genetically inherited IQ some fifteen points lower than that of whites, was published in the *Harvard Educational Review* (1969) and was taken seriously by many in the scientific community (see Kamin 1974; Loehlin, Lindzey, and Spuhler 1975). In the 1970s, when the feminist movement was exposing the oppression of women in our society, sociobiology, popularized by Edmund O. Wilson, Richard Dawkins, David Barash, and others, was used in this same fashion—to rationalize inequality and injustice. Sociobiology claims that certain human behaviors and forms of social organization are explicitly programmed in our genes because they are adaptive. These genetic tendencies include territoriality, racism, xenophobia, conformity, male aggressivity, female passivity and nurturance, and dominance hierarchies. Barash claims that sociobiology relies heavily on the biology of male-female differences and that nature itself appears to be "sexist" (Barash 1979, 283). Therefore, according to Barash, "it may be that human rapists in their own criminally misguided way are doing the best they can to maximize their fitness"— that is, to leave as many offspring as possible (pp. 30, 31, 55). Once again, like social Darwinism and the IQ studies, sociobiology provides the comfortable message that injustices and inequalities, racism and sexism, oppression and wars are natural and inevitable accomplices of human evolution, providing confirmation for those who find comfort in the status quo and its legitimation by science.

In addition to the popular reshaping of science to reaffirm the status quo, some scientists have themselves distorted and even fabricated data to perform these functions. For instance, investigations of Burt's studies of the genetic basis of IQ in his famous twin studies (1955, 1958, 1966) reveal that his findings were contrived (see chap. 3). Burt was a hereditarian and eugenicist. He was convinced of the rightness of his ideas and was exceedingly careless with the data. For instance, Burt's twin sample grew in each of the studies, from twenty-one pairs to fifty-three. The correlation between IQ and twins reared apart was given as 0.771 for all three studies and 0.944 for identical twins reared together through three different sample sizes—a virtual impossibility (Gould 1981).

Another case in which unconscious manipulation distorted the conclusions of a scientific study is found in the data from craniometry, a popular science of the nineteenth century. From his 1830 study of the relative cranial capacity of different groups of the human race, Samuel George Morton concluded that the largest average cranial capacity (and hence intelligence) was to be found among Caucasians, followed by Indians and then by black peoples. Women's brains were, of course, inferior. A reanalysis of the data shows that there is actually no mean difference between any of these groups and that Morton arrived at his conclusions not by the conscious manipulation of data but through a series of unconscious slips, inconsistencies, omissions, and miscalculations. Gould (1978) speculates that the unconscious manipulation of data may be a scientific norm rather than an exceptional phenomenon.

Is the bonding research part of this tradition of rationalizing the status quo by manipulating data to fit intuitive notions of how things are or should be—in this case, that women's biology determines their mothering behavior? The answer to this question is extremely complex. Certainly there was no attempt to defraud or deceive on the part of bonding researchers. Yet this research is like all scientific research in that it is socially influenced—by assumptions held by researchers of which they are unaware; by prevailing and unquestioned research paradigms; by the pressing need to find solutions to social problems; and by the dictates of professional groups. Kuhn has argued that the evidence scientists normally draw on is dictated by an overriding contemporary *paradigm,* a term he uses here to describe the guiding theoretical concepts of a science. The paradigm will shape the way in which any given generation of scientists construes a research problem. If the body is construed as a machine, it will be investigated as if it were separate from the mind, with its parts in mechanical relation to one another. The guiding theoretical concept underlying the bonding research is, of course, evolution, the idea that animal models are pertinent to the study of human behavior and that biologically based behavior is "good" because it is adaptive. More specifically, bonding research was embedded in the attachment paradigm, which helped to establish the supposition that it was *adaptive* for mothers and young children to be in close proximity to one another. Therefore, the problem of mothers who failed to care for their infants was addressed as a biologically based survival mechanism by researchers trained in psychology and medicine. (Had they been sociologists, they might have focused on the socioeconomic conditions that make it difficult for parents to raise their children, using the sociological paradigm to decide the questions to be asked and the methods used to investigate them.)

Interestingly, the bonding thesis was not primarily the result of an empirical discovery but rather of the researchers' need to solve a problem in pediatrics. In the mid-1960s, because of advances in medicine and medical technology, premature and sick infants were increasingly able to survive, their survival depending in part on their staying for long periods in neonatal intensive-care units separated from their parents. Many of these parents were also experiencing considerable poverty and social isolation. The discovery of bonding allowed parents into the previously off-limits NICU and promised to prevent subsequent problems of parenting. Bonding was also useful in addressing another growing problem: the critique of hospital childbirth leveled by the natural childbirth movement. Bonding served as a scientific rationale to free infants from isolation in the nurseries and give parents more access to their babies. Thus it helped to retain the alienated obstetric clientele. Bonding, then, was a product of conducting normal science within the maternal deprivation paradigm. New sociomedical problems were construed as a piece of the maternal deprivation puzzle. Maternal deprivation, as will become increasingly clear, is indeed a conservative fiction.

Conflicting Research Communities: Mediators of Science

The bonding research and its demise are the products of two differing paradigmatic communities. Most of the bonding studies were done in pediatric research units and were initiated, directed, and ultimately defended by medical professionals, primarily pediatricians interested in the newborn. Peter De Chateau, Hales, Kennell, Klaus, Korsch, Lipper, Betsy Lozoff, Minde, Seigel, Sosa, and O'Connor are all pediatricians.[1] Yet most of the criticisms of the research were initiated by psychologists or psychiatrists. Campos, Susan Goldberg, Herbert, Hwang, Lamb, Myers, Gail Ross, and Wladyslaw Sluckin are all psychologists. Chess, Leiderman, and Thomas are psychiatrists. Svejda is a Ph.D. in nursing. Note also that bonding research was first published primarily in pediatric medical journals. In the 1970s, the notable exception was a study published in *Child Development* by A. D. Leifer and co-workers that was an extension of the Stanford study started by Klaus in 1964. Its publication in a psychology journal may be in part explained by the fact that Leifer is a developmental psychologist; Leiderman had been trained as a research psychologist and did work in comparative psychology before he became a psychiatrist. Their methods were therefore more acceptable to those with psychology backgrounds. Leiderman also claims that developmentalists who had been trained in the 1940s and 1950s (and were heading the research journals in the late 1960s and 1970s) lacked good clinical training and were therefore suspicious and even jealous of the training of pediatricians and psychiatrists, especially in physical science[2] (personal interview with Leiderman, May 1990).

It was not until 1978 that *Child Development* published a bonding study by Kennell and Klaus that incorporated more of the criteria acceptable in psychology (Ringler et al. 1978). Child psychology journals opened up to some of the bonding research, although it remained primarily in the pediatric literature. Moreover, about two-thirds of the critiques of the bonding research were published in the psychology rather than pediatric journals. Lamb makes the point that the critiques were important not so much because of what they said but because of where they appeared. Herbert and Sluckin, who published an entire book criticizing bonding research, had little influence in the United States because they were British. Indeed, in 1989 Klaus claimed never to have heard of their book (personal interview, April 1987). The point is subcommunities in science (and their institutions) are mediators of scientific knowledge by determining what is acceptable. They influence what is considered a problem, structure the socialization of young scientists, and provide regular, organized outlets for the announcement of innovations through conferences and publications. Interestingly, according to Kennell when he and Klaus began their research on bonding, the pediatric community was eager to have information on neonatology and therefore had no difficulty publishing in pediatric journals. But for the bonding phenomenon to be accepted, it was essential to establish a biological basis and use a controlled design with statistical analyses. The standards of journals like *Child Development* were rigorous, much more so than those of the pediatric journals (personal interview with Kennell, June 1990). Leiderman claims pediatricians were generally not able to publish in the developmental journals because "developmentalists didn't believe in the pediatric paradigm. They didn't work with live sick people, or even at that time, with families." Moreover, Leiderman asserts that as a psychiatrist, he did not have to prove that there was a biological basis for bonding in order to have bonding accepted within the psychiatric and child development research communities (personal interview, May 1990).

In the same vein, according to Lamb, most developmentalists initially did not accept the research. At first they "ignored the claims and hoped they would go away" (personal interview, May 1990). They felt the claims had been greatly exaggerated. Kennell, in retrospect, also feels that they worded things in a way that was a little exaggerated. Their prime concern was to help mothers (personal interview, June 1990). The first published critic of the research, Ross (1980), had just received a Ph.D. from Harvard in human development in the late 1970s when she became concerned about the bonding research. A research psychologist specializing in attachment, she was connected with a regional NICU in a New York City hospital and became alarmed at how much bonding was being applied as a doctrine there. She was concerned for mothers who had had cesarean sections and for those with ill babies: "They had enough upsetting problems without being told there was something else they had to do, or as often, had failed to do. There was so much pressure! If women hadn't held their babies, they were being given Polaroid photographs to look at so they could 'bond.'" When she examined the bonding research, she felt it was "really not very scientific" (personal interview, May 1990).

Lamb claims that he had become alarmed in the late 1970s in talking to perinatal practitioners who said they were being "inundated by this bonding material." He found that "nurses were using bonding as a cudgel to beat OBs about the head" in an attempt to humanize their practices. "Medical professionals didn't have a training that encouraged them to be critical consumers of research." Lamb therefore began his assessment of the bonding research with this group in mind (personal interview, May 1990). He was joined in this endeavor by Swedish psychologist Hwang, then engaged in a study of early contact. Hwang claims that he was struck by the contrast between the rigorous standards required of his own research and the poorly derived data of the bonding research, for which such exaggerated claims were being made (personal interview, May 1990).

If Lamb was concerned about the pressure on perinatal practitioners to practice bonding, his criticism was also tied to the professional and status needs of developmental psychology. According to Lamb and Hwang (1982), "exaggerated claims about the importance of mother-infant bonding may well contribute to skepticism about the subdiscipline of behavioral pediatrics, a young subspecialty that currently needs to demonstrate its value to a somewhat hostile parent constituency. Behavioral pediatrics needs to demonstrate the standards and cautions widely respected in the scientific community." Korsch, a physician, closes her editorial commentary on Lamb's critique in the *Journal of Pediatrics* by stating, "There is also no indication that the credibility of behavioral pediatrics has been threatened by the work of Kennell and Klaus as was suggested by Lamb" (Korsch 1983).

The criticism, then, appears to have been the response of one scientific subcommunity to the politics of research in another subcommunity. In addition, the disagreement about the research is rooted in the divergent paradigms of these scientific subcommunities. The models of what is relevant to study and how to proceed in studying it are apparently related to the differing agendas of medicine and psychology.

Medicine and Psychology: Conflicting Paradigms

Medicine

What then of the controversy regarding research design and analysis? Why did the medical community consistently construe this matter differently from the psychologists? The pediatrician's training, first of all, emphasizes biomedical rather than biosocial research, empiricism as opposed to theory. Some of the early research by Klaus provides a useful illustration. Klaus was co-author of about a dozen, well-recognized studies on various aspects of hyaline membrane disease, a major cause of mortality and morbidity in the premature newborn. One of his early studies examined the composition of surface-active material isolated from beef lung (Klaus et al. 1961).

An excerpt from the report suggests some important characteristics that distinguish the paradigm.

> Beef lungs were perfused with saline via the pulmonary artery and ventilated with intermittent positive pressure via the trachea. After a short time, a thick white foam poured out of the trachea. The foam was washed with distilled water to remove most of the serum proteins and then dried at 5 degrees C. The dried powder was spread on isotonic saline in a modified Wilhelmy balance and surface tension was measured during compression and expansion of the surface film. This powder lowered the surface tension to less than 10 dynes/cm when surface area was decreased.

The first thing that strikes one in reading this is how concrete the elements of the experiment are. One action here results in another action there, both of which can be measured with precision. This biochemical research also represents a pervasive practice in science—the use of a simulating model to test and develop theories in domains that are clearly distinct from the domain of the model. In medicine, perhaps the most important simulating models are those involving animals and laboratory cultures. They have played major roles in helping us to understand disease processes and the effects of new therapies. In psychology, animal models have often served a similar function, although the boundaries of comparison have usually been less clear and more debatable than in the more circumscribed physiological models. For instance, laboratory animals, especially rats, were often used in American psychology, especially in the 1940s and 1950s, to study learning processes. The original impetus of this research was the desire to understand evolution more fully by comparing the behaviors of a wide variety of species. But the most frequent comparisons were made between rats and humans, a pursuit that was eventually attenuated because of its limited fruitfulness. (See Hilgard 1987, chaps. 10 and 11.)

Simulating models, analogous to the subjects they model, differ significantly from theoretical models. Molecular biologists think of their theoretical models as exhibiting genuine molecular structures and consider them to be realistic representations. In medicine, scientists make no claim that cattle or rats have anatomies or physiologies sufficiently similar to ours to serve as representations. They claim only that animals share enough relevant similarities to permit the testing of hypotheses that—because of ethical, legal, or time constraints—cannot be tested on humans (Albert, Munson, and Resnik 1988, chap. 6).

Yet models are essential. They can help to extend and modify theories to account for new phenomena. For instance, the billiard ball model of the kinetic theory of gases was responsible for advancing our understanding of the action of gases. The original analogy made the claim that billiard balls in random motion were like gas particles. This is not to say that they are in all respects like gas particles. They are hard and shiny, of differing colors, painted with numbers, and so forth. In fact, the properties of billiard balls that are not like gas molecules constitute a *negative analogy*. Motion and impact, however, are properties of billiard balls that we can ascribe to molecules in our model, and these constitute the *positive analogy*. Those properties we do not know about for certain form the *neutral analogy* and require further investigation. Thus, from a knowledge of billiard balls we may be able to make new predictions about the expected behavior of gases (see Hesse 1963; Leatherdale, 1974; MacCormac 1976).

In the case of bonding, scientists worked with the analogy between human and animal maternal behavior in the postpartum period. The discovery of mother-infant bonding sprung from Klaus's perception of an analogy. At the time he began to work with Leiderman, Clifford Barnett, and Rose Grobstein, he already had a special interest in sensitive periods regarding biological matters. If the mother took steroids during a certain period in fetal development, for instance, it seemed to interfere with the fetus's lung development. Klaus also pursued the research literature on the behavior of animals, especially goats, that would reject their offspring if postpartum separation occurred. He claims that what inspired him was the startling analogy with the behaviors of mothers of prematures who did not seem to see their babies as their own after they had been separated. He claims it was just like the animals he had been reading about (personal interview, June 1990).

Animal studies were being used to advance our understanding of mother-to-infant behavior. Yet both the neutral and negative analogies were quickly lost sight of in favor of a politically appealing, positive analogy between animals that reject their infants after a brief period of separation and human mothers who also reject their infants after a brief separation. From the start, however, the negative analogies were abundant. Klopfer, for instance, one of the animal researchers whose work with goats apparently sparked Klaus's hypothesis in the first place, wrote in 1971 of his attempts to identify the variety of complex hormonal and environmental mechanisms accounting for the bonding behavior of one type of goat. Klopfer makes no claims of parallels in humans. In fact, he underscores the complexity and variety of biologically based mechanisms that could account for the behavior of just one type of goat under investigation.

Presumably the editors of *American Scientist* who included a picture of a goat butting her kid away with the headline, "Portrait of a rejecting mother," believe that the description will sell copies since people will want to know more about rejecting mothers, thus contributing to the distortion of Klopfer's work. Klopfer points out, however, that a goat is one of the species of ungulates (one of the animal groups most likely to exhibit mother-infant bonding) having stable, specific, and rapidly formed bonds. Among roe deer, conversely, females will naturally adopt alien fawns while fallow deer do not. Moose mothers, particularly when they have lost their young, are prone to adopt aliens; they may even kidnap the offspring of other females. Although female goats generally limit their solicitude to their own kids, such behavior varies within species. According to Klopfer, these variations reflect experiential differences, while the differences between goats and moose represent phylogenetic adaptations related to different ecological and physiological demands. When feeding habits require great dispersion, as in moose or deer, there may be less occasion to exclude alien individuals than when the social group is compact (goats) and the animals are compelled to maintain a great deal of contact with one another. Given the extent to which the negative and neutral analogies abound even among ungulates and even within a single species of goat, it is astonishing how freely the positive analogy was extrapolated from the animal research.

Much of the research conducted by physicians involves the clinical assessment of the effects of some intervention or treatment on subjects who are ill. Often the treatment is partly derived from the simulating models. For instance, Klaus and his colleagues conducted a study in Singapore on twenty-seven newborns suffering from hyaline membrane disease (Chu et al. 1967). The authors attempted to define various aspects of the disease further and to develop an appropriate method of application and the correct dosage of two substances that they hypothesized would remedy the condition—dipalmitoyl lecithin and acetylcholine hydrochloride. Detailed scale drawings were presented of the equipment that was applied to the infants and a host of readings reported for each subject, together with dozens of tables. Statistical treatments, of course, are the only hope of successfully describing such data, and indeed the authors used three types of statistical analyses. Standard matters of research design—selection of subjects, selection of outcome measures, blindness, and so forth—are tied to the physiological treatment and assessment needs of the study and are described by the authors.

These physiological measurements present technical difficulties because it is important that procedures should not imperil the infant. Many methods were designed to be used within the incubator to ensure minimum manipulation, but these methods are therefore not standard. Also, any manipulation may alter the disease. For instance, one measurement required that the researchers stimulate the infant to cry; they had no means of assessing how this may have affected their results.

In spite of the myriad of charts detailing physiological and biochemical functions, all carefully assessed through statistical analyses, interpretation of outcome is based as much on clinical inference as on any statistically significant outcomes. The authors have sufficient knowledge of anatomy, physiology, and biochemistry to know which variables are of clinical significance regardless of statistical significance, and to some extent they use the research to illustrate what they feel they already know from their clinical analysis. (In clinical research, response to treatment, if pronounced, can be a form of evaluation in itself. Controls and statistical analyses, for instance, are not essential if the patient shows clear signs of recovery.) Indeed, in this study the authors cautioned against the overinterpretation of statistical significance as their measurements involved many complicating factors.

Most important, the clinical research is motivated by the wish to understand and treat disease. In this study, the subjects could literally live or die as a result of the treatment. The research depends on accurate, systematic, detailed observations of immediately occurring physiological processes. The researchers try to standardize the treatment as much as possible so that inferences can be drawn from it, but the focus is on saving the life of the patient. Their concern is to find out what works in their patients and how, which may involve changing procedures in midstream. They are not trying to establish universal laws for all subjects under consistent conditions. In fact, uncontrolled clinical observations concerning the signs, symptoms, natural history, and responses to therapy constitute a primary source of facts in clinical medicine. Clinicians are not always able to collect systematically all necessary data on a question and to follow a structured and rigorous approach before reaching a decision. They are often forced, in fact, to make rapid decisions based on incomplete data. Klaus's Singapore study illustrates some of the exigencies of clinical medical research.

Given the sheer complexity of the pulmonary ischemia study and the precision with which it was conducted, it is surprising to look back at some of the criticisms of the bonding research conducted by the same investigator and see that they refer to such matters as the selection of subjects, small sample size, double-blindness, the biased selection of outcome measures, performing numerous statistical tests but reporting only the significant ones, and artificially combining variables to create composite scores of questionable meaning. The Lamb group concluded that the Kennell and Klaus group "appears to have a weak understanding of some of the more thorny aspects of research design and analysis." After looking at Klaus's research on respiratory distress, one could hardly maintain that he lacked sophistication regarding research design and analysis. Yet the bonding studies are rife with methodological problems. How can these be accounted for?

One contributing factor may have been the mistaken assumption that conducting research to find typical patterns of behavior in adult humans requires an approach comparable to diagnosing and treating the physiological problems of young humans. Isolating a possible "pathogen"—separation in this case—and then treating mother-infant pairs by putting them together and observing the outcome is not like isolating pulmonary ischemia, treating it with surfactant and vasodilation agents, and measuring the outcome. The causes of mothers' behavior are at least as complex and varied as differences in personality, culture, health, socioeconomic status, education, and the dynamics of love and responsibility. The sources of children's development can hardly be confined to the behavior of their mothers; such things, moreover, are not visible in an experimental situation.

Using animal models to simulate discrete physiological processes is not the same as using animal models to explain the behaviors of human adults, who are capable of composing operas, orbiting satellites, and having nightmares. The concept of a sensitive period in fetal development that affects the development of the lung is physiologically based, and the variables are tangible and even quantifiable. A sensitive period affecting maternal behavior in a particular species of goat mother exhibits considerable variation, and the variables are not clear or quantifiable. To establish the existence, let alone influence, of a sensitive period in a human mother requires considerable analysis of evidence that is not concrete or discrete and is highly complex.

Case Studies

The work of Klaus's partner may also shed light on the problems of the bonding research. Before his alliance with Klaus, Kennell was concerned primarily with aspects of the doctor-patient relationship that were becoming increasingly important to pediatricians: how to deal with the parents of infants and children regarding psychological matters. In a 1960 *Pediatrics* report, "Discussing Problems in Newborn Babies with Their Parents," Kennell and Rolnick presented five illustrative case studies. The report is based on part of a wider study of childrearing directed by Benjamin Spock. Pediatricians, psychiatrists, child therapists, a psychologist, and a nurse functioned as counselors and medical consultants to twelve families, attempting to clarify some of the psychological factors of everyday problems about which parents commonly turn to pediatricians for help. According to the authors, the pediatrician always faces the dilemma of telling the parents of a newborn too much or too little about the child's medical problems. Clinical experience showed that early problems have a grave impact on the parents in how they handle the child and consequently affect the child's adjustment.

The case studies involved infants whose births were abnormal and illustrate the difficulties pediatricians have in knowing how to allay parents' fears, since people differ widely in their ability to express and handle anxiety. The following case illustrates how parents can displace and deny their fears about a premature infant's survival.

Case 2: The mother [asked,] "Isn't the head big?" When asked why she thought so, she mentioned a friend who had given birth to a hydrocephalic infant. She could then be reassured that her baby's head was appropriate for the size of the body. On the following day the pediatrician told her the baby had slight inward rotation of the feet. Her reaction was to enumerate infants she had heard of who had deformed feet and needed surgery. For the next 2 or 3 days she focused her attention on the child's feet exclusively and had to be assured that their condition did not warrant anxiety. . . . She was told that she could visit her child, who had been placed in an incubator in the premature nursery, as soon as she felt like it. She refused to do so until the infant had been fed. (There are some mothers who appear almost disinterested in first contact with their baby. Experience shows that in almost every such case this is due to great anxiety. This mother may have thought that her small baby would possibly look and be stronger after a feeding.) . . . Once she began feeding and holding her, however, the mother's fears seemed to subside.

After presenting summaries of the five cases, the authors express their opinions about the management of neonatal crises, based primarily on experience with many similar cases in the past and on the closer observation of the study cases. Among their recommendations are the following:

It has proved particularly helpful for the pediatrician and mother to look at the baby together. This gives her a chance to ask revealing questions, which often are not the ones the pediatrician had anticipated. The mother should be permitted to see the baby as soon and as often as possible as she receives reassurance from this far greater than words can give her. Treatment should be discussed in a simple manner. If a parent asks questions about tests, the pediatrician should satisfy the parent's curiosity but use terms they can comprehend. Almost every parent has been brought up in such a way that he [sic] reacts with guilt when something is wrong with his baby.

Kennell's advice is based on his personal interpretation of his experiences. The evidence for the validity of these principles is suggested only by the case studies. Case studies, however, are a prevalent form of gathering and disseminating information in medicine. They serve as forums in which doctors can state their opinions, based on experience, intuitive reasoning, and a host of idiosyncratic factors. Such opinions stand or fall on the basis of the confirmations or challenges that come from the experiences of other practitioners.

In 1966, Kennell (and Mary Bergen) published another report in *Pediatrics* that may also shed light on the problems of bonding research. Continuing to use information from the Spock long-term study of childrearing, the authors observed the reactions (primarily crying, clinging, and the intensified use of a comforting object) of young children to separations from their mothers in the course of ordinary family life (vacations, the hospitalizations of the parents, mother's employment). The mothers each met with a counselor for an hour every two weeks. Their accounts of the behavior of their children and direct observations of the babies by the counselors were discussed in weekly staff meetings. All of the children in this middle-class sample showed "conspicuous reactions to separation" no matter how close or how distant the mother-child relationship, the type or length of the separation, or whether it was the first or the fiftieth. The authors cite the work of Bowlby and Ainsworth as well as animal studies illustrating the importance of mother-child proximity in the early years. They do not describe specific cases that illustrate the damage done by separations. (One nine-month-old infant was hospitalized for depression, the apparent result of separation, but no further information about the cause or length of separation was given.) They claim, however, that separations have a "disintegrative effect." Part of the separation problem appeared to be mothers' failure to understand the separation reaction as well as their tendency to mistake it for spoiling. The researchers were also concerned about mothers who wanted to get away from their children—telling the counselors how satisfied they were to stay at home—then suddenly going to work or off for a week's vacation without consulting the counselor, who was their adviser in these matters. The authors interpreted their findings as suggesting that "separations of more than one or two days during the first year and a half to two and half years of a child's life are harmful" to the child, who is not meant to handle extended separations, "including full-time employment of the mother."

This study of separations is curious. It appears to involve something like a case study approach, but only the briefest excerpts of cases are presented. There is no discussion of how many children were separated or for how long. The interpretation of the separation reaction appears to be through the lens of the medical or disease model; the child's attachment behaviors, crying, clinging, and so on—seem to these authors to be signs of pathology. Yet there is no evidence presented to indicate what behaviors are actually pathological or why three days' separation or full-time employment of the mother constitutes a pathogen. It is not clear whether the standards for reporting on such research are lax or whether the research itself is lacking in criteria of assessment.

In an interview (June 1990), Kennell describes what he calls "the Cleveland syndrome of the 1950s and 1960s." He explains that it was standard at that time for mothers to stay at home and raise their children. However, because Cleveland was a rather dreary place with little sun and long winters, mothers often were depressed and their family physicians often recommended that they get away to Florida with their husbands for a couple of weeks. Kennell claims that while this was great for the parents, he would be faced with an eighteen-month-old child who would be terribly upset. The child would get angry, clingy, would not eat well, and would regress to an earlier level of development. Then the mothers would think what a "little stinker" they had. Kennell knew that this was really just the child's reaction to the separation.

In talking about the changes in standards and the sophistication of research, Kennell admits that those cases based on the Spock studies would probably not get published today.

The 1960 and 1966 Kennell publications are examples of clinical thinking; the cases are used primarily to illustrate what the doctors feel they know from their practice. (In this instance, Kennell's intuition is also primed by the maternal-deprivation paradigm. Without knowing the context in which these opinions were derived, it is hard to evaluate their relevance or validity. Kennell's diagnosis and treatment were based on clinical observation, informed by attachment theory, and by a particular clinical situation. Whether his conclusions can be verified or extended to other situations cannot be gleaned from the information given. One has to take it on faith.

Psychology

The attempt to diagnose and treat disease through physiological research, clinical studies, case studies, and observations appears to be the main element of the pediatric paradigm. Research is often a response to pressing problems of illness and doctor-patient relations. Research in developmental psychology, however, stems from an entirely different set of premises, although it should be noted that pediatricians and developmental psychologists have often worked together.

Child development research emerged at the turn of the century as part of an attempt to shed light on the process of the evolution of the species by studying the growth of individual members. The primary goal of child development research was simply to define normative, age-related behaviors for each stage of development. The research of Arnold Gesell in the 1920s, 1930s, and 1940s typifies this approach. Studying hundreds of children from a few weeks of age to adolescence, Gesell found that maturation proceeds in an irreversible order of stages—a child crawls before walking, walks before running, and so forth—and that these stages occur at regular age intervals. Of course, the overriding question of developmental psychology is, what shapes the behavior? How much is due to biological factors—maturation, genetics, instinct—and how much can be accounted for by environmental factors, by learning?

Broad principles of learning in children were portrayed, for example, by the work of J. B. Watson in the 1920s and 1930s. Watson proposed manipulating environmental stimuli and then measuring the behavioral responses of the subjects. He made great claims for the capacity of conditioning to shape behavior. In the 1940s and 1950s, psychoanalytic thinking was also applied to an understanding of child development and parent-child relations. Principles of breast-feeding, toilet training, and guidance through the Oedipus complex were advanced, based on a knowledge of universal psychosexual stages of development. In the 1960s and 1970s, the focus shifted to cognition with the work of Jean Piaget, who described the stages of intellectual progress proceeding in invariant age-related order. Also in the 1970s there was a burgeoning of infant research, using sophisticated new laboratory methods, which began to uncover the remarkable capacities of neonates to take in and respond to their environment. All of these research theories and methodologies were applied to the task of mapping child behavior, which was thought to unfold in universal age-related sequences and to be rooted in the evolution of the species. The ultimate goal was not only to identify and understand these age-related characteristics but also to tailor age-appropriate childrearing and educational practices based on the knowledge of broad principles.

Because of the concern with age-related behavior, much research in developmental psychology has been longitudinal, following the same children over a number of years. In addition to controlled experimental studies, sometimes involving a microanalysis of behaviors, research in developmental psychology typically has included naturalistic observation, often in the home and school and sometimes case studies, although case studies are more common in child psychiatry, a field that intersects both child development and pediatrics.

Child psychiatric research more closely resembles the pediatric paradigm in that it is clinical, attempting to define, diagnose, and treat disease. Case studies are often used, and clinical inferences are made based on both the tenets of psychodynamic theory and a standardized classification system of disorders in which a comprehensive approach to etiology and treatment is provided.[3] The most empirical side of this paradigm is in the realm of psychological testing, where standardized inventories are used to diagnose personality problems.

In looking at the problems of the bonding research, it appears that Kennell and Klaus and their pediatric colleagues may have been operating out of assumptions different from those of their psychologist critics regarding what constitutes legitimate research. It may be that in transferring their biomedical research training and experience to research that addressed emotional matters they did not realize that the laws of evidence so trustworthy in physiology and biochemistry were inadequate to assess the psychosocial complexities of individuals, which are less immediately evident or manipulable. It also may be that for practicing physicians, carefully constructed research is secondary to knowledge based on clinical inferences, which is the art of medicine. Research may be used to back up or illustrate what doctors feel they already know. Although Kennell's previous research did address the more psychological realm of parent and child psychiatry and doctor-patient relations, it appears that the criteria for knowing were rooted in problems of practice rather than an assessment of universal behaviors. Pediatricians generally do not have much training in research design and analysis unless they specialize in research. Klaus was specially trained in physiological research at the Cardiovascular Research Institute in California in the 1960s. Kennell, however, had the standard medical education of a pediatrician, with no formal training in research design (personal interview with Kennell, June 1990).

Certainly the pediatric paradigm, as practiced by Kennell and Klaus, was inadequate to address the problems they were trying to solve. Motherhood and family relations were treated as if they could be reduced to biologically based phenomena, varying quantities of which could produce regular changes in people's lives. Each mother-infant pair was also treated as if it were a clinical case for which a medical treatment could be prescribed based simply on the opinion of the doctor. The emotional problems of parents, however, do not have straightforward solutions like the physiologically based medical problems that pediatricians are trained to treat. The problems Kennell and Klaus were addressing were not likely to be solved by developmental research; they needed immediate solution, not years of research to establish broad principles. Kennell notes that when he and Klaus would attend meetings with pediatricians and developmental psychologists, the pediatricians were always looking to apply new research information to their patients. Developmental psychologists, however, had a terrible time thinking of applications (personal interview with Kennell, June 1990). The need for a truly hybrid paradigm, a behavioral pediatrics, is evident.

The Problem of Analogies

If the pediatric paradigm was not adequate to the task of dealing with the complex emotional and social problems of human beings in the bonding research, certain theoretical aspects of the model also got in the way of assessing the soundness of the research. All scientific theory is based on analogy; it gives to one set of phenomena (the body, for instance) a name or description that belongs to another (the machine, for instance) based on a proposed set of similarities between the two. In this case, the semantic and iconic properties of the analogy overpowered the paradigm so that bonding was eventually mistaken for the things it was first thought to resemble in some respects—animal instinct and glue.

The use of animal models in medicine can be deceptive when the simulating models appropriate for physiological processes are assumed to have equally valid simulating properties for human behavior. Both Kennell and Klaus still believe that there is a biologically based sensitive period in women immediately after birth when they are primed to accept or reject their infants. They still find the animal models compelling—the studies of Rosenblatt with rats and the studies of ungulates previously cited. They also believe that new studies monitoring hormonal shifts in women postpartum, noting the relation of oxytocin and estrodial to the letting down of breast milk and the expulsion of the placenta, could be useful in establishing the existence of bonding in women. They add that they had several reasons for not monitoring women's hormones in their original studies. One was the great difficulty of doing so in a real-life hospital setting; another was that they did not know which hormones to monitor. Finally, they were initially surprised by the group differences they found and felt them to be sufficient evidence in themselves (personal interviews, May–June 1990).

The profound effects that physiological interventions can have in the neonatal period may also have primed the doctors to find similarly critical psychological effects in this period. Klaus claims that he saw the biological basis of bonding to be a system very much like the first breath of the neonate: there are multiple biological switches that turn it on, just as there are multiple switches that lock mother and infant together for the survival of the species. In the same vein, there are multiple switches that lock mother and infant together for the survival of the species. Klaus also indicated that he was inspired by the comparative information about birth practices in other cultures, about which both Leiderman and Barnett (an anthropologist) were knowledgeable. The three met regularly as a kind of study group to talk about perinatal problems and practices. Klaus was spurred by the anthropological examples to bring to the group examples from animal studies. The three were, in effect, building a theory by analogy to explain the strange problem of mothers rejecting their newborns (conversation with Klaus, June 1990).

In addition to the "instinctual" analogy, bonding is metaphorical in another sense. It refers to the connecting of molecules in certain chemical reactions, as in the adhesive action of glue. Inferentially, the bonding-mechanical parallel is therefore also drawn, which is quite different from the instinct-based comparison rooted in biology and evolution yet similar in that both metaphorical roots suggest automaticity. Underlying this similarity is probably the fundamental characteristic of technological society—the pursuit of efficiency.

Finally, there is also a connotation deriving from anthropology, which refers to social connections between people based on kinship, social roles, economics, and group survival functions. This connotation broadens the bonding metaphor even further, suggesting that, like other human relationships, bonding is the result of social connections rooted in some mutually beneficial social function.

Science contributes to the shape of our thinking, but society's attitudes and demands upon the work and thought of scientists in turn help to shape the scientific enterprise. Models and metaphors in science must therefore function to help scientists organize and analyze data, but they are also essential to the scientist's credibility: her or his ability to communicate scientific ideas to the public that will be acceptable.

In the contemporary case of mother-infant bonding, the instinctual, the mechanical, and the anthropological analogues have overpowered their subject and blinded both the professional and lay community to the ways the relationship between mothers and their infants in the postpartum period is *not* like that of nonhuman animals, *not* like the mechanical action of glue, *not* like the connecting of molecular particles, and *not* like the functional underpinnings of social relationships in general.

The Didactic Function

The concerns of philosophers of science with the uses and misuses of metaphor in science seem particularly apt when one considers the role metaphor has played in organizing and popularizing modern science. Over the past century, science has increasingly supplanted religious authority as a source of understanding. This new system of authority has provided modern social thought with a vocabulary and a supply of images to explain, justify, even dictate, social categories and values, and provide clear ideal social types.

Popular analogues have been especially useful in establishing child-rearing advice. At the turn of the century, pediatric advice shifted from a sentimental and indulgent attitude toward children to one of regimentation and sternness (Stendler 1950, 122–34). According to Stendler, the key to producing an ideal adult was regularity, imitating the rhythm of industrial life. America was entranced with the industrial system, which could produce goods in massive quantities with less labor, make trains that ran on time, and create machines that could do the work of many. Scheduled feedings and developmental milestones became essential features in pediatrics and developmental psychology, partly because they evoked the efficiency, power, modernity, and progress of American industry.

Bonding also worked as a didactic and explanatory metaphor because both the mechanical and the biological metaphors are well suited to the principal means by which twentieth-century Americans comprehend their world. Bonding derived social authority from its ability to address certain contemporary sociomedical conflicts: the unnaturalness of hospital childbirth—which should be governed by women's biology yet retain the benefit of technological advances; the ability of medicine to ameliorate the difficulty of childbirth yet not being able to; and even the disintegration of the nuclear family while retaining its empirical authority. The formula, however, ends up being a rationalization. It dodges the conflict between medical authority and parental control over childbirth and the socioeconomic and psychological causes of family failure and child abuse. It does not, however, cost money or jobs and essentially preserves the status quo.

The case has been made that science could not proceed without models and metaphors. According to some philosophers of science, however, a metaphor goes through a series of stages. At what might be called birth, the metaphor makes a very unconventional analogy. Keeping babies with their mothers from the moment of birth (instead of taking the babies immediately to the nursery to protect them from infection) is not simply a matter of allowing mothers to hold their babies and get to know them. It is like goats and glue—mothers and babies are bonded, imprinted or glued. An automatic process has occurred as a result of the proximity. When the metaphorical distinction is lost—indeed, when the metaphor becomes a new term—the metaphor is dead. Mothers are not just holding their babies and getting to know them; they are getting bonded. The word is no longer a metaphor; it is a new word. Its history and the neutral and negative analogies are lost. The vagaries of a mother's love for her child and her motivation to love, as well as the probable outcome of that love in terms of the child's character, are no longer presumed to elude understanding or control. Does this loss of distinction enhance the progress of knowledge by helping us see the phenomenon in a new and more useful way? Or does it trick us into thinking that we know something we do not actually know? Do we know something fundamental about mothers and infants that other cultures do not know?

Our concept of the maternal-infant relationship is not universal. The Balinese infant is at first called "caterpillar" or "mouse," an analogy derived from the observation of nature. If it lives for three months, it is given a human name (Mead and Wolfenstein 1955). In Western Europe, up to the fifteenth century, babies were not named until they had survived the first year (Ariès 1962). In twentieth-century America, infants are named at birth if not before. In fact, increasingly, the establishment of parent-*fetus* relationships is becoming integral to the standard childrearing process. How did this twentieth-century belief in the importance of parents establishing a close relationship with their infants at the earliest possible moment arise? Is it distinguished from other customs as being a truth, rightly overturning previously held beliefs based on improved evidence? Is this early acceptance on the order of the discovery that the Earth actually revolves around the sun rather than the previously held opposite belief? Or is it simply a culturally relative custom, as useful as the threat of jinnis or the evil eye in keeping the energies of parents focused on taking care of their babies? The problem in answering the questions, for the moment, is that the analogy has become so established that no one is interested in seeing where the similarities end—how mothers and babies are not like goslings or goats or glue—how fathers are not like mothers, families are not like hospitals, and so forth.

Every aspect of the life cycle, from birth to puberty to sickness and death, demands meaningful explanation. These universal realities inevitably find explanations consistent with a society's worldview. In Europe and America, these explanations have assumed increasingly scientific forms since the seventeenth century. Almost every American social problem has attracted scientific discussion: the role of women, ethnic differences, sickness, the effects of poverty, even how to rear children. So our contemporary framework for understanding the education and treatment of infants derives not so much from observing nature, as in the analogy of the little worm or bug, nor from the spiritual realm, as in the case of jinnis and the evil eye, as from science. There have always been ideas about protecting children from harm. One cannot help but wonder if our notion of mother love, which appears to have migrated so far from our understanding of complex human feelings and a network of human relationships, has not joined the realm of cautionary tales and folklore.

Jinnis and the evil eye may be useful beliefs in a nomadic society in which toddlers could easily lose their lives by wandering off or even be snatched away by strangers. Large numbers of children in our society fail to thrive and are neglected and even abused by their own families, where divorce is also frequent. Often these children grow up to be destructive to themselves and to others. Moreover, twentieth-century American society increasingly sees its children as burdensome. Perhaps bonding constitutes a custom that reminds us to bind ourselves to one another for our childrens' sake in a time when there is great danger that our relationships will come apart and that our children will therefore suffer.

Overinterpretation of the bonding analogy supported established traditions in medicine and psychology and helped to resolve, at least temporarily, certain pressing social conflicts concerning the organization of hospital childbirth and the prevention of infant abuse. Perhaps most important, however, bonding enhanced the idea of mothers as the all-powerful sculptresses of their infinitely malleable infants. Ultimately, bonding is highly efficient, the fundamental goal of a technological society. As a conservative fiction, bonding is embedded not only in science but also in the ongoing social construction of motherhood and infancy. It has ultimately been accepted because it fits so well with these idealizations.

Although I have examined here those essential processes of reasoning in medicine and psychology that contributed to the controversy regarding methodology and real distortions of thinking, I return to the question I raised at the beginning of the chapter about the unconscious distortion and interpretation of data. The belief that infants and children are so profoundly shaped by their mothers that a few hours of contact with them could inoculate the babies from harm—even enhance their lives for years to come—would seem to border on magical thinking. Yet the idea was readily embraced as a scientific truth because it fit so perfectly with the presuppositions about women and infants that had been socially constructed over the course of a century and a half and were threatening to come undone in the early 1970s. Bonding had an intuitive appeal and the data may well have been gathered to confirm it.

Constructing Motherhood and Infancy

The research on bonding was a response to situations created by the practice of medicine. The solutions to those problems were conceived within a tradition of scientific inquiry that necessarily restricted the focus of reasoning and was ultimately inadequate to the task. In addition, the thinking of the bonding researchers was also influenced by a pervasive ideology of motherhood that formed the basis for powerful misconceptions regarding the sources of their patient management problems. A genuine redress for their problems under these circumstances was impossible as the researchers confused the solution to real institutional, social, and economic conflicts with prescriptions for the behavior of women.

Our understanding of the relationships of mothers and children rests far more on a set of ideas that are shaped by our culture than by empirical evidence. Ideas of motherhood and infancy have shifted in content from culture to culture and in our own society from century to century, even decade to decade. For instance, in Japan, especially before World War II, it was considered the traditional task of the mother to shape her infant's too-independent nature into a more cooperative dependence. In adulthood, the individual should subordinate himself to the group; interdependence was and is valued in the adult world. The American infant, by contrast, is considered too dependent, needing to be artfully guided toward separation and independence. In adulthood, the individual stands out from the group—individuality and autonomy are valued (Kagan, Kearsley, and Zelazo 1978, chap. 2).

In America childrearing experts of the 1920s and 1930s said that a mother was endangering her infant's development if she picked the child up and cuddled her when she cried. Such behavior "spoiled" her, even trained her to continue to cry. Her own nature was not to be trusted. Inspired by the efficiency and productivity of American industry, the experts proclaimed that the mother's goal should be to teach her child discipline and regularity from the start by scheduling the child's behavior (Ehrenreich and English 1978, chap. 6; Stendler 1950; Wolfenstein 1953). In the 1940s, a dramatic shift took place when it was "discovered" that infants required constant affection and proximity to their mothers who should respond to their every need. A mother's failure to provide such responsiveness, it was said, would cause neurosis and even criminality in her child later on. In the 1920s and 1930s, motherhood had to be learned. Women were encouraged to seek higher education in order to prepare themselves adequately for motherhood. In the 1940s, the opposite was true; it was common sense and instinct that would guide them.

Such variable constructions of motherhood and infancy are inevitable. Every society needs models of perfection to serve as moral guidelines for behavior. Before the twentieth century, such ideals originated in the Puritan religion; in the twentieth century, the authority by which such models are established has been science. Yet, as we are beginning to see, science does not exist in a cultural or historical vacuum. As researchers pursue the issues of early maternal child togetherness, they do so from the vantage point of a long-standing mythology regarding the proper role of women and their relation to their children, which began in earnest with the nineteenth-century cult of true womanhood, in which women were supposed to be guardian angels of the hearth.

The Cult of True Womanhood

The ideal of the hearth angel first appeared in the 1830s, largely in response to the industrial revolution and the increasing commercialization of society. Until this time, there was no stigma attached to women who owned businesses or managed farms. Although the colonial woman bore an average of eight children, the care of infants was not necessarily the work of the biological mother. Wet nursing could be done by strangers. Even though the care of infants was treated as a physical, impersonal, and natural process, the raising of children was virtually reduced to an economic one. Once children possessed the ability to follow directions, they were dressed as little adults and put to work for the household in jobs appropriate to their sex. Active parenting, then, was not women's work exclusively but was shared by the sexes. And since parenting essentially involved putting children to work at the jobs they would perform as adults, parenting was often conducted by nonfamily members outside the home (Matthaei 1982, 38–39).

The increasing industrialization of a previously agrarian society had caused a split between the domains of men and women. The traditional productive skills of women—textile making, garment making, and food processing—passed to the factory system along with the men who left the home for industry. What then, was to keep women from entering the world of industry and leaving the home behind? There were proposals for communal dining halls and housekeeping and child-care services so that women, too, could join the wage labor force. The factory system was brutal, and it was feared that these commercial services would turn out to be extensions of the hated factory system. Moreover, to take women from the household would be to take away the only thing that cushioned men from psychic destruction in the rough world of the marketplace (Ehrenreich and English 1978, 23).

As women were not to be paid for their work at home, it was important that there be a credible and compelling rationale for their staying in the home. Gender identity provided the perfect incentive (Degler 1980; Ehrenreich and English 1978; Lasch 1977; Welter

1979; Wishy 1972). Increasingly, women were persuaded that their femininity was contingent upon their being the angel in the house. Creating a haven in a heartless world was their appropriate vocation. The public world of commerce and willful self-interest was said to be separate from the private world of the home, which had become the repository of puritan values and the special domain of women. Accordingly, these polarized values began to be attributed to gender; men were rational, competitive, and self-interested, while women were altruistic, tender, and intuitive.

In her study of the cult of true womanhood between 1820 and 1860 in America, historian Barbara Welter (1979) describes the emergence of this ideal and its relationship to economic and social changes in the society. In this era the nineteenth century man was "a busy builder of bridges and railroads, at work long hours in a materialistic society." The religious values of his forbears were neglected, and "he occasionally felt that he had turned his new land, this temple of the chosen people, into one vast countinghouse. But he could salve his conscience by reflecting he had left behind in woman all the values he had held so dear and treated so lightly" (p. 177). In the cult of true womanhood presented by the women's magazines, gift annuals, and religious literature of the nineteenth century, there were four cardinal feminine virtues: piety, purity, submissiveness, and domesticity. Woman would be "another better Eve, working in cooperation with the Redeemer, bringing the world back from its revolt and sin" (pp. 177–79).

The true woman's place was unquestionably by her fireside. According to Mrs. S. E. Farley, writing in one of the women's magazines, "the true dignity and beauty of the female character seem to consist in a right to understanding and faithful and cheerful performance of social and family duties." Sacred scripture was used to confirm these views. "St. Paul knew what was best for women when he advised them to be domestic," said a Mrs. Sanford in another magazine. From her home, woman performed her great task of bringing men back to God. *The Young Ladies Class Book* was sure that "the domestic fireside is the guardian of society against the excesses of human passions." *The Lady at Home* expressed its convictions in its title and concluded that "even if we cannot reform the world in a moment, we can begin the work by reforming ourselves and our households—It is woman's mission." (p. 187).

Woman would be elevated too, by her role as mother. "My friend," wrote Mrs. Sigourney, "if in becoming a mother you have reached the climax of your happiness, you have also taken a higher place in the scale of being." The Reverend T. N. Danforth pleaded in *The Ladies' Casket*, "Oh mother, acquit thyself well in thy humble sphere, for thou mayest affect the world." America depended upon its mothers to raise a generation of Christian statesmen who could say, "all that I am I owe to my angel mother." The mothers must do the inculcating of virtue since the fathers, alas, were too busy chasing the dollar. Or, as *The Ladies' Companion* put it, more effusively, the father, "weary with the heat and burden of . . . [the] acquisition of wealth, the advancement of his children in worldly honor—these are his self-imposed tasks." It was his wife who formed the infant mind as yet untainted by contact with evil "like wax beneath the plastic hand of mother" (Welter 1979, 195).

Women who asked for greater scope for their gifts were not considered women. "They are only semi-women, mental hermaphrodites," according to the Rev. Mr. Harrington, who knew the women of America could not possibly approve of such perversions. But even while the women's magazines and related literature encouraged this ideal of the perfect woman, forces at work in the nineteenth century impelled woman herself to change, to play a more creative role in society. The movements for social reform, westward migration, missionary activity, utopian communities, industrialism, and the Civil War all called forth responses from women that differed from those she was trained to believe were hers by nature and by divine decree. Real women often felt they did not live up to the ideal. Although some women changed, the mystique of true womanhood persisted through the Victorian era, leaving considerable guilt and confusion in its wake.

The emphasis on gender differences was echoed in the period's growing concern with childrearing. For the first time in American history women were singled out as the primary agents in the development of their children's character. In Jacksonian America, as fathers increasingly left the home for work, a reappraisal of American family life was taking place. In the accompanying tide of domestic reform, each woman was to "acquire a discipline and knowledge preparing her for a great calling." The mother was the obvious source of everything that would save or damn the child; the historical and spiritual destiny of America lay in her hands (Wishy 1972, 28).

Although the new focus may have been on mothers as agents of their children's destiny, mothers were not exactly left in charge of their children's upbringing. They received abundant advice from the primary source of childrearing expertise of that time—the clergy. Throughout the eighteenth century and into the first half of the nineteenth, parents turned to the church for advice about how to raise their children. If motherhood was a constantly emerging cultural construction, so too was the infant whose very nature was said to necessitate redemption through the Christian church. During the eighteenth century the prevailing puritan view was that infants were born full of the devil. As Jonathan Edwards put it, they were "little vipers." Happily for children, by the early 1800s, a revised view held that infants were born pure and innocent. In the first case, the clergy would help parents discipline their children's ungodly willfulness and even "beat the devil out of them." In the second case, clergy would help parents to protect their children from corruption by an evil and increasingly secular society (p. 11). In either case, infants were seen as creatures in need of redemption, and the authorities who claimed to know how to guide this process were members of the clergy. Parents were especially receptive to these childrearing strictures because parenthood had been idealized by the church and also because Christian belief assumed one's own lack of self-worth and constant striving to improve oneself (Dally 1983, 92).

In the 1830s, the new emphasis on women's home and child-minding role inspired an increasingly secular advice literature (Wishy 1972, 29). The first widely popular guide for mothers was published in Boston in 1833 by the Reverend John S. Abbott. Called *The Mother at Home,* it was still permeated with the Calvinist view of children as little tyrants. The aim of rearing was to break their willfulness and force them into a mold of high conscience, piety, respect for authority, and a deep sense of responsibility. *The Mother at Home* represented a shift in disciplinary method from the use of physical punishment to that of withholding love (Wishy 1972). Another repository of the new "nurture" literature was *Mothers' Magazine,* founded in 1833 to show "the best method of regulating the temper and disposition of children and to communicate to mothers the full importance and responsibility of their tasks." A major goal of this and similar magazines was to "tie the child to the mother as tautly as possible."

The American mother was now placed under the sternest pressure. She was to give up wealth, frivolity, and fashion, conquer weakness, sloth, and insensitivity, and acquire a discipline and knowledge that would prepare her for her great calling. She was to be "constantly at the center of the child's life and take the most minute interest in all his activities (p. 32). By 1840, maternal associations formed by women who had embraced the ideology were encouraging rededication to the holy, healthy hearth. *Parents' Magazine* and *Mother's Assistant* published frequent glowing reports from members who were convincing their children of their sinfulness. One story told of a poor convict fated for prison since youth because his mother had not had the help of a maternal association (p. 28).

If the church was the authority by which infant character was "known," a coincident influence propelled a concern with rearing Christian infants properly: the growing fear, engendered by the French Revolution, of "atheism, licentiousness, and the intemperance of the time, the increasingly lax discipline in the home, and the overemphasis of intellect"—all seen as causes of the French Revolution. To the Puritans, they seemed to be the cause of the growing "maladies" (such as pride and materialism) of an increasingly secular American republic. As late as the 1840s Americans were warned that they could avoid atheism and radicalism only by "seizing upon the infant mind and training it up" under moral and religious influence (p. 12).

The ideals of femininity, of the virtuous mother as architect of her child's future and angel in the home, and that of her alternately

depraved and innocent infant, had been established in this period
by religion as a response to social and economic change and even
out of fears created by a different (nonpuritanical) culture and its
revolution. If modern conceptions of American motherhood stem
from the early 1800s, modern conceptions of childhood stem from
the second half of the nineteenth century, when the child had
become the redeemer rather than the one in need of redemption
(p. 17).

The Child As Redeemer

As America became more industrial and commercial, there was a
growing conflict between the traditional Calvinist ideals of asceticism
and piety, and the commercially inspired, strong-willed individualism and pursuit of worldly goods and pleasures. According to Wishy,
nurture experts at midcentury, who were increasingly secular, were
faced with the task of reconciling this conflict. They had to suggest
a way to develop the child's will that would do justice to the
American ideals of individualism while at the same time keeping the
child from indulging in the corruptions plaguing American society
(p. 17).

The experts managed to create a rationale for resolving, or denying,
the conflict by proposing that the character of children was especially
flexible. If children were properly guided, their will and conscience
would not be in conflict. Psychohistorian Glenn Davis, in his survey
of this literature, refers to the period from 1840 to 1880 as the
period of the *psychic manipulation* of children. "As the birch rod was
replaced by the carefully modulated tongue," new strategies of childrearing were developed placing responsibility for the outcome on
mothers. *The Son Unguided: His Mother's Shame* (1848) is emblematic
of the new view of the child: "Its character is as yet of wax."
According to Davis, key words such as *impress, mold, form,* and
shape, indicated the importance of the new role for woman as the
maternal sculptress (Davis 1976, 45).[1]

A child could be raised for worldly success without sacrificing
Christian faith and morality; people could have it both ways if only

they would follow the experts' advice. Child nurture expertise in the latter half of the nineteenth century became an obsession, perhaps as a means to avoid the actual conflict. Increasingly, the child was viewed as the principal means by which the society would progress; the child would be the redeemer (Ehrenreich and English 1979, 182–210; Wishy 1972, 81–113).

As the century drew to a close, the authority of the church had been eclipsed by a more secular authority. Social reformers at the turn of the century, addressing the effects of growing secular evils such as child labor and the tenement conditions caused by sudden waves of immigration to the cities, became the new authorities on childrearing (Wishy 1972, 11). They continued to advise mothers to model virtue so that their children might learn through imitation the ways of courtesy, honesty, industry, and charity. Instilling moral character in children was still considered to be the proper goal of childrearing at a time when the increasingly commercial and immoral character of the adult world continued to be a source of concern to so many (Stendler 1950, 125). Although these experts had little authority to support their expertise, they drew more and more on the evidence produced by scientific theory.

Darwin's Theory: Science Directs Moral Progress

By the turn of the century, Darwin's popularizers had managed to identify evolution with progress and Christian morality. The laws that science was discovering would turn out to be the expression of God's will. Science could therefore provide moral guidelines. According to scientific experts, the child was the potential link to a higher plateau of evolutionary development. In *The Century of the Child,* a best-selling book published in 1909, Ellen Key, a eugenicist, claims that only by dint of a total focus on children for several generations could women hope to bring forth "the completed man— the Superman" (p. 2). On the basis of Sir Francis Galton's application of Darwin's theory of evolution to humans, Key and other eugenicists believed that the selective breeding of human beings could create a super race. Eugenicists thought to help this process along by encouraging those most adapted (those most like the upper classes) to breed, while discouraging those least adapted from doing so (a philosophy that reached its apogee in the policies of Nazi Germany). For many, such extensions of Darwin to social thought became a new religion capable of saving the race. As Ellen Key asserted after lamenting the inability of Christianity to subdue man's basest war-mongering qualities: "My conviction . . . is that nothing will be different in the mass except insofar as human nature itself is trans-formed . . . when the whole of humanity awakens to the conscious-ness of the 'holiness of generation.' This consciousness will make the central work of society the new race" (Key 1909, 2–3).

The religious motive had become so deeply entwined with the scientific motive that, as one American woman told an international conference on *scientific motherhood* in 1908: "The goal is nothing less than the redemption of the world through the better education of those who are able to shape it or make it. The keeper of the gates of tomorrow is the little child upon the mother's arms . . . and that child's hands a woman holds" (Ehrenreich and English 1978, 190).

The infant was seen as a kind of evolving protoplasm through which the society adapted and progressed. Darwin's theory proposed a constantly evolving race, led to its destiny by selective adaptation to the environment. His discovery prompted some to study the ontogeny or evolution of individual humans, especially in the early years of growth, to uncover ways in which the adaptation process might be enhanced, not by breeding, but by education. From this concern for scientifically directing the course of human evolution toward a superior race, the field of child study or child development was born, and the new childrearing expertise came more and more to be derived from the authority of this new psychological science. By learning how individual infants evolved, or developed, childrais-ing could be scientifically tailored to the evolutionarily based course of development.

Science also found motherhood to be biologically based and pro-claimed it women's evolutionary duty to obey the newly discovered laws of nature. In the latter half of the nineteenth century increasing numbers of women began to strain against this puritan-Victorian role of virtuous exemplar in the home. Rapid economic growth had produced an increase in the number of middle-class families and some middle-class women, freed economically in a society that presumably valued individualism and freedom, were motivated to expand their roles into areas outside the home. They became involved in movements for humanitarian reform, improved educational opportunities, and (more covertly) birth control. Not coincidentally, it was at this time that medical theories about women's restrictive biology rose in opposition to this threat to the social order (Rosenberg and Rosenberg 1984, 15).

Women, it was claimed, were biologically destined to be mothers, and women who gave their energies to anything else were more prone to illness and more likely to produce defective offspring. Until the twentieth century, it was almost universally assumed that characteristics acquired in the form of damage from disease and improper life-styles could be transmitted through heredity. A woman who lived "unphysiologically," perhaps by reading or studying to excess, by wearing improper clothing, by long hours of factory work, or by a sedentary, luxurious life, could produce only weak and degenerate offspring (p. 14). Education, it was thought, was causing American women to deteriorate by using energy that was needed for reproduction. Medical authorities insisted that during puberty a girl's vital energies must be devoted to the development of the reproductive organs: 'The girl who curtailed brainwork during puberty could devote her body's full energy to the optimum development of its reproductive capacities. A young woman, however, who consumed her vital force in intellectual activities was necessarily diverting these energies [and] would become weak and nervous, perhaps sterile . . . capable of bearing only sickly and neurotic children" (p. 15).[2]

In 1873, Dr. Edward Clarke of Harvard published a review of the medical theories of female nature, concluding that higher education would cause women's uteruses to atrophy. The book went through seventeen editions in a few years (Ehrenreich and English 1978, 127). The uterus, it was assumed, was connected to the central nervous system in such a manner that shocks to the nervous system might alter the reproductive cycle or damage a fetus. The reverse was also true. Any imbalance, exhaustion, infection, or other disorder of the reproductive system could cause pathological reactions in seemingly remote parts of the body (Rosenberg and Rosenberg 1984, 13). Clearly, women's health was dependent on their reproductive system, and they needed to reserve all their energies for the hazardous task of motherhood.

In the twentieth century an understanding of biology rather than a knowledge of Christian teaching became the basis by which moral virtue and the redemption of humanity could be achieved. The critical thread that tied the two eras together was the concept of evolution, which had been transformed at the turn of the century into a theory of moral progress. The importance of the mother-child relationship continued to be a central assumption regarding the proper roles of women and their relation to the goals of society.

The Cult of True Womanhood Becomes the Feminine Mystique

It was not until the mid–twentieth century that the mother-child relationship took on critical proportions once again. Dramatic changes were taking place in the 1940s that threatened to alter radically the nature of social relations, especially women's role. Before its final demise in the 1970s, the cult of true womanhood resurfaced with renewed energy in the form of the *feminine mystique,* a term coined by Betty Friedan (1963) in her investigation of the growing malaise among middle-class women in the early 1960s. Friedan concluded that femininity had been a mid-twentieth-century construct of medicine, psychology, and the social sciences; that it was, in fact, a myth. Femininity according to these scientists was rooted not in Christian virtue but in women's biology.

The concept of an instinctual feminine basis for mothering was filtered through a growing misogyny in the 1940s and 1950s. It was the product of many factors, not the least of which was the growing burden of polarized sex roles where men were aggressive and logical and women were passive and emotional (see Dally 1983; Lasch 1977; Riesman 1961). The concept of femininity was also influenced by the aim of psychoanalysis and medicine to root out pathology and cure disease. It was found that women's subconscious (instinctive) urges could infect a generation of children with the germs of mental illness unless, of course, the new clergy of psychologists and social scientists saved them. The late-nineteenth-century concept of the detrimental effects of brainwork on women's biology was also reactivated in this era. According to one typical adviser, Margaret Ribble, the prospective mother should avoid "mental activity during pregnancy, lest she produce a nervous infant. . . . The more educated the woman is, the greater the chance there is of sexual disorder. . . . The greater the disordered sexuality in a given group of women, the fewer children do they have" (1943, 107).

At the same time this noble ideal of the natural instinctual mother was being honed and polished, there were those who found that it harbored a "viper," a concept articulated by novelist and social commentator Philip Wylie in his 1942 best-seller, *Generation of Vipers*. "Megaloid momworship has got completely out of hand," he proclaimed (Ehrenreich and English 1978, 237). According to Wylie, mom's true nature was cunning, ruthless, and power-hungry. Such ideas were increasingly reflected in the "discoveries" of psychomedical science, which shared a strange coexistence with the romanticized view of mother love. The prevalent view of disturbed children was that mothers caused all their problems, from autism to delinquency. In the early 1940s, René Spitz had identified the "psychotoxic diseases of infancy" in which "the mother's personality acts as the disease-provoking agent." Such maternal attitudes as "primary anxious overpermissivenes," he said, produced the three-month colic; "hostility in the guise of manifest anxiety" was responsible for infantile eczema; "oscillation between pampering and hostility," for rocking in infants; "cyclical mood swings of the mother," for fecal play and coprophagia; and "maternal hostility consciously compensated," for hyperthymia in the child (Spitz 1965, 206).

Psychiatrist David Levy had also written an influential book entitled *Maternal Overprotection* in which he drew on case studies from the New York City Institute for Child Guidance. These case studies were selected to illustrate various types of overprotection; the children involved had been referred to the clinic for such problems as poor schoolwork, withdrawal from group activities, enuresis, quarreling, and disobedience. According to Levy, what determined whether a woman would lean more toward overprotection or rejection was probably the "strength of the maternal tendency" or the amount of maternal-type hormones she possessed. Curiously, Levy proclaimed that a woman could be both rejecting and overprotecting at the same time, an expression of her "unconscious hostilities." "Overprotectiveness" became an accusation hurled not only at individual women but at entire ethnic groups, such as Italians and Jews (Ehrenreich and English 1978, 234).

Freud and the Psychology of Women

The twentieth-century version of true womanhood derived its authority not from the tenets of Christian religion but rather from the strictures of psychoanalysis, which described a moral order in which neurosis was seen as equivalent to the wages of sin. In America, the theories of Freud were fashioned into a conservative ideology, one that rested largely on his interpretation of the psychology of women. In the 1920s, in keeping with the zeitgeist of the roaring twenties, Freud's theories were interpreted to mean that women could and should enjoy sex (Banner 1974, 151). Although Karen Horney and other psychoanalysts in the 1930s had begun to attack Freud's negative theory of femininity—suggesting, for instance, that womb envy rather than penis envy was a critical ingredient in male and female personality development—it was the Freudian pejorative view that came to predominate in the following decade. In keeping with a growing misogyny of the 1940s and 1950s, Freud's ideas were used to illustrate the inherent pathology of motherhood.

Through his clinical work, Freud was able to observe women suffering from two causes: sexual inhibition and great discontent with their social circumstances. He tended to see the latter problem as dependent on the former and to recommend female sexual fulfillment as a panacea for the symptoms of social unrest (Chodorow 1989, chap. 8). Yet Freud's understanding of the female personality is first of all biological and negative—a woman's identity results from her not being male and not having a penis. According to this view, little girls, at about age three, when genital drives become important, discover that they do not have a penis. Automatically they think they are castrated and inferior and experience their lack as a wound to their self-esteem (a narcissistic wound). The female first blames her mother "who sent her into the world so insufficiently equipped" (S. Freud 1962, 192). At first the little girl expects her father to prove magnanimous and give her a penis. Later, disappointed in this hope she learns to content herself with the aspiration of bearing his baby (even then, she might still succumb to this envy if she cannot find complete fulfillment in motherhood). To do this, she must give up her active (clitoral) sexuality and substitute a passive (vaginal) sexual mode. The girl-woman never does come to want heterosexual intercourse for itself; she wants sex for reproduction to make up for her narcissistic wound. Pregnancy is the proper resolution of the oedipal complex; it allows a woman to accept her femininity. She is always in danger of envying the penis until she acquires the penis substitute, a baby. Having a baby is her sexual fulfillment (Chodorow 1978; S. Freud 1962; Friedan 1963; Millett 1970).

The three most distinguishing traits of female personality are, in Freud's view, passivity, masochism, and narcissism. Again, these characteristics are said to be rooted in biology, not in the customs of society, and they are said to prescribe normal female behavior. Passivity is achieved with the abandonment of active clitoral masturbation and the onset of maternal craving in the oedipal stage, and this upsurge is "accompanied principally with the help of passive instinctual impulses" (S. Freud 1962, 128). The natural masochism of women is evidenced by the fact that they (must) enjoy passive domination by the male in intercourse, which Freud appears to believe is painful for women. Narcissism is also constitutional in women according to Freud and is also produced by penis envy: "The effect of penis-envy has a share, further in the physical vanity of women, since they are bound to value their charms more highly as a late compensation for their original sexual inferiority" (S. Freud 1962, 132).

Several female followers of Freud who became psychoanalysts expanded upon these theories. Marie Bonaparte elaborated on women's biologically based passivity, which is due to "the clitoris, her phallus, whose very size dooms her aggression. [Therefore] female aggression, like her libido, is generally weaker than the male's" (1953, 81). Helene Deutsch, established her reputation in the psychoanalytic world through studies of masochism and wrote a two-volume work on female sexuality that was regarded as a definitive statement of "true femininity" (Millett 1970, 206). She claimed (as did Bonaparte) that women were naturally masochistic, narcissistic, and passive. Deutsch claimed that a girl became masochistic when she discovered that her clitoris was an "inadequate organ" for the release of her sexual excitement and transferred her sexual pleasure to the passive vagina. This process leads to masochism because in order to feel sexual excitement in her vagina, the girl needs to be overpowered by a male. Related to this is Freud's notion that the girl is biologically destined to turn her aggression inward, a process that is helped by her resolution of her sexual desire for her father. When she learns that she will be punished for her desires, she attempts to renounce them, in part by becoming passive rather than by actively pursuing her aim. Freud called this a major component of female masochism, although he himself explained this pattern not as a fundamental enjoyment of passivity and pain, but largely as a consequence of the girl's fear of punishment by her mother and need to keep her mother's love (Caplan 1985, 18–19). In any case, women could achieve psychological maturity only by remaining passive and becoming pregnant. As Deutsch explained: "She passively awaits fecundation; her life is fully active and rooted in reality only when she becomes a mother. Until then everything that is feminine in the woman, physiology and psychology, is passive and receptive" (Deutsch 1944, vol. 1, 140).

Childbirth was for woman, then, equivalent to a sexual act, one in which the woman was in passive girllike relation to her husband and to the male obstetrician who assisted her in obtaining the penis-substitute child. According to Deutsch, a woman who had wanted autonomy, who desired her delivery to be an active accomplishment on her part, "had distorted her femininity into masculinity and would have birth complications" (p. 141). In fact, labor was likened to coitus, which could result in orgasm. One analyst, Helen Wessel, made the following explicit comparison: "In labor, the descending baby can be considered the equivalent of the penis in inter-course. . . . To continue the analogy, as the climax is reached in both situations, the woman utters involuntary sounds and per-forms involuntary pelvic movements. With the expulsion of the child, as in reaching the climax of the orgasm, the woman suddenly relaxes and there appears a calm ecstatic look on her face" (in Wertz and Wertz 1989, 189).

Anything a woman did besides motherhood potentially endangered her childbearing capacity. This natural mother was once again the sole architect of her child's future. Sigmund Freud's theory indicated that serious flaws in adult character were due to traumatic childhood events tied to critical psychosexual periods in early development. If a mother, through inept childrearing in infancy, tipped the delicate balance between the demands of the child's pleasurable instincts and her own communication of the reality demands of civilized society, she could create a child whose character was stunted or fixated at the oral level. The result would be, not so much a character that was immoral or ungodly, but one that was neurotic or maladapted. Once again, this was all part of a subtext regarding the moral behavior of adults. It was the improper regulation of instinct in childhood that made adults sinners—that is, neurotics.

Through her biological instincts this new libidinal mother would naturally fulfill her child's needs and find her own fulfillment in the needs of the child. "Mothering behavior is regulated by a pituitary hormone," psychoanalyst Therese Benedek declared (Ehrenreich and English 1978, 221). In the Freudian view, the importance of moth-ering in the infancy period is so profound that the maternal-infant interaction can shape the character of an entire civilization. Using the Freudian framework, Margaret Mead, in her studies of seven South Seas cultures, for instance, found that the passive Arapesh character was the consequence of infant feeding patterns in which food was continually set on the infant's mouth and the infant had only to let it trickle in. The infant never had to cry or coo or otherwise assert himself to get fed. The aggressive head-hunting Iatmul, on the other hand, in their infancy, had been teased and made to grasp and snap after their food in order to get it. Their entire character was said to be shaped in this early period by a mother (Mead 1949).

Hearth Angel versus Rosie the Riveter

This powerful and pathologized motherhood, from which the maternal deprivation idea emerged, developed at a time of major cultural ferment brought about by the war and dramatic changes in the economy that once again threatened to alter cherished cultural values thought to be located in the home and tied indelibly to women. Women were supposed to be suited only for the home and hearth, yet their labor was needed for the war industry. Between 1940 and 1945 women took over jobs that were well paid and that only men were thought to be capable of handling. Women did the work successfully, undermining the mythology and giving women a sense of power and satisfaction. A 1944 Women's Bureau study showed that 80 percent of the women who worked throughout the war wanted to continue in their jobs (Banner 1974, 223). The feminine mystique intensified as a means to control women's labor.

Initially, persuading women to take these jobs required considerable effort as well as a delicate ideological balancing act. The prevailing prescription for motherhood was stretched to the limit as part of an official propaganda campaign directed by the United States Office of War Information (OWI), which engaged in a massive effort to persuade Americans that married women should be hired in jobs drained by the enlistment of men (Honey 1984, 28). This propaganda was essential. A preliminary government survey had discovered that though 33 percent of childless wives said they would be willing to take a job, only 19 percent of wives with children were ready to do so. No more than 30 percent of husbands thought it acceptable for their wives to work (Degler 1980, 420). To meet the needs of the war industry, an altered domestic construct was required.

The newly idealized woman worker was young, white, and middle class, even though she was often represented in work sectors where poor and minority women actually predominated. Class (middle and upper) and race (white) were always an important incentive in the functioning of the feminine ideals. Poor nonwhite women may have aspired to these ideals and their attendant privileges, but fear of being like the lower classes and races was certainly a spur to white middle-class women to conform to the ideology. The American War Advertising Council, a nongovernmental group of business advertisers, in searching for ways to "bring the issues of the war down to a personal level," had recommended that the war be portrayed as threatening people with the "loss of something vital to their well-being" in order to "create a burning desire in every citizen to cooperate in the war effort." That something vital was the family, and in wartime propaganda it became the task of women to preserve the integrity of family life and keep an orderly home to which soldiers could return. As the embodiment of safety and tenderness, the mother and wife stood for the survival of the country's humane values and served as guardians of its spirit by holding the family together (Honey 1984, 133).

Curiously, women would preserve the home by guarding it through work in industry. The refashioned image these propagandists constructed was of women as guardians of the home front, a tradition harking back to the pioneer women who had loaded the rifles for their men as they fought off the Indians. For instance, an A—— ad referred to a female truck driver as a 'covered wagon girl': "'I got a job driving a truck when Paul went across. I'm hauling the stuff they fight with.' Hers is the spirit of the women who reloaded the long rifles as their men fought off the Indians . . . the courage that helped build the kind of America we have today" (*Saturday Evening Post,* 1944, in Honey 1984, 103).

Advertisers, directed by the OWI, conveyed the message that the employment of women would not disrupt the family (pp. 118–20). War workers were often shown in housewife-mother roles, taking care of children or doing housework in factory coveralls. The children pictured in these scenes cheerfully helped their mothers with household tasks, especially young daughters, who were frequently dressed in coveralls and kerchiefs themselves. A series of M——coffee ads, published in the *Saturday Evening Post* in 1944 portrayed attractive young middle-class women war workers in warm domestic scenes. In one, a woman is resting after a hard day's work at the factory, still wearing her coveralls and identification badge; her lunch bucket is prominently displayed on the dining room table. She is flanked by an older couple, probably her parents, and a little girl, her daughter, hugs her closely while she sips the coffee that her mother has just poured. All three are eagerly listening to her working-day tales and clearly full of respect for what she is doing (pp. 118–19).

It seems that mothers did indeed retain their role as hearthside nurturers as they kept their children at home with relatives or friends while working. In spite of the passage of the Lanham Act in 1943, which provided funds for day care,[3] social attitudes toward day care remained negative. In fact, wartime conferences on the family were filled with complaints not about the paucity of day-care centers but about the fact that some mothers were actually using them. Readers of one of the most prestigious social science publications, *"The Annals,"* learned that mothers who resorted to day care: "forget that there are many children who have a dangerous feeling of insecurity when they are away from their mothers from dawn to dark. . . . In this tug of war between children and jobs, the children are losing" (Boll 1943, 75).

While government and business waged their propaganda campaign to get women to join the workforce, social scientists and childrearing experts criticized women who were thereby neglecting their children. Mothers were charged with being "war work deserters" for neglecting their children and not providing "adequate care and supervision." There were even fears that the desertion of children might become habit forming: "Once having left the children to their own devices, and finding that it can be done over and over again, the mother may develop much satisfaction . . . from evading her accustomed responsibility" (Barber 1943, 170).

By emphasizing that women's primary duty was to the men in their lives, advertisers avoided showing war work as leading to new roles for women. In fact, there were propaganda strategies that contributed to an increasingly reactionary view of women at the war's end. By the spring of 1944, ads began to dramatize the unhappiness of children with their war-working mothers. A company that manufactured war material showed a mother in coveralls and a factory badge stopping on her way to work to answer her daughter's plaintive question: "Mother, when will you stay home again?" The text provides an answer for her: "Some jubilant day mother will stay home again, doing the job she likes best—making a home for you and daddy when he gets back." The ad goes on to discuss the company's plan to convert to peacetime production in a way that illustrates the postwar focus of advertisers on women as consumers rather than as producers: "She's learning the vital importance of precision in equipment made by A——. In her postwar home she'll want appliances with the same high degree of precision and she'll get them when A—— converts its famous Design Simplicity to products of equal dependability for home and industry" (Honey 1984, 124–25).

The wartime image of motherhood was a romance that rationalized the two conflicting needs for women's labor. Only the heroic woman could both work and manage the home during the war. When the need had passed, only the villainous woman would try to do both. As manufacturers began to convert to the production of consumer goods, advertisers intensified the attack on working mothers. There were strong political pressures to save money and reduce unemployment by pushing women back into the home. In one ad, in the *Saturday Evening Post* in 1945, a factory worker has to plead before a judge for her teenage son, who is labeled a "Victory Vandal," and a hysterical girl is carted away to a foster home because her mother has to work (p. 126). These tragic scenes contrasted dramatically with ads showing mothers at home with their children playing happily nearby. Women were given little real assistance in their awesome task of shaping their children, however. Moreover, virtually every mother's manual and magazine article of this period assumed that the baby in question was wanted, loved, and had two loving and relatively well-off parents. In fact, this period saw an enormous increase in illegitimacy, abortion, and baby battering (Dally 1983, 97). Such real-life phenomena, however, were ignored by the authorities, who seemed to be looking through rose-colored glasses.

In England, D. W. Winnicott was a major promoter of full-time motherhood and a supporter and popularizer of John Bowlby's maternal-deprivation theories. Winnicott's wartime radio broadcasts in 1944 advised women to stay at home with their children after the war and emphasized the central importance of mother love from earliest infancy. Drawing on Melanie Klein's psychoanalytic ideas, Winnicott urged mothers to stay with their infants during the early years so that the child would have the opportunity to "make restitution" for its early inevitable hostilities to the mother. Otherwise, juvenile delinquency might result as "children steal to mitigate an unrelieved sense of guilt" (Riley 1983, 80–84). At the end of the war Winnicott urged mothers to return to the home full time: "Talk about women coming back from the Forces not wanting to be housewives seems to me to be just nonsense, because nowhere else but in her own home is a woman in such command" (p. 88).

In fact, working mothers, as we have seen from the evidence of Bowlby's 1951 report, by being separated from their young children, were causing them to experience maternal deprivation. Bowlby had made a variety of recommendations in his report. He suggested that subsidies be provided to mothers to keep them from economic pressure to work and that family systems be evaluated and treated because they were engenderers of mental illness. But these remedies for maternal deprivation cost money; they even involved the possibility of changing the family system. The concept of maternal deprivation coincided with the need to persuade women to give their higher-paying jobs to the men returning home from the war and to preserve a family life that might provide a haven from the more harsh and uncertain public world of war, communism, and commerce. The idea became part of the propaganda. Maternal-deprivation studies were used as cautionary tales for mothers of children living in normal family situations. Popular books on childraising began to feature ominous references to orphaned animals and institutionalized children (see Kawin 1967, v). The research provided a tragic picture of the maternally deprived child—sunken eyes, wan cheeks, limbs thin and flaccid, prey to every passing infection—all presumably for lack of "constant attention day and night, seven days a week and 365 in the year" (Ehrenreich and English 1978, 231).

The postwar idea of maternal deprivation had a special appeal for the British. Until the late 1940s almost no member of the British middle and upper classes had experienced the continuous care of a mother "seven days a week and 365 in the year," as Bowlby had prescribed, because most of them had been cared for by nannies. Consequently, according to a number of theorists, motherhood was a highly idealized notion in Britain. When women were told that continuous mother love was essential to mental health, they tended to believe it because they had, in fact, never experienced it (Dally 1982, 93; Gathorne-Hardy 1972; Riley 1983, chap. 5).

With the war's end, traditional occupational patterns among women reasserted themselves. In America, from September 1945 to November 1946, 2.5 million women left work and an additional million were laid off, especially in the higher-paying manufacturing jobs, where dramatic gains for women had been made during the war. Of course, women did not disappear from the labor force; in fact, between 1940 and 1950, their numbers rose slightly, from 27 percent to 31 percent of all women. But the major increase came in spheres of work that were stereotypically women's, particularly office work (Rothman 1978, 224).

After the war, women's role received intense scrutiny; straying from its confines was found to be the cause of everything from infantile eczema to juvenile delinquency. The growing tension over women's role was actually the reflection of a variety of cultural and economic issues that faced the nation. Women and children came to stand for those cherished qualities that had been snuffed out by carnage and danger: innocence, gentleness, idealism, continuity, and safety. The deprivation of the war years made a close family life attractive. Marriage rates were high and the age of first marriage dropped while the size of families increased, creating the baby boom. College women were defending marriage and motherhood with Freudian arguments. In the 1950s, 60 percent of female undergraduates were dropping out of college to marry. The family was romanticized in movies, television, and popular magazines—indeed, a middle-class affluence made possible by the postwar economy reinforced the romance (Banner 1974, 236–37).

Regardless of the ideology of domesticity, however, there was a vast increase in the number of married women who continued to join the work force. In 1940, less than 10 percent of mothers with children under six held jobs; in 1950, the proportion was almost 12 percent; by 1970 it was over 30 percent and still rising (Degler 1980, 418). In 1984, 51.8 percent of women with children under six were working (Anderson 1988, 115). Since the 1920s women had been entering the wage labor force in steadily increasing numbers, threatening to change the nature of the family and attendant values. In 1900, 18 percent of the American labor force was female; in 1920 it was 20 percent; in 1930, 22 percent. The proportion jumped dramatically, however, from 25 percent to 36 percent between 1940 and 1945. Women returned to the home after the war, and the percentage dropped to 28 in 1947. But by 1951, 31 percent of the labor force was female, and by 1973 the figure was 42 percent (Banner 1974, 205, 219, 279).

The public debate over women's working continued, often bitterly, into the 1950s. For example, in 1952 one woman wrote to *Child Study,* a parent-oriented periodical whose advisory board included Benjamin Spock, René Spitz, and David Levy:

> I am a professional woman with a son five years old. . . . Though I keep planning to quit [work] so far I haven't . . . I'm not at all sure it would be wise for me to give up my work and try to be just a mother.

The response:

> You may want to get some professional help in finding out what has caused you to lose confidence in your capacities. It may be

that you're more the domestic type than you think and that under the right circumstances your powers as wife and mother could be liberated in the service of your child. (Ehrenreich and English 1978, 224)

The Reign of the Feminine Mystique

In the decade and a half after the war, a number of factors made the romance of the feminine mystique attractive. The fear of a recession, even another depression, gripped the nation as conversion of the war industry to a consumer industry caused inevitable unemployment and labor unrest. As the economy began to stabilize, anxiety accompanied a new prosperity and a new fear developed, a fear of communism (Degler 1968). Also, an intensified emphasis on consumerism altered the nature and function of the family, as well, which had become one of indulgence and spending—the opposite of the old Puritan values of thrift and asceticism. Moreover, the old masculine characteristics of aggressiveness and strength were threatened by the necessity of corporate conformity and docility (Riesman 1950; Whyte 1956). The idea of motherhood as a powerful and almost sacred institution, and domesticity as a safe harbor in the worldly turmoil, appealed to both men and women, expert and layperson alike. Medicine and the social sciences forged a conception of femininity so intense and so at odds with women's actual experience that it was bound to come undone. All women were to derive total fulfillment from complete devotion to their children and husbands. To be a wife and mother was the biological destiny for which their instincts had prepared them. This mythologizing was also a defense against the loss of ideals that had come into being a hundred years earlier. The angel in the house, the ideal woman first created in the 1840s in response to the industrial revolution, had finally tasted the wages of the labor market; the fear was that she would not return to her pedestal. Indeed, she was quietly, steadily leaving it, a fact that did not come to public awareness until the 1970s.

The feminine mystique amounted to another cult of true womanhood, propelled by a flood of propaganda. This time, however, the ideal was twisted by a growing misogyny. Nothing since Victorian literature equaled the reverence with which women's magazines and related advice literature of the 1940s, 1950s, and 1960s extolled home and maternity. They read like a replay of Mrs. Sigourney's advice to true women during the 1840s. *Modern Woman: The Lost Sex* (1947) was written by Dr. Marynia Farnham, a psychiatrist, who based the book on her clinical work in psychiatry. With her collaborator, Ferdinand Lundberg, a sociologist (both were Freudians), they proclaimed that contemporary women "in very large numbers" are psychologically disordered. They claimed that the problems of modern society—including the war and the depression—could be traced to the fact that women had left the home. In their view, women had given up their femininity to compete in a futile battle with men, causing their children to become delinquents or neurotics and their husbands to become alcoholics or sexually impotent. They based their position on studies that seemed to show high rates of neurosis among army draftees and career women and increasing alcoholism and impotence among American men. The authors therefore advised that woman should be domestic and self-subordinating.

> [She should] devote all her efforts to improving it [the home] in every way. When she is not tending to the children, she should be an amateur interior decorator, chef, mender, home nurse, retail buyer and member of the local parent-teacher association. She should be ever ready, upon the homecoming of her husband, to be a spirited companion, tricked out like a debutante for a cocktail party. In order to be a good companion, she should give some time to reading a few current books and the newspapers. It would not do at all for her not to know what the conversation was about at dinner. It would be especially humiliating to her husband if she were unable to contribute to the conversation about some public matter in the company of friends.

Women should consider themselves a reserve labor pool:

> It goes without saying that she should be smiling about sending her men off to fight, asking no questions about the failures of the

statesmen that invoked disaster. . . . She should also take a job in war production, but she should be ready at the drop of a hatpin to give it up to a returning soldier. She should at the same time keep her home going and her children contented. To fail in any one of these requirements would leave her open to serious question. (pp. 1, 8–9)

Modern Woman: The Lost Sex served to popularize these ideas and was used as a textbook in college courses on "marriage and the family," "life adjustment," and other innovative courses (Millett 1970, 206). Its particular concern was the sexual revolution of the 1920s and 1930s, which had made woman a "lost sex." (There had been a significant feminist movement that gathered strength around the turn of the century and succeeded in securing women's right to vote in 1920 with the passage of the Nineteenth Amendment. After that goal was accomplished, the movement subsided.) Feminism in this account is likened to anti-Semitism, communism, nazism and the Ku Klux Klan because of the hatred it presumably preached. Echoing the puritan fear of French liberalism so prevalent in America a hundred years before, the authors condemn Mary Wollstonecraft, who began "the madness" (seeking equality with men) that was like "the fires of the French Revolution." Feminism, according to *The Lost Sex,* is the negation of femininity because "it bade women commit suicide as women and attempt to live as men." Through divorce, abortion, and contraception, the sexual revolution had undermined marriage, an institution that "protects women." Women should turn their backs on the "brave new facade of modernity" and return to the old instinctual ways of submission, which they describe as "supporting manliness . . . to achieve erection, the male must be master" (pp. 207–10).

In 1946, Dr. Edward Strecker, a psychiatrist and consultant to the surgeon general of the Army and Navy, found that the almost 3 million men who were rejected for military service because of psychiatric disorders (including five hundred thousand draft evaders), and who "lacked the ability to face life, live with others, think for themselves and stand on their own two feet," were all suffering from "momism." According to Dr. Strecker,

> mom is sweet, doting, self-sacrificing . . . takes no end of trouble and spares herself no pains in selecting clothes for her grown-up children. She supervises the curl of their hair, the selection of their friends and companions, their sports and their social attitudes and opinions. By and large she does all their thinking for them. . . . It is the perfect home. . . . Failing to find a comparable peaceful haven in the outside world, it is quite likely that one or more of the brood will remain in or return to the happy home, forever more enwombed." (Strecker 1946, 52–59)

In spite of the accusations leveled against the all-too-loving and insufficiently loving mom, popularizers of Freud continued on an even wider scale in the late 1940s and 1950s. Benjamin Spock was a Freudian and, in fact, had been analyzed himself. He too asserted that how the mother treated her infant and young child would determine the adult personality. By this time infant care had become more technical, and mothers were required to be able to diagnose a range of both psychological and physical ailments. The professionally trained physician and psychiatrist had taken the place of the family and community as a source of authority, as women now felt the knowledge of their friends and relatives was not sufficiently modern. Contributing to this dependence, women were increasingly separated by frequent geographic moves, and owing to a rising standard of living, more private but isolating housing.

Spock was embraced by this generation of mothers, in part because he sounded reassuringly old-fashioned, telling mothers to use their common sense and do what was natural at the same time that he was telling them every step of the way what the modern physician recommends. Spock was especially concerned that mothers not re-create the authoritarian personality, that is, the personality of a Nazi, by frustrating their children or being too authoritarian. He advised permissiveness and the avoidance of conflict with children. The mother's goal was to create in her child a congenial, well-adjusted personality (Zinsser 1986).

Motherhood was becoming, once again, a total way of life. *Life, Look, Redbook, The Ladies' Home Journal,* and other national magazines proclaimed that the college-educated woman had not "matured" into the recognition that feminism had been a "disruptive trend," but soon they would find the right perspective. As in Victorian medical theory, motherhood was said to be woman's natural, biologically based fulfillment, the means to mental health for her and for the whole society. According to psychiatrist Joseph Rheingold, in a book entitled *The Fear of Being a Woman* (1964): "When women grow up without dread of their biological functions and without subversion by feminist doctrine and therefore enter upon motherhood with a sense of fulfillment and altruistic sentiment, we shall attain the goal of a good life and a secure world in which to live."

The feminine mystique lived on into the early 1960s. Even 1961 presidential candidate Adlai Stevenson echoed the old cult of true womanhood, advising woman to "inspire in her home a vision of the meaning of life and freedom . . . and to help her husband find values that will give purpose to the specialized daily chores. This assignment for you as wives and mothers, you can do in the living-room with a baby on your lap or in the kitchen with a can opener in your hand" (Wertz and Wertz 1989, 182).

The bonding research of the 1970s came at a time when recognizing that women could not remain at home was finally unavoidable, both by women and their guardian experts. Bonding became a craze in the 1970s, a last gasp of the ideology regarding the all-powerful maternal sculptress. Now almost a third of mothers were already in the labor force; only 13 percent of American families fit the ideal of a two-parent family, where the man works and the woman stays home (Anderson 1988, 147). By that time constructs of motherhood and infancy had created a pat ideological superstructure into which the findings of the bonding research easily fit and onto which the conflicts of society could be once again projected. Doctors naturally reached for this form of redress for complex problems as it was by now part of their professional equipment. Women grasped it too as a means to address their own growing conflict, of being "liberated" to work outside the home and feeling entirely responsible for the psychological health of their children. Full-time motherhood was out of the question, yet bonding provided the possibility of having it both ways in case the old ideology were true.

Although the architects of bonding were no doubt unaware of the legacy of assumptions that guided their scientific project, a powerful group of people were becoming aware of the mythology surrounding women's sex role and were beginning to actively dismantle it. The feminist movement of the early 1970s sparked by Friedan's feminine mystique and elaborated by the theories of Germaine Greer (*The Female Eunuch*), Kate Millett (*Sexual Politics*), Elizabeth Janeway (*Man's World, Woman's Place*), and so on, identified the source of women's systematic oppression as the mythology surrounding women's sex role. The ideology of motherhood was thoroughly demolished by feminist theorists. Curiously, women inspired by feminism helped to precipitate a reform movement that actively embraced bonding, which was a vehicle for the old myths. Their failure to see how extensively bonding reestablished the old maternal sculptress rationalization can be explained in part by the power of a more palpable enemy of women's liberation: the medical profession. Insofar as bonding could oppose this conservative institution, it seemed a welcome idea.

How we perceive motherhood and infancy, whether our means of knowing is religion or science, is also a means of conceptualizing the goals of society. The idea that biological and psychological factors of motherhood and infancy will redress the complex social, economic, political, and cultural problems of poverty, corruption, pollution, violence, and nuclear threat, is a means of trying to transcend those problems. It is also a form of scapegoating, of blaming relatively powerless groups for the sins and fears of the whole. Although ideals are necessary in every society, when they are far out of touch with the realities of peoples' lives, they are dysfunctional.

Medicine Frames Motherhood and Infancy

Motherhood and infancy were once considered normal phases of human life. As medicine expanded and specialized, however, motherhood and infancy were increasingly reframed as pathological and within the province of physician care. At the turn of the century, 95 percent of America's infants were born at home; by 1940, half were born in hospitals; by 1979 the figure was 99 percent (*Research Issues*, 1982, 2). What had once been the province of midwives and the occasional physician became exclusively the domain of obstetric physicians whose special skills were primarily surgical and pharmaceutical.

In the early part of the century, the needs for infant milk stations and child welfare clinics mandated the pediatric specialty. As the specialists expanded their services to the middle classes in the 1930s and 1940s, they allied themselves with psychology and began to define the parameters of normal child behavior, once again bringing into the sphere of medicine clients who had not before been considered in need of treatment. The characteristics of neonates also became the subject of investigation by pediatricians as newborns were increasingly observed in hospitals. By the 1960s new technology also brought a large population of premature and sick newborns into the sphere of medical management. Not all of these developments represented progress in medical science and treatment nor an advantage for these new patients. Whatever their actual capabilities, obstetrics and pediatrics sold their services to women, and in the process reshaped our thinking about the nature and meaning of these aspects of our lives. Women came to see them as potentially pathological—not just physiologically but behaviorally as well.

For instance, among American obstetricians in the 1940s, the claim was made that women's natural, biologically based postpartum behavior toward their infants was potentially so pathological that mothers and infants should be separated after birth, an idea that appeared to require critical physician management of both women and infants. Bonding, of course, is a new version of the same notion. Women's natural, biologically based postpartum behavior toward their infants is so potentially constructive (or destructive) as to enhance (or damage) children's intelligence and prevent (or cause) child abuse. These assertions are not so much the product of medical research or successful treatment as they are professionally convenient beliefs. They are part of a tradition in which medicine has increasingly defined the nature of patients in order to enhance market needs and its own status and to fashion some kind of redress for the problems created by the practices of the profession itself.

Obstetrics: The Fiction of Pathology

The profession of obstetrics, for instance, unlike most specialties in medicine, did not result from technological imperatives or the accumulation of scientific advances. It did not even come into being from a widespread popular mandate or a push for health reform as pediatrics did. In fact, it had to capture its clientele from midwives, who were the most commonly sought expert attendants at birth until the end of the nineteenth century.

By the first decade of the twentieth century, American obstetrics had largely eliminated the midwife as a competitor in the childbirth process. That battle began with the invention of forceps in the early seventeenth century by an Englishman, Peter Chamberlen (who kept them a family secret for more than a century) (Wertz and Wertz 1989, 34). The barber-surgeons, the first men called by midwives to assist in difficult births, had kept the construction and application of forceps a trade secret. Forceps were an improvement over the other instruments used by surgeons because it freed the fetus without killing it. The men who first used them generally received brief "training." In England, in the early 1700s, often using a leather dummy with a beer-filled bladder, a cork, and a wax doll, a Dr. William Smellie taught the use of forceps to male barbers and sometimes even butchers in as few as nine lessons (Wertz and Wertz 1989, 40–42). These men apparently regarded the forceps as a talisman of their ability and a panacea for every difficulty of birth. As a consequence, overuse of the forceps caused an outcry by British midwives in the 1740s. Even so, they continued to be used throughout the nineteenth and even the twentieth century. Female midwives did not use instruments, in part because their tradition of seeing birth as a natural process did not encourage it. Money was also a factor; the cost of obtaining forceps was prohibitive for most midwives.

After 1750, American men receiving their medical education abroad began returning with a knowledge of what they called *midwifery*, which involved the use of instruments. In 1765, the Medical College of Philadelphia was founded, followed by King's College (later Columbia) Medical School in 1767, and Harvard in 1782. Obstetrics, or (male) midwifery, was the first medical specialty in those schools, preceding even surgery, for it was assumed that every graduate would attend birth as part of his practice. Midwifery itself provided only a small income, but it opened the way to a more lucrative family practice since those who had seen a doctor "perform" successfully were likely to call him again (Wertz and Wertz 1989, 49–55). From about 1750 to 1810, American doctors conceived of the new midwifery as an enterprise to be shared with trained (female) midwives. In the early 1800s, however, schools for midwives attracted only men, in part because women did not feel the need for formal training and also because the prescriptions of the Victorian era limited the proper role of women to homemaking. But the primary reason women began to disappear from American midwifery in the nineteenth century was because the growing population of newly educated male doctors needed a sustained medical practice, which attendance at birth could help them to establish.

As the practice of medicine became more institutionalized in the first half of the nineteenth century, men attempted to bring childbirth within the medical model of disease and to treat it as other diseases were treated, using forceps and such measures as bloodletting, the application of leeches, and drugs (Leavitt 1985, 84). The shift away from a theory of birth as a natural process and toward more reliance on artful intervention by males in the 1820s, is evident in discussions as to what doctors should call themselves when they practiced the new midwifery: *male-midwife, midman, accoucheur,* and even *androboethogynist* were suggested. In 1828 an English doctor suggested the term *obstetrician,* from the Latin meaning "to stand before." It had the advantage of sounding like other honorable professions such as that of electrician or geometrician, in which men variously understood and dominated nature (Wertz and Wertz 1989, 66).

The introduction of ether in 1842 to eliminate the "unbearable pains" of childbirth made it necessary to have a person skilled in the use of medical instruments in attendance while the mother was eliminated from effective participation in the delivery, thus furthering the need for obstetricians (Leavitt 1985). Male obstetricians advanced the process of taking over childbirth by maligning female midwives and actively excluding them from medical education. Female midwives were not organized, in contrast to (mostly male) American doctors who began to develop social and professional organizations. By the end of the nineteenth century female midwives served primarily poor and rural women (Arney 1982, chap. 2; Wertz and Wertz 1989, chap. 2). As the number of midwives diminished, middle-class women found fewer respectable trained women of their own class to assist in childbirth and so turned to male doctors.

According to many theorists, it was the surgeon's exclusive use of forceps that enabled physicians to challenge the midwifes' traditional role as an attendant at all normal births (Arney 1982, chap. 2; Leavitt

1985; Wertz and Wertz 1989). Physicians used forceps to create an atmosphere of danger and to cast themselves as experts in saving women from danger. In the mid-nineteenth century, for instance, Walter Channing, professor of midwifery at Harvard Medical School, was said to have told doctors to "appear to be doing something": to intervene in birth, using forceps or administering medicine, in order to give the appearance of doing something midwives were unable to do, even though, in fact, nature could take its course just as well on its own. As this display of esoteric power became more widespread, women came to anticipate difficult births (Arney 1982, chap. 2). As a result, middle-class women who wanted "the best" and "the latest" began to demand these interventions whether they actually needed them or not.

It was the hospital, however, that proved to be the strategic organizational resource for the emergent male practitioner (Wertz and Wertz 1989, 127). Before the twentieth century, *lying-in* was the name given to the event of birth and recuperation. The midwife attended delivery along with women relatives, neighbors, and friends, some of whom stayed with the new mother for the first three or four weeks after the birth, while she kept to her bed with her infant (Wertz and Wertz 1989, x). Lying-in hospitals were established in the nineteenth century and were primarily for indigent women, although some reserved a few beds for women who were better off. These hospitals gave medical students access to their "material" so that they could learn about birth. In the Victorian era, the upper classes started using the (more expensive) medical students and set the fashion for doing so among the middle classes as well (Arney 1982, 46; Leavitt 1985, 84–89; Wertz and Wertz 1989, 64). Moreover, the men who attended upper-class women in the hospital gained notable reputations because they were said to be providing the most advanced care. Ironically, as more women were attended by doctors, they acquired puerperal fever, actually caused by the unhygienic practices of the doctors themselves. Because of the danger of spreading puerperal fever, all women had to be treated as if they were diseased, which contributed even further to the control of childbirth by doctors (Wertz and Wertz 1989, 127). Thus, as part of hospital routine, the personal effects of expectant mothers were taken away, their pubic hair was shaved, and they were given enemas.

In Victorian America there was one major obstacle to the widespread (middle-class) adoption of the male accoucheur: Victorian prudery. As both men and women balked at the idea of male accoucheurs, male obstetricians developed an ideology that concerned the relative importance of safety over the constraints of modesty and made an extreme case regarding the danger of childbirth. As Dr. Charles Coventry eloquently put it in midcentury, testifying for a professor of obstetrics at the University of Buffalo who had permitted his students to observe a delivery, he could "conceive of no purpose, that has for its object the saving of human life, [that could] be either indecorous or immoral" (Arney 1982, 42). In order to build up an ideology of the relative importance of safety over modesty, medicine had to have a theory of childbirth that declared it unsafe, contrary to the general view of birth held by midwives. The profession recognized that this was a political task, not a scientific one. At a lecture on obstetrics at the University of Pennsylvania in 1838, Dr. Hugh Hodge said, "If females can be induced to believe that their sufferings will be diminished or shortened, and their lives and those of their offspring be safer in the hands of the profession, there will be no difficulty in establishing the universal practice of obstetrics" (Arney 1982, 43).

At the turn of the century, the state licensing of obstetricians was established and obstetricians became the official guardians of safety for women in childbirth. At this time, obstetricians were still primarily responsible for "abnormal deliveries," while midwives were clearly responsible for normal births. Obstetricians were also in competition with general practitioners. Thus, in an attempt to establish their specialty even more firmly, obstetricians had to extend the notion of abnormal births—despite their knowledge that "primitive" peoples delivered unassisted or with minimal assistance and that many women from the so-called lower orders successfully gave birth attended primarily by midwives. Even among the upper classes, whose natural ability to endure the pains of childbirth supposedly had been eroded by the advance of civilization, some women could deliver without the application of sophisticated obstetrics. Obstetricians therefore decided that birth should be watched for signs of impending pathology (Arney 1982, 54). This framework gave them the license to intervene in childbirth in a variety of ways, from speeding labor with drugs to doing routine episiotomies (an incision in the perineum, the area between the vagina and the anus, to enlarge the opening through which the baby will pass).

In spite of their claims of expertise, obstetricians were still poorly trained. In 1910, the Flexner report revealed that chairs in obstetrics were occupied by men who had relatively little experience and that students could graduate from medical school without ever attending a delivery (Leavitt 1985, 88). Among its recommendations, the report advised that a campaign be mounted to drive midwives from the childbirth sphere of medicine and to promote obstetric physicians by raising fees in order to attract able men (p. 90).

As late as 1910 midwives delivered about 50 percent of all babies, particularly among rural residents and disenfranchised blacks and immigrants (*Research Issues,* 1982, 3). If poor women continued to seek midwives for their confinements, student doctors would have no one on whom to practice and midwives would continue to constitute real competition. A renewed attack on midwifery became part of a growing move toward hospitalization for all childbirth. The hospital was also the place where physicians' growing knowledge of biology and microbiology could be applied to the management of pregnancy. In the next decade the word *midwife* was hardly ever used without appending words like "ignorant and dirty" or using slurs such as "mammy," "grannywoman," "hag," or "crone" (Edwards and Waldorf 1984, 153). In fact, although the preparation of midwives was poor, it was not much worse than that of physicians at the time, and some immigrant midwives received excellent training in their own countries (Leavitt 1985, 88). The campaign, however, was a success. Although public health advocates attempted to convince the medical profession and laypeople that properly training and regulating midwives would help reduce mother and infant mortality rates, the physicians were better organized. After 1930 only midwives from recognized schools were allowed to practice, and the traditional midwife was replaced by the obstetrically educated and supervised midwife (pp. 87–89).

A problem remained, however. Because childbirth was usually a normal process, what would compel a woman to seek an obstetrician? Throughout the midwife debates of 1910–30, the views of a famous American obstetrician who introduced the concept of prophylactic forceps delivery, predominated. Yet even Joseph DeLee's polemic in favor of prophylactic forceps, which appeared in the first issue of the *American Journal of Obstetrics and Gynecology* in 1920, made it clear that he felt birth was only potentially pathological. DeLee's articles set the standards for the obstetric management of birth, making routine such procedures as forceps extraction, episiotomy, manual extraction of the placenta, and the lithotomy position (mother supine, with knees up). Once again, however, as with the concept of prophylactic forceps and other "preventive" interventions, physicians created an atmosphere of danger in order to advertise their power to manage birth. Once this power was brandished, it was also used. Many women were operated on after little or no labor. The number of cases in which manual dilation of the cervix, the use of forceps or version (turning the fetus), and manual removal of the placenta occurred was deplorably large (Edwards and Waldorf, 105).

The Problem of High Mortality Rates

In 1930, the American Board of Obstetrics and Gynecology was established, and obstetricians officially replaced obstetrically trained general practitioners as the appropriate physician birth attendants. The actual benefit of this new specialty to birthing women, however, cannot be easily discerned. In 1933, the U.S. Children's Bureau made an analysis of 7,537 maternal deaths, which showed that between 1915 and 1930 the maternal mortality rate actually went up by 40 percent and that 50 percent of this rise was a result of excessive interventions and poor prenatal care (Leavitt 1985, 91; Edwards and Waldorf 1984, 154). Even though obstetric intervention often made matters worse, middle-class women seemed interested in the latest type of intervention. Indeed, in the 1920s they were demanding that their obstetricians use drugs to create the new phenomenon of "twilight sleep" (Wertz and Wertz 1989, 181). The combination of morphine and scopolamine produced an amnesic-analgesic state, which became popular for a while in the 1920s (Speert 1980, 139–40).

The maternal mortality rate remained high in the 1930s, which led obstetricians to search for standards by which to manage labor. They wanted to see the patient as an amalgam of known processes to be kept on course by selective intervention. They therefore attempted to establish norms for the various aspects of the birth process, such as the mother's position, length of labor, and amount of pain. Of course, they recognized that there was tremendous variation in the ways women give birth. The establishment of one set of standards would nevertheless provide better guidelines for intervention (Arney 1982, 53).

Available ethnographies and observations of women left to their own devices during delivery suggested that squatting was more natural and more comfortable. But obstetricians chose the lithotomy position as the ideal birth position, claiming that the position aided asepsis. There was no evidence for this claim, but the lithotomy position did permit the doctor to survey his patient and intervene easily. It was prescribed as the standard birth posture; women were even strapped into their beds to keep them in that position (Arney 1982, 65).

Textbooks reflected the growing institutionalization of the practice; for example, Edward A. Schuman's 1936 obstetrics text says a woman will try to assume a squatting position in the second or expulsive stage of labor "in an instinctive attempt to increase the diameter of the pelvic outlet and to enable the abdominal muscles to exert their utmost contractile force." But in properly managed labor, the obstetrician will "eliminate instinct" and effect an order that simulates the natural order: "the squatting position may be simulated to some extent in bed by an exaggerated lithotomy position, the legs held in place by attendants" (Arney 1982, 63). In fact, one obstetrics text claimed that "restraint that will prevent any shifting of the patient's relative position by her own muscle actions is very desirable." Special beds were designed to accommodate the position, and by 1944 it had been firmly established. A woman delivers, the reader of the 1944 textbook is told, "lying on her back with her knees raised and abducted," to which is added, "an unruly patient may need anesthesia." Textbooks maintained the lithotomy position as correct until as late as the mid-1970s. Even at the height of the natural childbirth movement in the United States one obstetrician tried to revise the profession's concept of "normal physiologic delivery" to include delivery in the sitting or squatting position by proposing a bed that could be rotated 90 degrees, thus continuing to restrict a woman's ability to assume the position she preferred (Arney 1982, 65–67).

In the 1950s and 1960s research showed that the mother's contractions are stronger and less frequent (more efficient in obstetrician's terms) in the lateral position than in the lithotomy position. These studies appear to have had no effect on practice. In the 1970s, however, when women began insisting on alternative types of deliveries, obstetricians referred to their own research to back up what the women were advocating (Arney 1982, 67–68). Thus they appeared to retain their authority in the face of challenge.

The standards that obstetricians claimed to have established scientifically were central in shaping and maintaining a specific kind of doctor-patient relationship. In their history of American childbirth, Richard Wertz and Dorothy Wertz claim that certain strictures used by obstetricians, although without basis in fact, were used to condition obedience in patients. For example, women were told to keep their weight gain to twenty pounds to prevent eclampsia.[1] Those who did not were called lazy and lacking in self-restraint. The only evidence for this advice, however, was that in World War I it was found that women near starvation did not experience eclampsia. Many doctors had found that the scales were a convenient means of social control over the lives of patients. Research after 1970, in any case, contradicted the assumption (Wertz and Wertz 1989, 168).

Expanding Their Role: The Psychological Pathology of Women

Obstetricians were not content to confine themselves to matters of physiology in managing their patients. For instance, they felt enfranchised to criticize the work role of women during World War II. An editorial in the *American Journal of Obstetrics and Gynecology* decried the employment of women who were pregnant or who had "family ties": "How could a profession which for years had been working to make childbearing safer," argued the editor, "condone exposing women to the hazards of the workplace?" (quoted in Sumney and Hurst 1986b, 109).

Obstetrics strengthened its prescriptions for behavioral conduct by allying itself with Freudian psychology. And Freudian psychology claimed that women's essential nature was passive (see chap. 5). By the 1950s obstetrics and gynecology had expanded their scope to encompass the emotional care of women (Sumney and Hurst 1986b, 107). In fact, they even suggested that they should replace the psychiatrist. Women, said the profession, would never establish the rapport with a psychiatrist that they had with their obstetrician-gynecologist. Valuable time and continuity would be lost in making the change from one specialty to another, and psychosomatic disturbances of women demanded "a basic understanding of the sensitive reproductive and cyclic endrocrinological physiology of the female which is more properly the gynecologist's domain" (Sumney and Hurst 1986b, 108).

According to Freudian theory, either women were wives and mothers or they were maladjusted. If they questioned their doctors, they were competitive and suffering from penis envy. Even childbirth was bound to be psychologically pathological. In his presidential address to the American Association of Obstetricians, Gynecologists and Abdominal Surgeons in 1944, W. R. Cooke proclaimed: "Psychopathology is inherent in the woman, particularly the upper-class woman, because her urge to reproduce the species and her 'maternal instinct' conflict with her 'pregnophobia'" (Cooke 1944). A woman who advocated women's working for wages was guilty of pushing women away from their natural reproductive roles into "pseudomale life." A woman who would not welcome a return to the "haven of support by a husband" was "usually totally frigid and sexless or psychologically masculine [and] regards work either as does the average man or (unconsciously) as a substitute for a nonexistent sexual life" (Cooke 1944).

Such women were immature, dependent, passive personalities (which made them feminine, which made them sick). Women were considered to be predominantly pathological—everything from the symptoms of premenstrual syndrome to labor pains was labeled psychosomatic. Even the pain experienced during childbirth could be an indication of "deepseated unconscious fears." In fact, women's pathology was considered to be so profound that it was claimed that infants and mothers should be separated right after birth because the frequency of postpartum depression made mothers a danger to their infants (Zilboorg 1957).

Moreover, according to Freudian theory, women would naturally regress to a more childlike and passive state when they became pregnant. This regression was considered to be the only way a woman could overcome her penis envy, by reverting to her childlike relation with her father, allowing the father figure to give her a baby as a substitute for the envied penis and thus become a real woman. Interestingly, while the accompanying regression was thought to be necessary, it was also considered to be pathological by the medical profession. As one obstetrician wrote in a medical textbook: "Regression in the course of pregnancy is universal and normal, and pregnancy has aptly been called a 'normal illness.'. . . Just as the regression of the pregnant woman brings to the surface childhood fears, so we find the pregnant woman as suggestible as a child. . . . This is the reason for the success authoritarian obstetricians have with their patients" (Heiman 1965, 480–81). In this childlike state women were thought to be naturally tractable and therefore receptive to professional authority. In fact, the famous Dr. Benjamin Spock described women's greater willingness to take advice from professionals as one of the basic differences between the sexes.

This biologically based Freudian mother was, like women of the nineteenth century, encouraged to believe that her intellect would draw essential energies from the task of reproduction. Even the popular Grantly Dick-Read, the British obstetrician who started the natural childbirth movement, told women in 1947, "Brain work will exhaust the reproductive organs and make healthy birth impossible" (Wertz and Wertz 1989, 188).[2] Motherhood had become so instinctual and mindless by the 1940s that Winnicott advised mothers: "You do not have to be clever and you do not even have to think if you do not want to . . . It hasn't got anything to do with whether or not you are a good mother. . . . If a child can play with a doll, you can be an ordinary devoted mother" (Ehrenreich and English 1978, 224).

Specialization: Women Become an Anatomic Region

Interestingly, at the time the profession of obstetrics was claiming authority over women's psyches, it was experiencing the threat of the return of the midwife. With a plethora of postwar births, 3.5 million a year, the roughly two thousand certified obstetrician-gynecologists needed help. In 1954 there were 158 general practitioners and seventeen specialists for every ten thousand births; in the poorer states there were only ten specialists for every ten thousand births. In the 1940s obstetricians suggested that the midwife might have a legitimate role in obstetric care (Sumney and Hurst 1986, 109). Once again the profession redefined itself (and therefore its women patients) in an attempt to maintain its status. Defining obstetrics-gynecology by the population it served, namely women, would recall its lowly origins and identify it with the equally lowly specialty of pediatrics. Therefore, definition by anatomic region, in this case the female reproductive tract, placed obstetrics and gynecology in the forefront of new specialties developing along anatomic lines—orthopedics, urology, neurosurgery, chest surgery—surgical specialties that depend on extensive medical knowledge. "In this way," argued Howard Taylor, president of the American Gynecological Society in 1958, "the specialty is not on the precarious footing of a specialty like pediatrics defined by some general concept" (Taylor 1958).

The new obstetrics thereby reduced childbirth, if not women themselves, to an anatomic region. Women were essentially left out of the process; childbirth was a medical surgical event done to the patients in assembly line fashion. Moreover, procedures and regulations begun in the 1920s in the pursuit of safety had become by the 1950s inhumane, as women were anesthetized, drugged, strapped down, isolated, and generally divorced from participation in the birth process. It was at this point that natural childbirth became attractive to some as the only appropriate reaction to the conditions of hospital birth.

Natural Childbirth: Co-opting the Resistance

The medical profession's response to natural childbirth was largely negative. Obstetricians labeled their patients hostile if they proposed it and called natural childbirth the Rolls Royce method—a luxury absorbing too much of the doctor's time—or part of the "do-it-yourself craze." Mothers who chose the Lamaze method, which stressed autonomy, were told that they were dissatisfied women who wanted to complete their drive for masculine power (Wertz and Wertz 1989, 190–92). A review of research on the subject published in the *Journal of the American Medical Association* in 1950 concluded that there was absolutely no scientific evidence to suggest that natural childbirth was advantageous (Reid and Cohen 1950, 615–22); the same conclusion was drawn by two researchers in 1978, publishing in the *Journal of Obstetrics and Gynecology* (Beck and Hall, 371–79).

In the 1950s and 1960s, many obstetricians found a way to reconcile the demands of the small but growing number of women who wanted fuller involvement in childbirth with their own interventionist ideology. The "trained obstetrical patient," particularly the woman having her first child, was given physician-designed education about birth and the hospital, even physiotherapy and increased supervision in labor. She was, however, also given analgesia, anesthesia, and a low-forceps delivery. Training was considered good for women because it made them less anxious but did not affect obstetric practice

(Sumney and Hurst, 1986, 106–7). "Natural childbirth," in fact, was used to make those women more tractable patients.[3]

Blackwell Sawyer, a doctor who was using Dick-Read's natural childbirth method, characterized it as a "deliberate attempt to harness, direct, and control" women's "desperate" wish to have children. Women who are "handled in an unsympathetic way become frightened and out of control. When such a woman goes into labor, one must remember that her whole life up to this time has been in preparation for this event. It has been thought about, hoped for, prepared for. It is the fulfillment and culmination of all that the girl intended to do and become" (quoted in Sawyer and River, 1946).

Since the 1950s, there had been voices of dissent from the profession of obstetrics that embraced natural childbirth and later "family-centered care." A 1956 article explained:

> Considering the fact that, for the vast majority of married women, having a baby is the most important thing that they do . . . our domination of their pregnancy and delivery thus robs them of a considerable amount of the psychological satisfaction they might derive from the process. More and more we, and less and less they, are having the baby. Natural childbirth seems to reverse this situation, so that the women, despite the fact that we still play an important part, feel that they are having the baby and that we are simply auxiliaries to the fact. (Tupper 1956, 737)

Expansion: Women Are High or Low Risk

While the natural childbirth movement was quietly gathering force in the 1960s, obstetrics was once more expanding the scope of its authority by shifting to a new focus. As the popularity of Freudian psychology died down in the 1960s and the use of epidemiological studies became more widespread in medicine, obstetrics incorporated its patients into the latter paradigm, once again reshaping the definition of mother and newborn. The Freudian "girlmother," who regressed in proper resolution of her Electra complex, gave way to the "high- (or low-) risk" mother. The notion of risk was transformed from a dichotomy to a continuum. Originally, "high risk" referred to an epidemiological map of whole communities across which programs could be deployed. In the late 1960s a host of articles suggested ways to profile high-risk individuals using evaluations of a woman's fears, attitudes, hostilities, motivations, behavioral patterns, previous pregnancies, employment patterns, income, education, housing, race, marital status, nutritional status, and so forth. There was no set level at which the woman became high risk. Note that this concept did not allow for the identification of patients as "no risk" (Arney 1982, chap. 4). This epidemiological framework fit nicely with the growing idea of obstetric care as part of an "ecosystem." It extended to all parts of the woman's life, recognizing that all parts influenced each other and ultimately birth and motherhood. This idea led to a new focus on family-centered care. In many cases, fundamental concepts had not been defined. In 1970, the Committee on Fetus and Newborn, which had previously set regulations governing the building and operation of nurseries, met to set standards and guidelines for this fast-growing field. One of the tasks of this meeting was simply to define the new perinatal terminology (Friedman 1974, 258). The research on mother-infant bonding fit into this new risk model in which obstetricians headed a team of professionals who claimed the authority to evaluate a host of factors in a woman's life as a means of guarding and treating birth. "At-risk scores" for bonding failure meshed perfectly with this view.

New Technology Enhances the Appearance of Control Again

The 1970s was a time of great technological invention in obstetrics, and the image of childbirth fluctuated dramatically between the dangerous illness concept promoted by obstetricians earlier in the century and the normal or natural model promoted by the childbirth reformists. In 1976, *Newsweek* announced, "Dramatic advances have revolutionized the process of birth . . . Fetal monitors prevent cases of brain damage . . . Newborn intensive care units will halve the rate of US infant mortality . . . High-frequency sound waves are being used as a diagnostic tool during pregnancy." Drugs to start or stop labor would now aid even normal pregnancies. New machines transformed hundreds of labor rooms into "high-risk centers." There was enormous excitement over these "advances," which promised to lower the still high perinatal mortality rate of twenty deaths for every one thousand live births (Edwards and Waldorf 1984, 100).

With these new technological developments obstetrics found a new means of looking for (and often establishing) pathology. Not everyone agreed that the developments were beneficial, however. There was evidence that electronic fetal monitoring often indicated fetal distress when none existed and was therefore partially responsible for the increasingly high rates of cesarean sections (Arms 1975; Edwards and Waldorf 1984, 121; Arney 1982, 121; Wertz and Wertz 1989, chap. 6). Interestingly, while obstetricians, women's health advocates, and the government all had access to the same data, the various groups came to different conclusions about the usefulness of electronic fetal monitoring. Women's health advocates concluded that it was another invasive intervention. Government officials claimed that there was no clear indication for or against its use. Physicians, however, embraced it; in a 1973 study, obstetricians said that electronic fetal monitoring permitted the more accurate assessment and management of labor. It also reduced their anxiety about being sued.

In the 1970s, obstetricians felt themselves attacked from all sides: by other specialists who encroached on their territory and criticized their competence; by the government, which felt they did not regulate themselves and thus needed outside regulation; by the press, which repeated endlessly the relatively poor standing of the United States compared to other countries in infant mortality; and by women who wanted a redistribution of power from the obstetrician-gynecologist to the patient (Sumney and Hurst 1986b, 111–12).

As the decade progressed, physicians felt besieged by "unreasonable" consumer demands and by the threat of malpractice suits. Technology offered a means of tightening their control. The editor of a 1982 newsletter for the American College of Obstetricians and Gynecologists issued a warning to fellow practitioners: "If we are to avoid being done in by the malpractice problem, we must reassert our control over the patient and insist that we exclusively make the decisions . . . putting an end to non-physician interference" (Rhodes 1982).

Woman as Receptacle for the Fetus

In response to the challenge to its authority, the profession closed ranks to become even more specialized and clinical. There was a shift in focus from the management of childbirth procedures to monitoring and surveillance, and a shift from the woman as patient to the fetus. Women were once again viewed as a passive receptacle and even as a meddlesome and dangerous third party. The health of the fetus gave the obstetrician reason to extend his authority throughout pregnancy, a new point of intervention into problems of pregnancy, and a way of investing pregnancy with yet newer meanings, providing more reasons for medical control of the birth process. Obstetricians could leave their treatment of the mother-to-be out of the debate entirely, for now they had the fetus to defend against the potentially bad consequences of a more natural childbirth experience (Arney 1982, 136).

In the late 1970s, the *perinatal* concept emerged as a new specialty with its own journals, professional organizations, and board examinations. Its focus of attention was the fetus from the presumed point of viability (at about twenty weeks of gestation), through the neonatal period (the first four months) (Arney 1982, 153). Moreover, since the use of neonatal technologies was reimbursed at very high rates by insurance companies or by the state or federal government, innovation in these technologies has turned perinatal care into one of the most profitable aspects of the health care industry (Edwards and Waldorf 1984, 177). The new perinatal subspecialty gave doctors a new patient whose management only they could control.

The Premium Pregnancy and Bonding

Now that American parents were choosing to have no more than one or two children, they expected a perfect child at each birth, and the concept of the premium pregnancy appeared. Claims made by the medical industries led parents to believe that when intervention was used routinely, birth tragedies could not occur. At a conference on obstetric technology early in 1983, some obstetricians spoke of being forced to use whatever technology was required by the local medical community regardless of its advisability in individual cases. Otherwise, in the event of legal action, they could be convicted of having provided substandard care (Edwards and Waldorf 1984, 81). Doctors then began to view the technologies not so much as a service to patients as a protection for themselves and hospital administrators, whose best legal defense rested on their use of the newest obstetric innovations.

The aggressive promotion techniques of the pharmaceutical and medical equipment industries also contributed to the use of the technologies. In a letter published in a perinatal journal, author Suzanne Arms described how the companies that developed electronic fetal monitors employed nurses who made the rounds of medical meetings asserting that all labor was high risk and reminding doctors that a child injured at birth was legally entitled to sue the attending doctor for twenty-one years thereafter (Arms 1974, 13). In the 1980s, hospital childbirth seemed likely to become a high-tech event beyond the control of nearly all birthing women. Many manufacturers currently have a vested interest in birth practices that require an array of costly machinery, and connections between the industry and the profession have produced a formidable alliance, with the power to influence national policies.

If technology expanded the scope of medicine to manage birth, so too did bonding theory. It simply made falling in love with the infant another phase of pregnancy and childbirth. The theory suggested simple interventions that could correct a deviant process. Child abuse, for example, might be reduced just by encouraging parents to interact with their babies within the first twelve hours of life (ten Bensel and Paxson 1977). The doctor's job was no longer simply to deliver a laboring mother. It now included, as a column in the *British Medical Journal* explained, "Helping mothers to love their babies," in order to prevent problems of attachment that could result in abuse, neglect, or failure-to-thrive.

Pediatrics: The Public Health Mandate

If technology transformed obstetrics, it revolutionized the care of premature and sick infants. Yet knowledge about these infants was made possible only by earlier developments in pediatrics. Until the first quarter of the twentieth century, when pediatrics was becoming a medical specialty, most medical assertions about the relationship between mothers and infants concerned the nutritional aspects of feeding neonates by breast or bottle. Pediatrics originally developed as a response to social problems addressed by child welfare advocates. At that time the medical profession did not know a great deal about young infants, since most of them never saw a doctor. The few doctors who called themselves pediatricians focused on the study and dissemination of feeding information to help stem the high infant mortality and morbidity rates due to malnutrition and disease among infants of the poor and working classes. Throughout the country, well-baby clinics, growing out of the earlier milk stations, were established to provide these poor mothers with an increasing array of services from prenatal care to feeding instructions. It was out of this network of infant welfare clinics that the profession of pediatrics developed. Pediatrics came into its own in the second quarter of the century. In 1930, the American Academy of Pediatrics was formed. Almost every major city had a children's hospital and departments of pediatrics existed in most medical schools. In a growing number of teaching hospitals the responsibility for the care of newborn infants, traditionally the concern of the obstetric services, was being transferred to the pediatric service (Cone 1979, 203).

Research in pediatrics at that time consisted primarily of the description and classification of childhood illnesses (Fitzgerald et al. 1982, xv). By 1930 there were several thousand infant welfare clinics, which contributed to an increase in demand for pediatric services. Also instrumental in stirring public demand for pediatric care was a flood of advice from the Children's Bureau regarding the proper care of infants and young children (Halpern 1988, 90). About this time, the Society for Research in Child Development was formed, heralding the growing movement toward research establishing developmental norms of infant and child behavior.

During the 1920s and 1930s, pediatricians typically worked at infant welfare clinics part-time, and their constituency was primarily the poor and working class. As the demand for preventive child health care grew, however, it was possible to transfer the delivery of child-health supervision from free public clinics to private medical practices. The publicity campaigns of child-health activists and the example of the clinics stimulated the use of private pediatricians. In the process, pediatric clientele shifted from being predominantly working class to middle class, and the new profession was financially viable (Halpern 1988, 94). Moreover, the concern with infant mortality and children's diseases that had dominated professional rhetoric in the early 1900s gave way to a focus on children's growth and development, drawing liberally from the rhetoric of the child health movement. This growing demand for child health supervision placed the pediatrician in a new relation to the American family as a child management educator. The specialty's core tasks now included the dissemination of norms regarding parenting and age-appropriate behavior in children (p. 93). Motherhood and infancy, then, became normative processes, the parameters of which could be known by pediatricians who were in the business of telling parents what was normal.

In addition to the well-baby clinics and the public health emphasis on preventive child health care, the pediatric supervision of mothers and infants was stimulated by the fact that more and more babies were to be found in hospital nurseries as a result of the hospitalization of birth. During the first fifteen years of this century, with the exception of infant feeding studies and endless feeding advice, little scientific attention was directed toward the newborn infant, despite the remarkable progress of pediatrics during the period. But by the 1920s, interest in the neonate was heightened as the Children's Bureau, which was established in 1912, began to publish statistics showing that the mortality rate during the first month of life had remained constant for the first two decades of the century. Prematurity alone accounted for 24.1 percent of the deaths of infants under one year between 1918 and 1925, and it was prematurity that soon became a new frontier for medical science to address (Fitzgerald et al. 1982, xv).

In the following decades, several conditions helped to foster a new psychosocial or behavioral emphasis in pediatrics. During World War II, pediatric concerns were refocused on the treatment of serious infections because the discovery of antibiotics offered dramatic uses. Together with immunizations and improved milk storage, these achievements permitted the control of most life-threatening infectious illnesses. Consequently, in the post World War II era, pediatrics had more resources to give to the behavioral aspects of childhood problems (Fitzgerald et al. 1982). In the 1950s, processes internal to the specialty, combined with support from private foundations and state agencies, spurred the emergence of psychosocial pediatrics. The academic pediatricians who were leaders of this new movement claimed that pediatric residency programs provided inadequate training in handling behavioral and developmental problems of practice and that research in this area should be promoted. This resulted in a shift in emphasis from the preventive care of well children to the treatment of behavioral syndromes and developmental pathologies. At Case Western Reserve University Medical School, for example, a new, psychoanalytically oriented, family-centered clinic was established during this period. Inspired by Anna Freud's work with children, it drew Dr. Spock to its faculty in the 1950s, as well as Doctors Kennell and Klaus (personal interview with Kennell, June 1990). Moreover, medicine as a whole was placing greater emphasis on social-psychological phenomena during the postwar years, and pediatrics was influenced by this trend (Halpern 1988, 129–30). Spock's *Baby and Child Care,* first published in 1946, exemplified this stance. The book popularized psychoanalytically informed child-rearing practices while embodying the authority of the concerned, supportive, advice-giving pediatricians (Halpern 1988, 128). Little attention was paid to the emotional needs of the neonate at this time, however. Advice on the newborn was still focused on feeding and other purely physiologic matters. Even the attachment research of the 1950s indicated that infants under six months of age had little emotional or social capacity. It was not until the burgeoning of research in infant perception and social interaction in the 1960s that neonates were incorporated into the psychosocial pediatric paradigm.

The growth of behavioral pediatrics was facilitated by support from public agencies and private foundations. Beginning in the 1950s, the federal Division of Maternal Child Health provided grants to pediatric departments for education and research in behavioral medicine. Training grants and further increments in faculty positions continued to evolve in the 1950s and 1960s, supporting the emergence of more highly differentiated academic tracks and the consolidation of new psychosocial specialties. Support for these fields continued during the 1970s, and training grants in behavioral pediatrics were provided in the 1980s. By the 1970s, interest in general outpatient care had given way to more highly differentiated areas for patient care and clinical investigation, and a new generation of professional associations emerged. In 1978 the Society for Developmental Pediatrics was established, and in 1982 the Society for Behavioral Pediatrics (Halpern, 1988, 141–42).

Psychologists connected with pediatrics increased in diversity as well as in numbers. One new specialty with roots in clinical child psychology and developmental psychology was pediatric psychology, originally associated with the pediatric wards of hospitals. Pediatric psychologists work in specialized centers, clinics, intensive care units, in private practice, and as consultants to physicians, parents, school systems, welfare departments, and juvenile courts. Although they have clinical skills and an understanding of child psychopathology, their skills tend to be more behavioral, more research-based, and more concerned with measuring competency than with diagnosing and treating psychopathology (Peterson and Harbeck 1988, 5–9; also see Kagan 1965 or Wright 1967).

Specialization: Neonatology

If the inception of pediatrics as a medical specialty was primarily a response to social health movements, the subspecialty of neonatology was spurred by the hospitalization of the birth process and the technical innovation in the care of premature and sick infants. In 1922, Julius Hess founded the first premature infant center in the United States at the Michael Reese Hospital in Chicago, after several years in Germany and Austria studying the care and feeding of premature infants (Cone 1979, 187). At Michael Reese and similar centers subsequently established, the assistance of mothers in the care of their premature infants was not stressed. This exclusion was due in part to the example set by Dr. Martin Couney, who exhibited premature babies in incubators at fairs in the United States, England, and the Continent. The mothers did not participate in caring for these babies, and Couney sometimes had difficulty in persuading them to take the infants back (Moore 1971, 133).

The exclusion of mothers from central nurseries also reflected the rigid measures instituted to prevent infection in all areas of the hospital. During the first half of the twentieth century normal-birthweight infants, as well as premature and sick infants, were kept in central nurseries in order to control the spread of infection. It was thought that gowned, masked, and scrubbed personnel would maintain a sterile environment and that infants' unrestricted exposure to their parents and outsiders would cause infection. The central nurseries also facilitated the medical monitoring and management of infants without the complication of accommodating their mothers' needs and desires, which did not generally correspond to hospital schedules. These nurseries were established during the second quarter of the century; their growth required professional management, which in turn required knowledge pertaining to the development of the newborn. In a number of teaching hospitals, responsibility for the care of newborns, traditionally the concern of the obstetric services as long as the mother stayed in the hospital, was now transferred to the pediatric service.

Medical Staff Control: The Central Nursery

By the early 1960s, however, there were increasing numbers of studies showing that most newborn infections are acquired in the hospital, usually through cross-colonization in the newborn nursery. (For a review of this literature, see Young 1982, 235–42.) Some studies showed that staphylococci are transmitted among newborns, primarily through handling by staff rather than through the airborne route and that hand washing with hexachlorophene reduces this type of transmission. Some studies compared infection rates of rooming in with ward and private services, finding that the rooming-in rates of infection were lowest. There were also studies of the effects of requiring staff to wear masks and gowns on levels of staphylococcal colonization in the newborn nursery. These studies showed that the rates did not increase when the masks and gowns were not worn. It became clear from the research that the central nursery itself, not the family, was the major source of staphylococcal contamination. Although this information was eventually recognized by the American Academy of Pediatrics, hospitals were reluctant to change their practices. In 1971, the American Academy of Pediatrics stated that one of the four special features of rooming in was that it reduced the incidence of cross-infection between infants transmitted by nursery personnel (Young 1982, 241–42). However, the central nursery is still a fundamental feature of American hospital birth; it facilitates the control and efficiency of the medical staff.

The Challenge of Prematurity

During the second quarter of the century, one of the major causes of death in the first year of life was prematurity; the high morbidity and mortality rates of infants of low birthweight were emerging as great challenges to pediatricians. The perils infants faced during and immediately after birth were not so much those of infection as difficulties in the onset of respiration, handicaps brought about by congenital abnormalities, hazards of obstetric accidents, and other situations that require an understanding of normal physiology (Cone

1979, 220). Investigation of these problems was aided by the spread of the neonatal intensive care units in the 1960s, the result of tremendous technological advances, with smaller and more accurate pieces of equipment to monitor and treat the newborn. These were made possible, in part, by increased government and business funding for research into the problems and care of the newborn, which also enhanced the growth of the profession (Ensher and Clark 1986, 5). It is interesting that neonatologists in the early 1970s were eager to hear of any research in this area, which was then scarce and needed to enhance the growth of the profession (personal interview with Kennell, June 1990). The bonding research of Doctors Kennell and Klaus was therefore received with a special zeal. It was not until 1974, however, that neonatal and perinatal medicine was officially recognized by the American Board of Pediatrics with its own examining board and certificate (Halpern 1988, 111).

In the third quarter of the century, increasingly sophisticated technology was being employed to enhance infant survival, thus enhancing the role of the central nursery in promoting survival and requiring the considerable expertise of medical personnel in monitoring the new technology. In increasing numbers, therefore, mothers were excluded from the care of their newborns, especially in the neonatal intensive care units, where infants might be separated from their mothers for weeks and even months. Because of the extreme conditions of separation, the forbiddingness of the technology, the perilous health of these infants who were difficult babies to care for, and the disappointment that comes from having an infant who is not "perfect," it appeared that the mothers of premature and sick infants had more problems establishing a healthy relationship with their babies than did the mothers of normal infants.

The psychological well-being of these infants now became a concern of the doctors. About the same time that intensive care units were burgeoning, in the late 1960s, new investigative techniques in developmental psychology revolutionized scientists' ability to study infant behavior. As a result, it was found that infants were behaviorally and emotionally far more complex than had ever been thought possible. They discovered that infants' sensory equipment is wired to facilitate social responsiveness. Newborns turn their heads in the direction of human voices but not in response to artificial sounds. They gaze more at a drawing of a human face than at a geometric pattern (Fantz 1961, 66–72). They focus best on objects about nine inches away, which is also the typical distance between the eyes of a nursing infant and the mother. Within days of their birth, babies can distinguish their mother's facial expression, odor, and voice (MacFarlane 1978, 74–81). It appeared that neonates begin to develop their own important complex and malleable personalities as early as the first days of life. Their advocates began to focus on the behavioral and emotional health of neonates as well as their physiological health, and concern with their parents intensified.

The authority of the neonatologist to advise parents about the behavior of neonates soon became accepted. In the early 1970s, Dr. Spock's authority as America's premier child rearing expert was challenged by a neonatologist. Then chief of the Child Development Unit at Boston's Children's Hospital, T. Berry Brazelton developed an innovative scale to evaluate a newborn's interaction with his environment in an attempt to assess an infant's behavioral health. Brazelton produced a number of books, films, and magazine advice columns emphasizing the importance of the infant's early development and relationship to the parents. Prescriptions for maternal behavior were espoused that followed the old pattern. In Brazelton's view, the women's movement had devalued motherhood. "The maternal instinct," he claimed, "that capacity to really give and stay on the child's wave length—is a very precious thing" (Brazelton 1981).

Once again, in lieu of a real solution to a complicated problem, "women's instinct" was used to provide the medical profession with a formula for managing its problematic patients. The condition of these premature and sick newborns was indeed pathological, and their parents were often disappointed, worried, and stressed by many other problems. Moreover, it was often difficult to give an accurate prognosis for the child's future. Fears of retardation, deformity, and other abnormalities were difficult for doctors to allay or assess. Pediatricians seldom received training to assume the task of talking with parents about medical and developmental problems of their infants. Often they did not know how much to reveal of what they did know for fear of overburdening the parents, and did not know how much to reveal about what they did not know for fear of losing their authority and further stressing the parents and infants. Doctors were often faced with parents who did not visit the infants and seemed to lose interest in them, and later saw many return to the hospital failing to thrive and sometimes battered.

The necessity of bonding was an appealing notion. Not only did it require the involvement of parents inside the intensive care unit, but it soon promised redress for the more elusive problems of neglect and abuse that seemed to be outside the doctors' control. The Leiderman and Klaus study, begun in 1964 at the Stanford Premature Research Center Nursery, allayed fears of increased infection rates and opened the intensive care nursery to parents. This opening of the NICU allowed medical staff to help parents to care for their infants amid the forbidding technology and worries about their children's future health. The subsequent bonding studies, however, went far beyond this simple mandate and promised to solve the problems of neglect and abuse by discovering a new pathology of motherhood.

Mothers and Infants At Risk

The intensive care unit facilitated a model of the mother-infant relationship that was consistent with the epidemiological model becoming popular in medicine in the 1970s. A major concern of neonatology during this period was the careful delineation of factors that could be life-threatening in mothers or might result in problems in newborns. Mothers were said to be "at risk" for problems of attachment if they exhibited certain characteristics or were from particular demographic groups. Concepts of vulnerability and risk in infants were defined according to three main sources: environmental influences, such as restricted or aberrant patterns of interaction between the primary caretaker and the child; biological conditions in the infant that have been associated consistently with mental retardation or other developmental disorders; and medical conditions such as severe respiratory distress requiring periods of extensive medical support that often in the past have been related to later impairment (Ensher and Clark 1986, 7). When mothers were fit into this model, the sources of risk were linked to the old maternal deprivation and attachment categories that claimed to find indexes for risk in such factors as the mother's attitude toward the infant as expressed in various aspects of interaction (bonding).

Infants were also said to be at risk on the basis of biological factors. Medical facilities in given geographic regions of the United States were ranked on their ability to offer perinatal care. Those at level three had the ability to handle the full range of complications of pregnancy and of sick newborns. Most of these facilities are now associated with medical schools and many have been designated regional perinatal centers. They provide for the care of newborns with severe respiratory distress, cardiac diseases, and various surgical problems. This approach led to a decrease of nearly 50 percent in infant mortality during the decade 1975–85 (Ensher and Clark 1986, 7). In spite of the remarkable progress the decrease in infant mortality represents, it indicates the kind of struggle perinatologists are engaged in. Infant mortality and morbidity are directly associated with low birthweight. As of 1985, low birthweight infants (weighing less than 2,500 grams) are forty times more likely than normal birthweight babies to die before the age of one month and twenty times more likely to die before that of one year. Two-thirds of all infants who die weighed less than 2,500 grams (Ensher and Clark 1986).

Physicians felt they could have a longer term impact on the well-being of infants whose lives were being saved by new medical developments through the care of the behavior of the mothers. For this reason, physicians have suggested that careful attention to the needs of mothers has great potential impact on fetal and neonatal well-being (Committee on Perinatal Health 1976). In the early 1970s, researchers examining infant-parent relationships concentrated on families dealing with preterm and developmentally delayed infants. One of the recurrent areas of study was attachment and bonding, considering the effects of variables such as separation, prematurity, types of handicapping conditions, and congenital problems. The research of Kennell and Klaus awakened neonatologists to the premature infant's need for involved parental caregiving to ensure optimal development and became a doctrine by which separation policies were revised and by which parents were scrutinized (Ensher and Clark 1986, 178).

Although it was claimed that mothers who did not bond and certain groups, such as the poor, the addicted, and teenage mothers, were high risk for child abuse, the evidence was at best conflicting. Some studies showed a higher incidence of abuse in the NICU population, whereas others did not. All, however, suggested factors other than bonding as the causes of abuse.

The nursing profession struggled to preserve the humanity of women and infants and serve their psychosocial and physical needs in the face of physician-dominated medicine, which pathologized and dehumanized birth. The professional nursing of mothers and infants is a product of unique historical forces. American nursing is deeply rooted in the Christian ethic of commitment, caring for others, and personal sacrifice. In the nineteenth century it was one of the few professions through which Victorian women could seek higher education and remain respectable. Maternity, however, was not a specialty. Most births took place in the home until well into the twentieth century, and female midwives attended the birth while female relatives and neighboring women nursed the birthing mother and infant for days and even weeks.

The development of professional maternity nursing is associated with the hospital. In the nineteenth century the lying-in hospital and lying-in ward had been established as a charity for indigent women who bore children illigitimately. Nurses attending these women were responsible for moral and emotional guidance as well as physical care as such women were thought to be immoral (Rosenberg 1987, 269). At the turn of the century physicians were well on their way to capturing childbirth from female midwives. For economic reasons, however, physicians could not normally stay in the home for long hours like the midwife. The logical next step was to bring women to the hospital where the physician could delay his entrance until fairly late in the birth process. To win over patients from midwives it was not enough for physicians to create an atmosphere of danger, arguing the hospital was safer; they had to show it was more convenient and that better support was available. More care was then shifted to the nurse, whose professional qualifications served to enhance the physician's role (Bullough and Bullough 1984.)

Public health nurses also served as maternity nurses. In the 1920s, the newly established Children's Bureau, from a concern over America's high maternal and infant mortality rates, began a campaign to provide funds to educate poor women about prenatal and postnatal care, resulting in the Sheppard-Towner Act of 1921. Visiting public health nurses were soon dispatched across the country to poor women, providing prenatal care and education as well as birth assistance.

Middle-class women translated this national concern into a personal search for the best care they could find, which meant having a hospital birth. By 1940 half of all births took place in hospitals, 99 percent by 1979 (*Research Issues* 1982, 2). Maternity nursing was now entwined with medicine, which stresses knowledge and ability over the nursing tradition of commitment and personal sacrifice. Nurses found themselves in a hierarchy dominated by physicians. One way that nursing, as a profession, coped with the conflicting ideals and power imbalance was to emphasize its role in the assessment of the patient's needs, emphasizing the psychosocial aspects of birth (Bullough and Bullough 1984.) By the 1940s and 1950s hospital birth was regimented, surgical, and lonely, and maternity nursing found itself in conflict with the medical model of birth. Maternity nurses spent an average of ten days with their charges and had ample time to teach self-care and infant care and to assess the health of their charges. In their concern for their patients, however, they recognized the problems of women's isolation from their families and the complexities of integrating the new infant into family life. Gradually, in the 1960s and 1970s, nursing texts began to refer to "family-centered" care, attempting to restore some of the psychosocial support provided by the traditional nonhospital birth (see Pilletteri 1976). This family-centered approach also gave nursing a role in birth that helped to alter the balance of power with the dominating physician, who tended to manage most of the birth process in absentia. This family-centered approach became especially important in the subspecialty of perinatal nursing—a product of the burgeoning NICU's of the 1970s where psychosocial complications of family life were more prevalent. Bonding assessments gave nurses a critical role unavailable to physicians in guiding and predicting a favorable maternal child outcome. Unfortunately, in nursing's struggle to care for women and infants and achieve some kind of parity with doctors, they, too, contributed to the pathologizing of childbirth by using their assessments to measure "risk."

Mothers as Potential Abusers

The medical model of child abuse implies that child abuse is a form of disease inherent in the mother, the signs of which may be discerned long before symptoms emerge. This disease is often ascribed to the absence of postpartum bonding. Two American pediatricians, Helfer and Henry Kempe, have been in the vanguard of this medical model of abuse prediction. The establishment of screening procedures for child abuse rests upon the ability of researchers to isolate correlates of abuse. The method chosen by Kempe is a prospective investigation in which families are selected, scaled on certain attributes, and then followed up in order to establish which attributes distinguish abusive parents.

Although Kempe claims to have predicted 76.5 percent of the abuse, he adopted an extremely wide definition of abuse, including injuries due to inadequate care and supervision, injuries suspected of having been inflicted, cases of failure-to-thrive that seemed to be the result of deprivation, and cases where the children had been relinquished by their parents, placed in foster care, or kidnapped by one parent. He also listed injuries thought to be true accidents, children who were no longer in their natural homes, and data on whether the children had been immunized (Kempe and Kempe 1978). Montgomery (1982) claims that the "eclecticism" exhibited by Kempe and his associates reflects not only a "haphazard approach to research methodology" but a medical orientation in which they "employ the analogy with a serious disease as a basis for expanding the concept of child abuse." He claims that Helfer and Kempe have embarked not on a scientific disclosure of truth but rather on a political campaign or moral crusade in which they have expanded the definition of child abuse to support their claim of the ability to predict it. (Montgomery states that the frequency of abuse in children aged zero to four years is somewhere between 1.5 per thousand and 10 per thousand.) Therefore, either an extremely large sample or a very broad definition of abuse is needed to "catch" abusers.

Pediatricians have, however, taken on the responsibility for preventing abuse. As one pediatrician (Dubowitz) explains in a 1990 issue of *Pediatric Clinics of North America*:

> The field of pediatrics has a broad view that is concerned with the total health and well-being of children, resulting in a mandate that includes mental and social health together with the more traditional biomedical focus. The psychosocial problems of the "new morbidity" such as drug abuse, divorce, adolescent pregnancy, and child maltreatment have been recognized as substantial issues confronting many American children and pediatricians need to be responsive to the needs of these children. . . . As providers of primary health care, pediatricians are well placed to assess a child's family circumstances and to make appropriate recommendations to help ensure adequate care. Although our colleagues in mental health or social work often need to overcome the stigma attached to their disciplines, pediatricians generally enjoy a trusting and respectful relationship with families.

Dubowitz cites the difficulty of pursuing this kind of treatment:

> In addition to clinical acumen, a body of research exists that has identified risk factors associated with child maltreatment, providing helpful guidance to clinicians. Characteristics that appear to be strongly associated with maltreatment include the lack of financial resources, lower educational status, a maternal history of childhood maltreatment, and negative maternal attitudes toward [one's] pregnancy.

"Interventions" can be made even if the evidence for their effectiveness is not verified:

The most encouraging findings regarding the effectiveness of interventions are the efficacy of home health visitors and early and extended contact between mother and her newborn. . . . Even in these areas the research findings are not consistently positive. However, the lack of evaluations demonstrating the success of programs does not prove the lack of their success. Indeed, no specific pediatric interventions to prevent child maltreatment have been reported, although more frequent office visits have been a part of programs for high-risk families.

It appears that in their desperation to save children, pediatricians have found a new pathology in mothers that allows them (at least the illusion) of some control.

Twentieth-century pediatrics and obstetrics have allied themselves with psychology to redefine childbirth, motherhood, and infancy, searching out pathology and claiming to have established norms on which behavior should be shaped. These monolithic standards are powerful because they are cloaked in the authority of science, which is considered the only reliable source of "factual" knowledge. However, medicine has often concocted scientific information from extant research to suit the politics of a particular situation. As a result, our ideas about what mothers and infants are like have been shaped considerably by the status and market needs of the medical profession, which selects from scientific and not-so-scientific research, filtering the findings through the lens of its own politics. Maternal instinct, for instance, has continued to be part of the lore of what makes women mothers. This "instinct" was often constructed as a danger to women and their infants from which medical men would save them.

Bonding would not have been "discovered" if mothers and infants had not become the province of modern medicine. Bonding also provided a formula for addressing the problem of how to handle parents of sick and premature infants who were often disappointed, fearful, and sometimes even abusive. The research on bonding probably would not have flourished had it not been so useful in the political struggle between parents and doctors that raged in the 1970s over this maternal-infant territory. It is to the struggle between parents and doctors that we turn next in examining the science and politics of maternal-infant bonding.

The Reform Movement

I n the 1970s the concept of bonding played a major role in reforming hospital birth across the nation. In fact, it is doubtful that the study of bonding would have taken on real force had there not been a concurrent zeal for a reform of hospital childbirth that had quietly, modestly, begun to develop in the 1940s and 1950s when parents and health educators united to establish alternatives to surgical birth. The information they gathered and the organizations they formed provided a foundation for the movement for natural childbirth that swept the country in the 1970s and threatened to take routine childbirth out of the hospital altogether. Had it succeeded, a genuine revolution in childbirth management would have occurred and the practice of obstetrics would have been severely affected.

The "discovery" of bonding, however, helped to keep childbirth in the hospital where the new obstetric technology, represented by the electronic fetal monitor, served as a glittering reincarnation of the prophylactic forceps—reminding even the reformers of "impending pathology." In truth, few parents were eager to leave the "protection" of the hospital. Bonding provided a rationale for making the hospital more like home, appearing to give parents the best of both worlds.

It also helped to bolster the beleaguered authority of medicine. Because bonding seemed to enhance the position of each party to the struggle for control of birth it was widely embraced; for the same reason, fundamental change was avoided. A truly natural birth (it is estimated that about 95 percent of births could be natural), where labor is allowed to take its course without the intervention of drugs, instruments, or surgery, was lost to the medical model. Today, almost one in four women experience "birth" as the surgical removal of their infant (Wertz and Wertz 1989, 260). Pain-killing drugs, episiotomies, fetal monitors, restricted labor positions, and standardized laboring times are the norm. Family and friends, however, are now more likely to be allowed to be present at the birth, and mothers are more likely to be able to have their baby with them in the hospital when they wish.

The movement for reform was fueled in the 1970s by the counterculture, the feminist movement, and consumer rights activism. The central appeal of bonding was that it was *natural,* a term that acquired the connotation of being inherently good, even moral. Nature was seen as something innocent in need of rescue from man's treatment through pollution, indiscriminate development, chemical agriculture, and so forth. What was natural represented an existence free of commercialism and materialism. That bonding was the "natural" way was its greatest endorsement. Connected to this romanticized view of nature was a religiosity that fit beautifully with the earlier Christian underpinnings of the natural childbirth movement of the 1950s—a small but dedicated group for whom childbirth was a holy and heroic event rooted in the teachings of the Bible. In the 1970s, the moral goodness of what was natural inspired parents, childbirth educators, and other reformers to view bonding through the same rosy lens. Bonding suited the spirit of the reformers; it also served their ends. It appeared to ensure a more natural childbirth that could still take place in the hospital, where drugs and surgery were readily available if needed.

Bonding also suited the views of medical professionals. Obstetricians and pediatricians saw bonding as a kind of medical procedure, a product of their scientific authority and even a means of keeping and managing their clientele. Nurses, too, used bonding to enhance their authority, working it into the checklists by which they evaluated patients and taught them how to care for their babies. Although neonatologists and NICU nurses were not directly part of the competition for control over birth, bonding provided them with a reassuring formula for redressing some of the problems of the NICU. They felt relatively powerless to affect the behavior of parents who did not visit or did not seem to want to care for their infants. For them, bonding was a kind of medicine they could prescribe for these unmanageable adult charges. If child abuse occurred, it would be because the patients had not taken their bonding "medicine."

St. Christian's Hospital

A study of the role bonding played in hospital reform illustrates the adaptive characteristics of the bonding idea (Eyer 1988, chaps. 4 and 5).[1] In the early 1970s the obstetric services of "St. Christian's" hospital were scattered over three floors in a dilapidated wing of the hospital. Birth took place in a room designed for surgery, and medical interventions were routine. It was standard policy when a woman came in to give birth that she be put immediately in the labor room and prepped for surgery. General anesthesia was common. Husbands were not allowed to be with their wives during birth, and babies were kept in nurseries, to be given to mothers only according to a strict schedule. By the mid-1980s, however, obstetrics was located on a single remodeled floor of the hospital, and patients could choose from a half dozen birthing suites equipped with calico curtains, old-fashioned rocking chairs, and stereo systems, as well as electronic fetal monitors, IVs, and a set of stirrups hidden away in a trunk at the end of a homey-looking bed. The entire family—husband, grandparents, even siblings and "significant others"—could be present at the birth. Bonding would take place right after the birth for an hour in a separate "bonding room" equipped with a radiant heat lamp. If bonding was not possible at that time, then nurses would make certain that at least one hour of postpartum bonding took place as soon as the mother and infant were physically able. The total amount of time spent bonding was noted on a nursing chart. Middle-class mothers appeared to be informed about bonding and actively sought the bonding experience. On the other hand, poor, minority, and juvenile mothers seemed to have no knowledge of the process. They were actively singled out by the nurses, who made certain that they held their infants for the requisite time. There were plans to develop more extensive charts that would record such aspects of the interaction as the mother's alignment of her face with her infant's, whether she spoke to the infant in loving terms, and whether she had a positive attitude toward her birth experience.

The changes at St. Christian's were the result of a struggle among a variety of individuals and groups. One individual who sought to reform approaches to hospital birth was a young obstetrician who claimed that two experiences alerted him to the limitations of his recent obstetric training. During his medical internship in 1969, he had seen women, "counterculture types," handcuff themselves to their husbands in order not to be separated from them during the hospital birth. In the early 1970s, stationed in a military hospital in the Far East, he was surprised to find many women successfully giving birth without medical intervention. By the time he arrived at St. Christian's, he was "looking to do birth more humanely." He formed an alliance with a head maternity nurse who was a local childbirth educator, already crusading for "family-centered birth" and the more humane treatment of birthing women in the hospital. The progressive thinking of this doctor and nurse was supported by women in the community who were taking Lamaze classes and wanted to have their husband-coach with them during the birth. The medical staff eventually conceded that husbands who produced a certificate showing they had attended Lamaze classes could be present for a nonsurgical birth. The obstetric chief of staff at this time was so opposed to having husbands involved that he is said to have given general anesthesia to women in order to exclude their husbands. The head maternity nurse inherited a nursing staff that was also tied to surgical birth, in part because this meant that the patients were drugged and therefore "very manageable" (Eyer 1988, chap, 4). Infants, too, were more manageable in this system, where they were all located in the nursery and brought out only according to a strict schedule (the nurses' schedule).

The discovery of bonding gave real impetus to change. Lamaze instructors adopted the term, and the reform-minded obstetrician was delighted to have a scientific argument to back up what he already wanted to do. Reform-minded parents sought out this doctor, who sent them into the hospital with a written list of demands about how they wanted their birth to be conducted. While the older staff members continued to resist change, newer members inevitably were hired, and their ideas tended to be more progressive. Moreover, the popular media were full of accounts of other hospitals that were successfully implementing family-centered care. The women's magazines were presenting natural childbirth persuasively. (In fact, most subjects in this study first heard about bonding from these magazines. Even doctors, who made vague references to research, all mentioned the women's magazines as a primary source of their information about bonding.) Finally, in 1979, bonding became a policy at St. Christian's hospital on a six-month trial basis. Parents were allowed to bond for one hour in a special bonding room equipped with a radiant-heat lamp to regulate the baby's body temperature.

The critical factor in forcing the reform, however, was the increasing competition, owing to the declining birth rate, for obstetric business. Obstetricians had opened branch offices in outlying areas to attract patients by providing a more convenient location for their services. Pushed by reformers and the need to compete for obstetric business, St. Christian's embraced family-centered care and remodeled its obstetric facility to include a half dozen "birthing suites." The birthing suites were heavily marketed using the slogan "Have Your Baby Your Way." And "your way" included an early discharge program (it was now expensive to keep mothers in the hospital) called "There's No Place Like Home."

During the course of change, bonding had become a doctrine of almost religious proportions. At its height, one doctor is said to have fought with nurses to take infants off respirators in the NICU in order to get them to their mothers for bonding, thus jeopardizing the health of the infants. Nursing checklists were developed, and high-risk groups of mothers, especially teenagers, were actively bonded to their babies by "nursing interventions" in which their behavior was observed, recorded, and in some cases corrected. One mother said later, "It made me feel like a rotten mother when I didn't get to bond with my first two children. Made me feel they were going to go out and rob a bank." A lot of mothers felt, "I've got to do this or people are going to talk about me" (Eyer 1988, 284).

Bonding facilitated the almost inevitable change, in part because its meaning was so plastic that it could be shaped to the agendas of various factions in the struggle for power over birth. For example, doctors, and especially obstetricians, defined bonding as a medical procedure, an inoculation against family failure. Typical of statements by obstetricians is the following passage:

> After the baby is delivered I put the baby right on the mother, not necessarily skin-to-skin, a minute or two. The cord is clamped and cut. . . . The baby is given to the mom or to the father and held for approximately 1.5 hours in the bonding room. We are concerned here with family failure. . . . Bonding, natural childbirth, taking photos and videos may help promote a better generation. Divorce is a real problem. If we can involve fathers we can help create a better society with more family stability. The long-term goal is to make a better society in our own small way. (Eyer 1988, 263–65)

Nurses often referred to bonding as "getting the family off to a good start." The nurses in the birthing suites were especially enthusiastic. "It's important for both parents and children to begin that process of creating a family unit. Physical contact promotes that caring feeling" (Eyer 1988, 266).

The nurses who were charged with the postpartum care of mothers and the nursery nurses were less glowing. In fact, many of the nursery nurses, who had lost considerable authority over their infant charges, felt that there was no basis for "believing in" postpartum bonding.

I don't have any problems with the bonding after birth like some here. They can go out and bond. It doesn't bother me. It would be better if women could just say, "Could I hold my baby or stay with it for awhile?" Babies don't cry less or smile more because they've been "bonded." We almost make a joke of it. We've been bonded, like glued together. I'm sorry, but I think anybody can be with the baby for the first three or four months. (Eyer 1988, 266)

For mothers, bonding was generally a form of leverage with hospital staff to have their baby with them. Most mothers tended to see bonding as a means of being allowed to greet the baby, with no consequences for later development: "The importance of bonding? I was anxious to have him near me and not have him whisked away somewhere. The nurse was a little concerned that he was so calm, she wanted to take him. So I said, 'Shouldn't I be allowed to bond with him first?'. . . There's [sic] absolutely no consequences for the relationship later on. It's just a nice thing to do" (Eyer 1988, 278).

Bonding at St. Christian's, then, was spurred by a wish to reform surgical birth, a movement started by parents but picked up by childbirth educators and progressive doctors and nurses. The force that tipped the scales in favor of institutional reform was the hospital's need to retain its obstetric business by responding to consumer demands. These changes were part of a much wider movement for reform that swept the country in the 1970s.

Childbirth without Fear

A natural childbirth philosophy and several seedling organizations for this movement had begun two decades earlier. But the time was not then right for major reform as most women were not interested in challenging their doctors. Active dissent regarding surgical birth began in the late 1940s, inspired by Dick-Read's 1944 book, *Childbirth without Fear*. Dick-Read's natural childbirth theory was based on the premise that a woman's pain in childbirth was the result of fear and that education about the birth process and learning to relax would make normal childbirth painless. Interestingly, a hundred years earlier another British doctor, James Simpson, had attempted to eliminate the pain of childbirth by pouring a half teaspoon of chloroform onto a handkerchief and holding it over the nose of a woman giving birth. Simpson was attacked for daring to circumvent the biblical condemnation of women to childbed agony. In Victorian times, religious leaders proclaimed that birth pain was necessary to produce motherly love. In 1853, however, Queen Victoria asked for chloroform for the birth of her seventh child, Prince Leopold, whose subsequent sickliness was sometimes blamed on the drug (Dick-Read 1959, 3).

The necessity of feeling pain in childbirth was an idea that was revived by the psychoanalytic movement of the 1940s. As a woman's destiny was to bear and rear children, it was thought that the experience of pain would heighten her awareness of this sublime beginning. A flood of popular books on psychoanalysis after World War II showed that motherhood was a woman's fulfillment. Birth was supposed to be something like coitus, and women who were heavily drugged had missed an important experience. Helene Deutsch claimed that when women who have been drugged for childbirth awaken, they feel no love for the child, sometimes even declaring that the child presented to them is not theirs because they had not felt the birth (Wertz and Wertz 1989, 189). Moreover, the pain of childbirth was consistent with women's masochistic nature and their passive role in coitus, and childbirth was, after all, like coitus (which was also painful but pleasurable). (See Deutsch 1944, vol. 1.)

Dick-Read's ideas caught on among a small group of women, in part because he associated motherhood with essential piety, femininity, purity, and submissiveness—ideas consistent with the postwar glorification of motherhood and with the psychoanalytic assertions that femininity rested on women's identifying with motherhood. He believed that birth was a woman's moment of ecstatic fulfillment. According to Dick-Read, without good mothering, "a nation of gladiators" would arise and more wars would occur. "Give us back the Victorian mothers of seven and ten children and we shall again be swayed by the quiet but irresistible goodness of true motherhood" (Dick-Read 1959, 346).

In 1947, the Maternity Center Association of New York brought Dick-Read to America for a series of lectures.[2] In Chicago, nurse Margaret Gamper, who had given birth using what she herself had gleaned from reading Dick-Read's book, was encouraged by an article in *Collier's* to organize classes to train women in the Dick-Read method. The article, entitled "Motherhood without Misery," discussed Dr. Blackwell Sawyer, who had been using the Dick-Read method of prepared childbirth in rural New Jersey since 1943. Sawyer was enthusiastic about the results of the training, which included making patients more tractable (Edwards and Waldorf 1984, 18; and see chap. 6). Dick-Read appeared in Chicago during his 1947 visit and attendance at Gamper's classes boomed. The Chicago newspapers wrote about the classes, and in 1949 Gamper produced the first of five films on the relaxation method (Edwards and Waldorf 1984, 20–24).

The movement for natural childbirth was enhanced by a postwar religious revival, which fit perfectly with Dick-Read's ideas (Wertz and Wertz 1989, 188–90). "In the Christian religion . . . childbirth is fundamentally a spiritual as well as a physical achievement. . . . The birth of the child is the ultimate perfection of human love. In the Christian ethic we teach that God is love" (Dick-Read 1959, xvi). Dick-Read had declared that a woman had to be a believer, since childbirth was a spiritual as well as a physical event (p. 6). "In motherhood the fearless woman advances to the dais of the Almighty to receive the prize of her accomplishment" (pp. 24–25). He saw childbirth as part of an evolutionary perfection in this life.

Motherhood offers all women who have the will and the courage to accept the holiest and happiest estate that can be attained by human beings. That we, as obstetricians, can help and guide them is our greatest privilege, for with each succeeding generation we may establish the foundations of a new race of men with a clear vision of the future that holds a practical philosophy and a purpose worthy of fulfillment.

The leaders of all manner of religious organizations, sects and denominations recognize the holiness of motherhood and the basic value of the newborn child. We do not forget the significance of Christmas or the manger in the stable of the wayside inn. (Dick-Read 1959, 5, 7)

Dick-Read pointed out that in addition to being a glorious holy event, childbirth received an unfair legacy from the Bible:

Many women read and study their Bible carefully . . . and it is not unreasonable that . . . [they] should believe that childbirth is a grievous and painful experience. They read of its sorrows; we teach of its joys. They read of its pain; we teach that pain is avoidable. . . . Unfortunately . . . Genesis 3:16 quotes the Lord God as having said to Eve: "I will greatly multiply thy sorrow and thy conception; in sorrow thou shalt bring forth children."

This passage, known as the "curse of Eve," rests on the authority of translators in the time of James I, an interpretation that Dick-Read challenged. "Being interested in this subject for many years, I have acquired in my library a considerable collection of ancient Bibles and find that some of the translations differ. . . . The Hebrew word *Etzev*, which is usually translated as "sorrow" and "pain" has obviously been misconstrued. . . . Etzev can mean [many things, including] 'labour'. . . 'concerned' or 'anxious' but not 'pain'" (Dick-Read 1959, 94, 97).

Natural childbirth appeared to women as a heroic Christian act to save their babies, who might otherwise be damaged by anesthesia. In addition, Dick-Read had described childbirth as an athletic contest in which one either succeeds or fails and in which, of course, the doctor is the judge of success. Some women actually pretended not to feel pain lest they be judged inadequate (Wertz and Wertz 1989, 187–91).

Dick-Read also suggested that the natural process was better emotionally and physiologically for both mother and infant. Breastfed babies were more placid and less colicky because the child develops better on natural food and becomes familiar with the comfort of being cuddled.

> When a mother takes her child to her breast immediately after she has witnessed its arrival, not only does the sound of its cry or the touch of its hands give rise to an emotional reaction, but a beneficial physical influence is established within the woman herself. This activity hastens separation of the placenta and closing of the blood vessels in the part of the uterus to which it was attached. The feeding of the child induces certain conditions in the mind of the mother. There is a complacent, peaceful sense of achievement associated with the knowledge that she is giving herself to her beloved possession. (Dick-Read 1959, 244–47)

Stirrings of Protest

In the post–World War II era, women seldom challenged the need for submission to medical control. For example, in the *Ladies' Home Journal* a popular feature entitled "Tell Me Doctor" (1951) by Henry B. Stafford responded to one woman's query about whether her doctor would stay with her during her labor: "If he's a busy man he may have other patients to serve at the same time. . . . It won't be much help to have him sit by the bedside and hold your hand." To "Can I have my family with me?" the response was, "Certainly not. . . . One of the very good reasons for being in the hospital is to get away from well-meaning but uninformed advisers. That sounds sort of cruel. It's not. It's kind." He went on to describe what would happen to her next in the expert hands of her doctor:

> Let's say that we have reached the point where the patient feels great pressure in the region of the outlet [sic]. . . . She must be taken to the delivery room. . . . There she is placed upon a specially devised table equipped with stirrups which sustain her legs with knees flexed in an appropriate position for the delivery. Her hands are also effectively restrained. [Here the woman interrupts to protest the thought of being bound hand and foot.] . . . In all probability you will know nothing or feel nothing until you

suddenly awake and hear, coming from what will probably seem a great distance, a lusty little Wa-a-ah! (Edwards and Waldorf 1984, 30)

Childbirth in which a woman was efficiently removed as an intelligent being was most common during this period, and this kind of birth and the dehumanizing attitudes surrounding it eventually became the focus of reform.

The first movement to humanize maternity care in hospitals was a movement to reverse the separation of mother and infant from each other and the family by means of "rooming in." There were a few hospitals in the 1950s that had begun to adopt more humane policies. The best known of these was Grace-New Haven Hospital. Under the direction of Herbert Thoms, head of obstetrics and gynecology, women were prepared using Dick-Read's methods and a rooming-in project was designed. This project was described in the *Ladies' Home Journal* in 1960 in the article "The Challenge to American Obstetrics" (Edwards and Waldorf 1984, 31–32). The challenge did not go unnoted. Some doctors began to see natural childbirth as a threat to their control. *Time* magazine quoted an article from a medical journal in which obstetricians pictured women chatting over a game of bridge about childbirth, entertaining each other with the vivid details of an undrugged labor, including (the doctors wrote with an apparent shudder) "the ecstasy of the unassisted expulsion of the placenta." They claimed that the Dick-Read method could do serious harm because it was a "psychobiological lobotomy" that hid other fears of childbirth, such as "deep-seated anxieties . . . [about] increased responsibility, loss of personal freedom, economic hardships, and overcrowding of the home." Other obstetricians used the tenets of psychiatry to attack the motives and even the sanity of women who sought a prepared natural childbirth. Psychiatrists themselves disagreed on the origin of such an inclination; some insisted it came from the desire to prove authentic femininity, while others declared the root was quite the opposite, a drive for power or "psycho-masculinity" (Edwards and Waldorf 1984, 41).

In 1956, the La Leche League was formed to defend a belief in the

value of family life and the role of lactation in preserving it at a time
when women were being told to bottle feed their infants. Its members
claimed, among other things, that because the breastfed baby is held
more by the mother, it is psychologically closer to her. New mothers
who wanted to breastfeed had few sources of support or authority
at the time. The league promoted breastfeeding and provided information and counseling.

Few women demanded natural childbirth in the 1950s and 1960s.
An article published in 1957 in *Harper's Bazaar,* however, provided
another impetus for change and marked the beginning of a shift
away from the methods of Dick-Read to the coached breathing
methods of Lamaze (Karmel 1959, 6). Marjorie Karmel, an actress
and playwright, described her experience of "painless" childbirth
under the tutelage of Dr. Fernand Lamaze, whom she had met on a
trip to France. A year later the full story of her experience was
published as a book, *Thank You Dr. Lamaze.* In the Lamaze system,
as in Dick-Read's system, natural childbirth was a contest. The
expectant mother went into training, using the scientific methods of
conditioning developed by Pavlov. "'Remember, you are entering a
competition that you are going to win,' Ms. Karmel's 'monitrice'
admonishes her. . . . 'I had faith in Mme. Cohen [the monitrice]
and Dr. Lamaze, faith in Pavlov and most of all faith in myself. I
was looking forward to the championship match, confident that I
would win'" (Karmel 1959, 66).

With Elisabeth Bing, a New York childbirth educator, Marjorie
Karmel created an organization for the promotion of Lamaze methods that would involve physicians as well as nurses and laypersons.
Although the American Society for Psychoprophylaxis in Obstetrics
(ASPO) advocated prepared birth using "psychoprophylaxis," it also
admonished women not to challenge their obstetricians. "If he himself [the doctor] suggests medication, accept it willingly even though
you don't feel the need for it. He undoubtedly has good reasons for
his decision" (Bing 1969, 11). In time, Lamaze came to refer to any
of the general aims of natural childbirth: consciousness while giving
birth, a minimum of medication, spontaneous as opposed to forceps
delivery, prenatal education of the parents, and participation of the

father. In the early 1970s, when Lamaze classes were mushrooming in every community, there seemed good reason to hope for major changes in hospital birth. The need for change is vividly illustrated by women's own accounts of their experience of hospital birth in the 1950s, as published in some of the women's magazines.

Labor was often actually arrested until the woman's doctor could be present (or speeded up to suit his schedule.)

> My obstetrician wanted to get home for dinner. When I was taken to the delivery room my legs were tied way up in the air and spread as far apart as they would go. . . . I was left alone.

Another charge was that births were often held back to wait for the doctor's arrival.

> The doctor went out to make a house call. One hour later my legs were released in the stirrups and held together by a nurse who sat on my knees upon the delivery table, mind you, because the baby was coming so fast.

Women were also left alone for long, frightening periods during the first stages of labor.

> With leather cuffs strapped around my wrists and legs, I was left alone for nearly eight hours until the actual delivery. (Edwards and Waldorf 1984, 55)

In the 1960s, a federation of parent groups advocating family-centered rather than hospital-centered birth became the International Childbirth Education Association. The group envisioned birth as a profound experience for both husband and wife. Although several professionals were invited to serve as consultants, among them Margaret Mead and Ashley Montagu, the work of ICEA member groups was done largely by parent activists. By the late 1960s, it had begun to merge with the counterculture in California, where, at a meeting in 1968, there was discussion of using encounter groups in childbirth education classes and midwives to deliver infants at home or in alternative birth centers. A strain of consumerism seemed to be emerging as well. Parents were encouraged to take responsibility for getting the kind of care they wanted by actively pushing for it (Edwards and Waldorf 1984, 63–66).

The Influence of Feminism

At about the same time, the feminist movement was also gathering force. In 1963 Betty Friedan, a journalist, published *The Feminine Mystique,* an investigation of the widespread malaise among middle-class women who were (in increasing numbers) taking tranquilizers, spending years in psychoanalysis, and complaining that they were discontented. Many experts postulated that their problem was "over-education." Friedan claimed the problem was "femininity" and that femininity was a myth, the *feminine mystique.* During the 1960s, women all over the country met to raise their consciousness about this myth. The feminist analysis of motherhood centered around what Adrienne Rich, poet and feminist, referred to as the *institution* of motherhood as opposed to the *experience* (Rich 1976). The institution was patriarchy: literally rule of the father. In feminist terms, patriarchy means the control of women by men through a blend of legal and extralegal means (including violence), and with women's consent, by socialization (see Millet 1970). Patriarchy defined women according to the institution of motherhood. Defining a woman's role as something other than a mother was considered by the feminists of the 1970s as central to freeing women from the confines of patriarchal oppression.

The phenomenon of bonding entered the feminist arena of discussion in an article by sociologist Alice Rossi in 1977: "A Biosocial Perspective on Parenting." Rossi suggested that feminists had gone too far in their rejection of women's nurturing role. She argued that because the biology of males and females has, throughout the history of our species, meant that females nurture, "there may be a biologically based potential for heightened maternal investment in the child, at least through the first months of life, that exceeds the potential for investment by men in fatherhood. Significant residues of greater maternal than paternal attachment may then persist into later stages of the parent-child relationship" (p. 24). Rossi, of course, cited the bonding research to back up her claim for this "biosocial perspective." Although she was not suggesting that only women should mother, many feminists were angered by this argument, which could once again be used to confine women to the mothering role (Eisenstein 1983, chap. 7).

Rossi's analysis was, however, consistent with a new direction that some feminist theorists had taken in the late 1970s. Although feminism had begun with a critique of the oppressiveness of women's sex roles, now many theorists saw women as carriers of the more laudable qualities of human civilization. The "feminine" traits of gentleness and nurturance had been denigrated by men, who had kept for themselves the dominating and managerial roles. But now it was suggested that what society (fraught with violence and nuclear threat) needed were the very qualities women had (see, e.g., Miller 1976; Chodorow 1978.) Rossi's argument and bonding coincided with this latter tack.

A prime goal of the feminist movement was to free women from the feminine mystique of the postwar era. To become free, a woman had to make her own rules about her reproductive capacity. In childbirth, this meant being in charge of birth—having her husband, friends and family present if she liked, being awake and aware if she wished to be, choosing medical procedures in conjunction with medical professionals rather than at their command. The feminist critique of childbirth centered around the fact that it was a fragmented process in which the woman was shuttled from place to place and from one doctor to another in a system that standardized and processed her pregnancy in assembly line fashion and withheld pertinent information from her.

In 1969, a consciousness raising group on the East Coast inspired the formation of the Boston Women's Health Collective. This group became a guiding force in the women's health movement, which works to reform the medical care system and to provide women with the information necessary to demystify medical authority. These women had first called themselves "the doctor's group," as they were brought together by feelings of frustration and anger about doctors who were so often "condescending, paternalistic, judgemental, and non-informative" (Boston Women's Health Collective 1973, 1). They began to develop a course for women to educate themselves about their own bodies and out of the course a book was born. The changing titles of both the group and the book reflected the growing philosophy of the collective—from "Women and Their Bodies" to "Women and Our Bodies" to, finally, "Our Bodies, Ourselves." They had come to realize the extent to which their identity was tied to their bodies (1973, 1976, 1984).

Our Bodies, Ourselves discusses every aspect of women's biological experience from menstruation, pregnancy, and childbirth to masturbation and rape. The continued popularity of the book reflects women's growing awareness of how limited and distorted their knowledge of their own bodies had been and the power this knowledge represented in terms of women having control of their lives. To these women, a prepared natural childbirth attended by chosen loved ones seemed as though it would put women in control of their giving birth. In the 1973 edition of the book there is no mention of bonding. The related maternal deprivation idea did not appeal to these feminists: "We believe it is a myth that the infant will be psychologically damaged unless the mother is always present. Studies of stunted children who have grown up in orphanages are often cited in an attempt to prove that infants need one constant caretaker (usually construed to mean the mother) rather than several" (Boston Women's Health Collective 1973, 212–13). They pointed out that the research was being questioned as behavioral scientists discovered how much these infants were products of institutional problems, such as a lack of stimulation and emotional warmth.

In the 1976 edition, although the word "bonding" was not used, the authors felt compelled to state, "You may not experience that 'gush' of motherhood you've heard so much about [right away]. Don't feel guilty. It takes time. . . . And besides, you may feel overwhelmed by all sorts of emotions" (Boston Women's Health Collective 1976, 296). In a section titled "How Medical Institutions Shape Our Childbearing Experience," however, the authors lament the fact that "We don't know enough about the earliest signs of a mother's inability to parent." They cite Kennell and Klaus's review,

"Mothers Separated from Their Newborn Infants" (1970). Then: "There is evidence that prompt presentation of the baby to the mother after birth (on the delivery table) is important for the mental health of the mother." They cite the 1972 study by Kennell and Klaus in the *New England Journal of Medicine,* in which they note that studies of other mammals suggest that a delay interrupts mothering impulses and may bring on rejection. They lament the hospital routine in which "the hospital staff acts as if the baby belonged to them. . . . It may well be that our hospital routines are partially responsible for the depression women feel after birth. . . . We must . . . offer . . . support to new mothers . . . and thereby stop a potential national health problem (mothers' inability to parent, babies' failure-to-thrive, battered child syndrome)" (Boston Women's Health Collective 1976, 308–9).

By 1984, the authors of *The New Our Bodies, Ourselves,* describe the continuing need for a women's health movement, citing the increasing grip of the medical model on women's lives.[3] The authors continue to doubt that the maternal deprivation and attachment research means that mothers should stay at home with their young children (p. 412). Regarding bonding, they now advise,

> Right after birth, hold your baby close. S/he's your own; you have waited all this time and labored hard. At home, in birth centers and in some hospitals, you can hold your baby right away. . . . You'll want to caress, touch, talk to her/him. Enjoy this slow time. If you are exhausted, your partner can hold the baby against you or close to him/herself. So much has been written about this moment. We want hospitals to respect how crucial it is for us, our partners and children to be close to our babies and in this way, begin (and continue) a family together. Most babies have the capacity to form a strong attachment to another human being right after birth. Yet this process, called "bonding," cannot be forced or created just by going through the motions. As [social anthropologist] Sheila Kitzinger said in one of her talks, "Some hospitals act as if it's a special glue that can be sprayed on and will take in five minutes. After that they think

it's too late." One mother fighting separation from her baby was told, "You're bonded to her now, so what's the problem?" And if for some reason the first moments after birth don't turn out the way you want, you will have many ways of becoming attached to your baby and her/him to you. "Bonding" in humans is an ongoing process.

They add: "*There is no medical reason to separate healthy mothers and babies after birth. It is your right to keep your baby with you; s/he belongs to you*" (Boston Women's Health Collective, 1984, 374–75). Kennell and Klaus are not mentioned. For the women's health movement, then, it seems that bonding is primarily embedded in the issue of a woman's control over her birth experience in the face of an opposing medical authority.

The Ideology of the Natural

Although many feminists were suspicious of biological explanations for women's behavior, the idea that there were biological underpinnings to the mother-infant relationship fit in with the growing feeling that everything should be "natural," from foods without preservatives to childbirth without drugs. The alliance of the natural with maternal instinct was an assertion of the experts that caught on. In 1969, Brazelton popularized the notion in *Infants and Mothers*. A consistent theme of Brazelton's was that infant and mother are biologically destined to shape each other: "There is some deep biological principle that abhors the imposition of one person's will upon another— even when one is mother and the other infant, or vice versa. The deepest principle is mutuality, and it begins early" (Brazelton 1969, xiv).

The women's magazines played a major role during the 1970s in popularizing and even advocating the all-natural and once again instinctual childbirth. In the article "Instinct and the Origins of Love" in the December 1970 *Redbook*, Margaret Mead declared: "The cues . . . parents give children and children give parents are built on innate responses. . . . The infant's gesture—frail, yet very firm—is a biologically determined way in which the new human being 'asks for' recognition. . . . The adult response contains, in addition to an innate, biological component, all that the adult man or woman has learned about the helplessness, the need and the appeal of infants."

Those favoring a return to the natural also found support in information suggesting that medicated birth is harmful. In "What Childbirth Drugs Can Do to Your Child," in the February 1971 *Redbook*, Brazelton described the deleterious effects of drugs on the newborn and especially the mother, who is disappointed by having a sleepy baby during this sensitive period. Brazelton also makes a link with Bowlby's ethological ideas: "The noted naturalist Konrad Lorenz has observed the 'imprinting' process among animals. He made proper 'mother goose' noises to goslings as they first hatched and found that thereafter they followed him about as if he were their mother. The British psychiatrist John Bowlby has recently pointed out that there is an imprinting process for human babies too that must take place if a firm, positive mother-infant relationship is to be established." He concludes that thanks to such groups as the International Childbirth Education Association, natural childbirth is "staging a comeback." These ideas regarding the importance of the mother-infant relationship, the instinctual bases of behavior, and the superiority of natural and family-centered birth continued to be echoed in the following years by the popular media and their experts.

Self-Fullfilment and Control

An article in the March 1973 *Parents* illustrates another important facet of the reform movement: the focus on adult self-realization and growth, the phenomenon that earned the 1970s the title of the "me decade." Childbirth was supposed to be an experience of self-gratification, especially for the mother, a phenomenon enhanced by the low birthrate, which contributed to the uniqueness of childbirth. Parents who were likely to have only one or two children could afford to focus a lot of attention on the premium birth experience. Now the birth was a peak experience for the pleasure of both parents. In "It Takes Two to Have a Baby . . ." the author complains that she was not the center of attention during her first birth experience: "Although I had received efficient care, the staff had seemed entirely disinterested in my role as a new mother. In the crowded labor room, I had been ordered around as if I were the least important participant in the birth process."

Her second birth experience takes place in a hospital that provides the new family-centered care, promoted by ICEA, which now also incorporates the experience of husbands: "When we talked with classmates from our prenatal course, all the fathers who had been present in the delivery room were immensely gratified by the experience. . . . The advantage of family-centered care is its flexibility. The baby can spend as much of the day in his mother's room as she wishes; or he can be cared for in the central nursery."

If the parents' pleasure is not sufficient reason for family-centered care, however, then science can provide the decisive rationale. The author concludes that most hospitals do not yet offer such services but they should do so, especially because "recent research indicates that close physical contact between mother and baby during the first few days of the infant's life may set a positive pattern for their later relationship."

In the September 1979 *Redbook,* Dr. Brazelton, too, describes natural childbirth as a means by which women are given a *sense* of control:

> Even if she must have medication or a cesarian section at the end and must face the disappointment of not having done it *all* by herself, she can still feel the sense of confronting pain and labor in the process of becoming a mother. Natural childbirth, then, has been enormously helpful in backing up women to feel in control as they experience a major developmental event in their lives. This is so much so that I see the movement for natural childbirth as parallel to the feminist movement in encouraging women to feel more competent in their roles.

Again, bonding is seen to aid this process: "Drs. Marshall Klaus and John Kennell . . . have demonstrated that when mothers are supported in this way [that is, allowed to hold the baby after birth] at the time of delivery, there tends to be better mother-infant bonding and significantly better developmental performance in the infants at one year and at two years." It appears that even in the 1970s some doctors viewed natural childbirth (and bonding) as a means to make women more tractable patients, giving them a sense of control while retaining the power to define and manage birth for themselves.

The Return of the Midwife

The women's magazines continued to reflect the move to reform and even reported on some of the more revolutionary forces that were gathering on the West Coast and a few other areas around the country. The October 1972 issue of *Parents* carried the article "The Midwife Returns Modern Style." People were beginning to turn to midwives because they were seeking a more natural, humane, and low-cost childbirth. They complained that obstetricians were too rushed to participate fully and consistently in the birth. One place where midwives were becoming more prevalent was California. There, counterculture parents were choosing home births, neighbors attended neighbors, and a new-age midwifery came into being, always on the edge of the law and in spite of active campaigns by established institutions to discredit them. One influential midwife was Pat "Raven" Lang, who had her first child in 1968 at Stanford University Hospital and found that when "another mother's baby" was brought into the maternity ward crying, her hormones triggered her milk letdown. When she was handed "her own infant," she insisted it was the wrong baby. Indeed, the other infant *was* hers— the nurse had made a mistake. Struck by this power of her woman's biology to *know,* Lang became a lay midwife and founded an alternative birth center run by lay midwives in Santa Cruz in 1971 (Edwards and Waldorf 1984, 59).

Local physicians in Santa Cruz became increasingly antagonistic toward the birth center, although its record of safety was immaculate. Lang moved to Canada and in 1972 published a book that became influential in the natural childbirth movement. The *Birth Book* advocated home births, and bonding was an important aspect of the book's philosophy. The book included a short essay on imprinting and maternal affection suggesting that mothers and infants should be together after birth.

Between 1974 and 1982, the midwives of Santa Cruz, as well as other regions of California, were persecuted by the medical profession and were eventually convicted of practicing medicine without a license. Their attorney maintained that birth was a normal process, not a disease, and that therefore attending a birth could not be called practicing medicine. The Santa Cruz center finally disbanded in 1978 (Edwards and Waldorf 1984, 156–72). The attack on midwives continued across the country, wherever midwives were threatening obstetricians' business.

In a discussion on midwifery that appeared in 1978 in the *American Journal of Obstetrics and Gynecology,* one physician explained how midwifery and alternate birth practices threatened obstetrics: "If we cannot have everything, we must make a decision as to whether we are going to give away 'normal' obstetrics. If we are, then I think the time will come that we must also decrease residency programs by a third or by 50 percent. We cannot flood an already saturated system. A survey in Ohio that asked people what they really wish reveals, at least in Ohio, that patients really want doctors" (Zuspan 1978).

Indeed, in 1981 the American Medical Association (AMA) voted to oppose federal funding for training nurse practitioners and midwives. However, in England, for instance, around 80 percent of babies are delivered by midwives, and within the National Health Service doctors usually handle only complicated deliveries. In America, on the other hand, midwifery is almost synonymous with home birth since in most states midwives are not allowed to deliver babies in hospitals (Kitzinger 1987, 107–8). In other industrialized countries, midwifery plays a major role in birth. In America, nurse midwives, of course, remain generally subordinate to physicians by virtue of their being nurses.[4] The American College of Obstetricians and Gynecologists currently remains opposed to all deliveries in nonhospital settings, in spite of the natural childbirth movement and the spread of birthing centers and midwifery.

Bonding and the Reform of Hospital Birth

While out-of-hospital birth continued to be assailed, the fight to reform birth in the hospital gathered strength. Even Dr. Spock advocated reform through bonding. In the May 1976 *Redbook,* he encouraged parents to pressure hospitals to reform their practices to allow for this more natural kind of childbirth, citing Kennell and Klaus's recommendation that all babies be brought to the parents for an hour right after birth for examining and fondling. Although the reader might by now be skeptical of all the phenomena attributed to women's instincts, Dr. Spock has some vivid examples in the long tradition of cautionary tales designed to frighten women:

> A new chimpanzee mother treats her first baby tenderly if she has had a labor of normal duration. But if she has a sudden, precipitate delivery, she is frightened by the baby and climbs up out of the cage to get away from it. You can see why the psychologically minded obstetricians, pediatricians, psychiatrists and nurses who heard of these observations 30 years ago pushed natural childbirth and rooming-in so that mothers could be conscious as they went through the stages of labor to begin the initial care of the baby.

Dr. Spock talks about some of the research of Kennell and Klaus in Guatemala where babies are carried close to their mothers' bodies all the time and experience constant motion, which he claims may keep the babies from being colicky. This reminds him of the studies by Harry Harlow in which infant monkeys preferred cloth dummies to milk-giving wire dummies (showing the importance of body contact) and exhibited bizarre behaviors resulting from isolation in infancy (*maternal deprivation*). Next he mentions "a psychologist named James Prescott [who] has speculated as to whether the high rate of violent crimes in our society may be related in part to the infrequency of close contact between babies and mothers." Perhaps recognizing the alarm that could be created by crediting such a claim, Spock adds: "We know that the majority of American children who have experienced the methods I've listed turn out to be bright and warmhearted. So don't rush—this minute—to pick up and hug and joggle your baby to try to make up for lost opportunities." To the long tradition of blaming the mother for juvenile delinquency (Bowlby), a nation of "gladiators" (Dick-Read), and "terrorists" (Brazelton), we may now add the "violent criminal" (Spock).

By this time bonding was an idea that needed little encouragement. Kennell and Klaus had been spreading the word across the country at professional conferences in which the doctors hailed a revolution in hospital childbirth. In 1977, a "Parent to Infant Attachment Conference" was sponsored by the Rainbow Babies' and Children's Hospital and the Department of Pediatrics at Case Western Reserve University, where Kennell and Klaus were on the faculty. Dr. Brazelton and his associates in Boston were also involved in organizing this conference. The proceedings were published in the Winter 1978 issue of *Birth and the Family,* a new journal promoting natural childbirth. At the conference it was declared that "there is a revolution occurring in the way in which mothers and infants are cared for in hospitals," and the proceedings focused on attachment or bonding as fundamental to a proper childbirth. At this meeting Dr. Klaus made a plea, one of many that he and Dr. Kennell would subsequently make, that people not reduce the bonding idea to a period right after birth (which he calls the "epoxy" bonding concept). By this time, however, the bonding idea was out of the control of its creators. In 1978, the American Medical Association had met and, according to Klaus, decided to make it part of its official policy that every mother should be accorded "at least ten minutes" of postpartum bonding. Even Dr. Klaus was aghast at the reductionism of this policy, about which neither he nor Dr. Kennell was consulted (personal interview with Klaus, June 1990).

Indeed, hospitals across the country had felt the pressure to reform in the name of bonding. In a 1978 article in the *Journal of the American Medical Association,* Annexton states that as early as 1973 consumers had apparently adopted the idea of bonding as a means to pressure hospitals to develop birthing rooms. A *Wall Street Journal* article on the rise of birthing rooms and the relaxation of hospital birth practices quotes the director of the National Association of

Parents and Professionals for Safe Alternatives in Childbirth as saying, "Hospitals that don't set up a birthing room will go out of business because of the competition" (Lublin 1979). Indeed, parents were taking their business elsewhere. According to a 1982 report by the Institute of Medicine and the National Research Council on Birth Settings, during the 1970s there was a "rising concern [among physicians] that births were increasingly occurring in places other than hospitals." The number of freestanding alternative birth centers (ABCS) grew from 3 in 1975 to 130 in 1982. By 1980 there were over 300 alternative birth centers both in and out of hospitals. Most advertised a homelike setting, a minimum of intervention (no routine preps, IVs, or fetal monitors), and welcomed family members, including the children and friends of women in labor. They provided a haven for nurse midwives and low-cost birth. In 1984, however, only 1 percent of all births took place outside the hospital, the same as in 1975 (Pearse 1987). In 1988, there were an estimated 150 alternative birth centers, 28 percent of them owned and run by doctors (Wertz and Wertz 1989, 285).

Although the bonding movement helped to promote reform, its overstated imperatives inevitably caused problems. By the late 1970s, a number of the experts published in magazines found themselves dealing with some of the casualties of these exaggerations. A note of caution was sounded by Ira J. Gordon, professor and dean at the School of Education of the University of North Carolina: In the November 1978 *Parents Magazine* he writes, "Bonding—is there a critical time? Parents . . . are often anxious about what they may have heard or read about 'bonding' or 'attachment.'. . . Although the first hours after birth are indeed a highly desirable time for mother and infant to begin the bonding process, there is no long-term data to support the notion that if this moment is missed, an irrevocable loss has been suffered."

In the September 1980 issue of *Parents Magazine,* Dr. Robert B. McCall writes:

A mother of a two-week-old infant reportedly burst into her pediatrician's office pleading "Doctor, bond me to my baby before it's too late!"

This woman had missed the opportunity for early skin-to-skin contact with her baby, which helps to initiate "bonding," a close, loving, attachment between parent and child. In one form or another, this practice has become widespread recently. While early contact is a good idea, this woman illustrates an undesirable side effect of this movement.

Although McCall believed that the early contact can be beneficial, he cautions against taking it too literally and concludes, "And in any case, remember that your love and concern are just as important when your child is six or sixteen years old as when he or she is six minutes old." Since practically every tenet of psychology emphasizes the importance of early development and mothering, this is an intriguing statement.

At the end of the decade considerable change related to bonding appeared to have taken place in hospitals, although not to the complete satisfaction of parents. In 1982, in the August *Parents,* the results of a survey on childbirth practices with sixty-four thousand respondents provided some perspective. According to the survey, husbands had finally gained admittance to the labor room, the delivery room, and even the operating room. Of the respondents, however, 77 percent were allowed to remain with their babies for less than an hour after the birth; one-third were with their babies for less than ten minutes after delivery; only 13 percent were allowed to remain with their babies for more than an hour; and 65 percent said they would have preferred to remain with the baby longer than they were allowed. Another study, conducted in 1984 in the Philadelphia area, showed that more than 65 percent of the area's hospitals had a birthing room in which women could labor and deliver in the same bed; 100 percent allowed a support person to be present during a vaginal delivery; 88 percent permitted a support person during any birth, even a cesarean (*Choice* 1984). If bonding helped to usher the family into the hospital, the more serious matter of the control of a natural course of labor fared less well.

In the battle over the use of obstetric drugs the pressure to bond was used by some persistent reformers in the 1980s as a rationale to take birth out of the hospital because of continuing excessive interventions. Yvonne Brackbill, professor of psychology in the Department of Obstetrics and Gynecology, University of Florida, conducted the largest review of obstetric drugs in American history, made public in 1979, which showed that obstetric drugs have lasting effects on the behavior of children. She also began to lobby in Washington. In her 1984 book, *The Birthtrap,* she claims:

> The medical establishment says that modern hospital delivery is safest for mother and child—and every year millions of new American parents believe it. . . . Instead of letting nature take its course, obstetricians take over through expensive, risky high tech intervention. . . . [But] *alternative birth environments promote the critical bonding experience. . . . Early separated infants may score lower on tests of intelligence and language. . . . [Separated mothers may exhibit] fewer protective and nurturing behaviors.* (pp. 1, 34, 129; emphasis added)

Although women's control over having their baby with them in the hospital was facilitated somewhat by the institution of bonding, the deeper issue of women having more control over the birth process with the prospect of less invasive practices took on some frightening dimensions. Toward the end of the decade, the battleground of childbirth had shifted from the hospital to the courts and legislature as the new technologies that had developed in perinatal medicine posed new challenges to those who sought a natural birth. Doris Haire, a member of the La Leche League and ICEA, testified as to how the obstetric pattern of interventions, from the use of pitocin to electronic fetal monitoring, distorted the physiology of childbirth so that it was transformed into pathology. The use of pitocin to speed up labor causes a more violent labor, which also requires more pain-killing drugs and induces more vaginal tears and makes episiotomy more common. The electronic fetal monitor often indicates problems where they do not exist. In 1982, several studies reported that EFM showed about a 75 percent false positive rate, indicating that the fetus was in danger when it was not, and a 13 percent false negative rate, failing to show the fetus in danger when it was (Edwards and Waldorf 1984, 119). In 1985, a study of thirteen thousand patients in Dublin showed no benefits from monitoring. Rather, it increased the use of cesarean section and forceps for presumed fetal distress. This confirmed the results of several smaller studies that had also showed no benefits from routine monitoring (MacDonald et al. 1985).

In spite of the growing research illustrating the deleterious effects of common obstetric procedures, the zeal to reform was subsiding along with the counterculture. The public relations departments of hospitals had adopted the rhetoric and style of those advocating reform, offering freedom of "choice"—the new buzzword that seems to have replaced "natural" as the sign of progressive practices. Soft-focus photos of mothers and infants along with the list of options regarding birth style made childbirth seem akin to a vacation package. The popular magazines began to reflect this illusion, suggesting that there was no real conflict, it had all just been a matter of perception. In the August 1985 issue of *Parents,* an article entitled "Which Birth Style Is Best for You?" claims that within the limits of safety, you can make choices that reflect your own personality." It describes the options women have.

> Giving birth in the 1980s can be a better experience than ever, thanks to advances made by medical scientists and consumer advocates for prepared childbirth. Though the two groups some-times find themselves in conflict (many obstetricians favor aggressive medical management of labor and birth while consumer advocates often press for minimal medical intervention) their objectives are really one and the same. . . .
>
> The best birth experience is one conducted as much as possible in accordance with parents' preferences, medical professionals are starting to discover.
>
> One authority who has studied this concept, Richard L. Cohen, psychiatrist . . . cites evidence that a satisfying birth experience can enhance parents' attachment to their newborn, which may influence the youngster's early development. His and other studies

suggest it matters less where and how you have your baby than whether you were able to draw satisfaction from the experience.

Dr. Spock, too, dismisses the conflict in favor of the idea that parents just need to feel good about their experience (Spock 1985). The real problem is that mothers will lack confidence.

> The babies may be in a nursery some distance from the mothers where they can be efficiently watched and cared for by the nurses and won't disturb their mothers' rest. But it isn't quite natural, from the new mother's point of view, to have her baby somewhere else and taken care of so completely for a number of days. It may give her the feeling underneath of being somewhat ignorant and useless. A mother who has had several children might laugh at this and say, "It's *wonderful* to have that long rest in the hospital and not to have to worry about the baby." But it's different for her; she has a lot of confidence in herself as a mother and takes the hospital in stride. (Spock 1985, 80)

Women and Work

If bonding will now merely help parents to feel good about their birth experience rather than cement family relations and prevent child abuse, it should not be taken to mean that women can rest easy about going to work. In 1985 Dr. Brazelton wrote *Working and Caring*. The book begins with an account of the plight of an apparently typical working mother who also serves to illustrate Brazelton's position on the subject. Dr. Brazelton advises, "Plan to breast feed him before and after work. You'll find it's so great to come home at the end of the day and be able to put him right to breast. You feel cemented to each other all over again" (p. xv).

The (typical) woman begins to cry. She is a lawyer but she doesn't want to go back to work at all. In fact, she has been counsel for a women's rights organization and "had bought completely into their beliefs." She continues, "After he was born I suddenly fell completely in love. I couldn't eat or sleep or think of anything but my baby. I don't care about work any longer. . . . I can't believe in the women's movement the same way I did in the past" (p. xvi).

Although Brazelton attempts to address the role of fathers and the plight of single parents, the old attitudes about maternal deprivation constantly resurface: "No matter what the situation is, the real issues [mothers] face is when to return to work without endangering their baby's development. Although financial and career needs may be pressing, these women cannot ignore their new roles as mothers in making the decision. Both the baby's needs and their own longing to nurture well are critical to their peace of mind as they return to work. Denial is a defense against the pain of giving up a small baby" (p. 55).

Net Gains for Women

If women had begun to think that bonding would facilitate their being good mothers to their infants while working in the paid labor force, the 1980s began to see the rise of another familiar twist to the tradition of mothering advice. It was a return in new format of the overprotecting or rejecting mother of the 1940s. It appears that women once again had followed the experts' advice too closely. One developmental psychologist, J. Belsky, discovered in the early 1980s that mothers were selfishly "overwhelming their infants with excess attention in order to alleviate their guilt" about working. In fact, he claims that these employed women were not only overstimulating their infants but, in so doing, were preventing fathers from having their share of playtime (Birns and Hay 1988, 60).

The reform movement changed some of the more inhumane medical practices of the past, yet the net gains for women in attaining control are plummeting. Even the gains related directly to bonding seem to be fading. Many mothers now emerge from the birth experience feeling groggy, exhausted, and out of control. Bonding is sometimes reduced to a ceremonial procedure in which tired women are expected to love their newborns on the spot. According to childbirth educator Sheila Kitzinger (1987), bonding has become just a ceremonial procedure in the hospital. "Feeling you have to bond in ten minutes flat or knowing that people are watching you to see if you are bonding correctly is unlikely to help you fall in love with your baby." Kitzinger wisely adds that many women do not fall in love with their babies immediately. They and their infants get to know each other over time (p. 282).

Bonding may have ushered the family into the hospital, but the new birthing suites have not reduced rates of intervention. Virtually all technologies except cesareans (which take place in an operating room) are used in birthing rooms. At least one out of five women who attempt birth in a hospital birthing suite is transferred to a traditional delivery room (Sullivan and Weitz 1988, 161). Most women, about four out of five, receive medication, though in reduced amounts compared to the pre-1970s norms. About 90 percent of women having their first vaginal delivery receive episiotomies. Induced labors and "outlet" forceps remain common (Wertz and Wertz 1989, 255). Hospital birth is moving even further from the possibility of a natural birth because of the threat of acquired immunodeficiency syndrome (AIDS). Already some hospitals are treating all birthing women as objects of pollution. Staff wear gowns, masks, gloves, and eye protectors lest they be splashed with the mother's possibly contaminated blood during birth. If the mother is black and poor, the fear is greater and the rituals are more carefully observed (Wertz and Wertz 1989, 257). Because of the technology of medical monitoring, which mushroomed in the 1980s, parents struggled with a whole new set of interventions that they had to learn about. Few however, actively opposed this new version of the medical model because of its promise to guarantee a perfect baby.

Today, as a woman prepares for a "natural" childbirth, her doctor will order the use of more technology than ever before. Long before she is in labor, ultrasound will be used to examine her fetus. Like the fetal X-ray before it, ultrasound may cause damage to the fetus. It has never undergone the large-scale clinical trials that would prove its safety, although there are over a hundred articles in the scientific literature suggesting that it may have some ill effects on the fetus, especially on the central nervous system (Oakley 1985, 98–105, 168–71). Curiously, while millions of dollars are spent on this dubious technology, prenatal care for poor women, which could prevent many serious birth problems, either cannot get funding, or when funded, is subject to endless testing.

About one in four women giving birth in a hospital can expect to have a cesarean (24.4 percent in 1987). The World Health Organization believes there is "no justification for a rate above 10 to 15 percent" (Sullivan and Weitz 1988, 36). The official reason most frequently given for first cesareans is "dystocia," which means that a woman has spent more time in labor than hospital regulations or doctors are willing to allow. But medicine has continually redefined the length of a normal labor into ever shorter periods. The rising cesarean rates are in large part a creation of medical regulations and redefinitions of normalcy; the rate of maternal mortality in cesareans is four times that for vaginal births (Wertz and Wertz 1989, 261). The high cesarean rate is also a product of the doctors' fear of lawsuits (a doctor can be sued for birth damage to an infant for up to twenty-one years after the birth). Moreover, obstetric insurance costs since the early 1980s are among the highest in medicine, leading 9 percent of obstetricians to cease delivering babies and restrict their practice to gynecology rather than pay up to $83,000 for coverage (Sullivan and Weitz 1988, 36).

As in the past, technology is liberally applied without medical justification. The fetal heart monitor has become routine in American births. The limitations that monitoring puts on a woman's mobility during labor are considerable—she must lie relatively still for the monitor to pick up the requisite information. Internal monitoring, for which the electrode is attached to the baby's scalp, may even force the woman back into the lithotomy position (Wertz and Wertz 1989, 257). The routine use of the fetal monitor is testimony to the underlying antagonism between doctors and their obstetric patients. From 71 to 95 percent of the babies delivered by cesarean section for presumed fetal distress shown on the fetal heart monitor are not in fact distressed at birth, which means that the cesarean was not necessary. Yet most doctors say they will continue to use the monitor routinely for fear of lawsuits (Wertz and Wertz 1989, 259–60).

Bonding had helped to usher the family into the hospital, but the family is more dependent than ever before on the medical expertise of doctors and nurses for the use of the technical monitoring devices. In fact, doctors have now shifted their focus to the fetus and are suing mothers for not meeting medically established standards of care for the fetus. By 1987 there had been eleven court orders for cesareans on unwilling mothers for the sake of the fetus. In one case, the mother was dying of cancer; the cesarean was performed, but mother and infant died. In another case, a poor woman with little education, living in inadequate housing with no health insurance, first sought prenatal care in her seventh month. When a severely retarded infant was born (who subsequently died) the doctor's response was to order the arrest and indictment of the mother for prenatal child abuse because she had smoked marijuana (Wertz and Wertz 1989, 270).

Parents reacting to overly medicalized birth controlled by doctors inspired a reform movement. Progressive doctors and nurses joined the ranks of the natural childbirth movement in the 1970s along with members of the counterculture and feminist movements. Bonding served as a kind of scientific seal of approval for these reformers. But in order for real change to take place, the profession of obstetrics would have had to give up some of its control and decrease its numbers. Parents, wanting the very best for their "1.7" children (the national average of children per couple) appear to have been reassured by the technology and homey decorating touches. Not far beneath the surface of this "reformed" hospital birth, however, is a level of antagonism among women, doctors, and medical institutions that suggests that childbirth is likely to be an even more fragmented and dehumanizing experience for women in the 1990s than in the period of the surgical birth.

Conclusion

Maternal-infant bonding is not just a passing fad. It is a reflection of deeply embedded problems within our society regarding the uses of science. Inevitably, this enterprise we call science is a social process, yet we have no model for managing the social and political forces inherent in research. Science is conducted by human beings whose interpretation of data is influenced by everything from high ideals to racism and sexism; from theory and laws of evidence that are useful for specific contexts to paradigms that are grossly inadequate.

Even when research is well constructed, once the findings are used as guidelines for moral behavior, there is great danger that the results will be shaped to suit variable social and political ends. In fact, the greatest danger is that we have made scientists into a modern clergy. We see them as the interpreters of texts that are handed down from some infallible authority, and we seek their guidance on matters far beyond the confines of those texts.

Unfortunately, women are in special danger of being victims of science. The myth that researchers are objective distances them from their subjects and creates a unidirectional flow of information that restricts information to the confines of the researchers' conceptions.

The fact is that subjects also have expert knowledge about their own condition from their own unique standpoint. Women who wanted to reform childbirth practices have claimed that the problems of birth were the dehumanizing practices of hospitals—not some phenomenon within women. To the extent that mothers of premature and sick infants were asked, they indicated a desire for more knowledge about how to care for their infants and more social support in the process of doing so. Their voices were subsumed into the agendas of those conducting the research. In fact, both medicine and psychology have a long history of colonizing women, first by idealizing them in ways that are highly restrictive and then by blaming them for not living up to those narrow ideals. Standards of femininity, motherliness, virtue, and mental health often have been unrealistic projections that attempt to redress social and professional problems by redefining women instead of taking the problems head on. Children, too, have been caught in this labyrinth of expectations. The ongoing discovery of their true nature turns out to be either a response to some salient feature of the adult world or an esoteric province best known to psychology and medicine, requiring their specialized treatment and interpretation.

Of course, the problem in escaping these uses of science is that science is esoteric. Even scientists themselves often fail to use their own language correctly or to understand their own rules, as evidenced by the bonding research controversy. How, then, can the consumers of such information be expected to interpret it correctly? Here, there is little hope unless those conducting the research themselves begin to ask more critical questions about the hidden agendas by which they operate. Consumers of this research can be aware of the history of medicine and psychology, of the ways in which it has been used as part of a political struggle for power, often conserving the status quo.

But we need to go beyond awareness. Women and men, I believe, need to do their own redefining. We are now at a critical juncture in the way we construct both sex roles and parenthood. As the gender barriers to women's professional work decline, women are in some ways being constrained as never before by new medical definitions of their reproductive responsibility. For instance, the new fetal rights advocates argue that fetuses have the right to be protected from their mothers, and they are attempting to create a new legal category of "fetal abuse." One husband has even successfully sued his own wife for damage to their fetal child because she had taken an antibiotic while pregnant that had discolored the child's teeth (Rothman 1989, 160). Once again, in protecting fetuses from their mothers, we are also using women as scapegoats for the tensions created by yet another social problem. Children are tremendously expensive now, and most people are having few of them. They therefore want each one to be perfect. But even children who are born perfect are not going to have lives that approach perfection unless our children become the priority of all of us. It is important for both men and women to reclaim their full responsibility for begetting and rearing children. Inherent behavioral differences between men and women are nil. Both sexes need to realize that the critical contributions to our children's futures turn on our willingness to spend time and money on them, not just in the earliest part of life, but throughout childhood and adolescence. We do not need science to tell us these things. We need to transcend the ideology of motherhood and do the right thing: recognize that women and men have equal capacity and responsibility in caring for our children.

Regarding the future of bonding, I would like to urge the impossible—that we discard the word entirely. Doing so would force us to recognize that strong relationships require many ingredients; they seldom endure automatically. Constructive relationships involve love, understanding, trust, time, money, sharing, giving, stimulating, and inspiring. Discarding the term *bonding* would force us to notice that children are not merely putty in our hands. They are born with vastly differing personalities and capabilities. Some of them are miraculously resistant to hardship; some are easily hurt. Children are profoundly affected by an array of people who interact with them, by the foods they eat, by the music they hear, by the television they watch, by the hope they see in the adult world, and by the institutions—especially schools—they attend. Children have fathers, brothers and sisters, and friends, as well as mothers. They have parents whose relationships are sometimes cordial and sometimes discordant, affected by worries about money, health, work, and recognition. Children and their parents live in communities that are sometimes peaceful and beautiful, sometimes violent and ugly. People can connect with each other intellectually, emotionally, through daily caretaking, through games, through music and art, through formal learning and from long distances. There are many, many dimensions to the nurturance of our children. To the extent that we have reduced these processes to a "bonding," we have done ourselves a disservice. To the extent that we continue to deify the maternal-child relationship, hoping it will issue us transcendence from the mundane problems of an unpredictable world, we are lost.

Notes

Chapter 1
Introduction

1. Brazelton even attributed the condition of youth in war-torn Cambodia to problems in the early mother-infant relationship. He added, "I saw it in Cambodia when I went over there; these kids who had been through that holocaust as adolescents sat there with vacant eyes." The same kind of assertion was made by Dr. John Bowlby with regard to war orphans in Europe in 1951. Bowlby concluded that their problems were due to the loss of their mothers, the devastating experience of war notwithstanding (see chap. 3).
2. One of the problems with bonding is that the definition varies greatly. In general, there are two related aspects of bonding: that related to hormonal changes in the mother as described by Kennell and Klaus, and the ongoing process facilitated by the postpartum bonding, which is said to be essential during the early years of a child's life.
3. Dr. Klaus did not suggest that extra contact alone could reduce the abuse, but he did say that it might be a significant contributing factor in the reduction.

Chapter 2
The Bonding Research

1. Damage during a sensitive period has slightly better chances of being reversed than damage during a critical period.
2. At one year a new set of investigators, this time reportedly blind to experimental or control-group membership, examined the mothers and infants (Kennell et al. 1974). Much data were collected in these visits, using time-lapse films, checklists, an interview, a physical examination of the infant, a child development test, and so on. Four differences emerged: Upon returning to work, more extended-contact mothers reported missing their infants; they spent more time standing near the table when their infants were being examined; they spent more time soothing their infants and kissing them when they cried. The extended-contact babies themselves scored an average of 5 points higher on the Bayley developmental test. These differences were said to indicate the positive effects of early contact. There was, however, a far larger body of data that showed no differences.

3. At two years, nine extra-contact and ten control mothers were compared (Ringler et al. 1975). The groups now differed in their linguistic behaviors. While speaking to the children, the extended-contact mothers used fewer content words, asked more questions, expressed fewer commands and used more words for each proposition than did the control group mothers. The experimenters interpreted these differences as indicating a style of speech that is greater in variety and elaboration, again suggesting better bonding. When the children were five, the same sample of nineteen returned with their mothers and were given tests of intelligence and language comprehension; the mothers were given an IQ test (Ringler et al. 1978). There were no significant differences between the groups on any of the tests. The researchers did, however, find a relationship between the mother's speech when the children were two and the children's intellectual and language performance at age five in the extra-contact group. They interpreted this to suggest that the extra-postpartum contact increased the level of association between mothers' and children's behavior by expanding on such early behaviors as looking en face.

4. Kennell and three associates also published a study of sixty low-income urban women in Guatemala (Hales et al. 1977). In this study the researchers compared three groups: mothers receiving routine care (first contact with clothed baby at twelve hours); mothers who had forty-five minutes of skin-to-skin contact twelve hours postpartum; and mothers who had forty-five minutes of skin-to-skin contact immediately after birth. Thirty-six hours after delivery, mothers who had early contact showed evidence of better bonding.

5. Statistically, something happens by chance 50 percent of the time: On any single toss of a coin you have an equal probability of getting heads or tails. In twenty tosses, however, the probability of your getting 16, 17, 18, 19, or 20 heads is close to zero. In fact, the probability of your getting ten heads is only .176. This is because random events tend to clump in various ways. In a series in which a coin was flipped several thousand times, it was found that long runs occurred when only heads or only tails turned up. The more times you toss, however, the more the variability in outcome will even out. If you toss the coin two thousand times, the probability that heads will show up 50 percent of the time is far greater than if you toss it two hundred times. When you apply this to the bonding research, you see immediately the problem with the small sample sizes. If you have ten subjects and you are assessing them for one hundred different behaviors, it is quite likely that some of those behaviors occurred by chance (i.e., were not the result of treatment). (See Spilker 1986, 10.)

6. Between 1970 and 1987, some 107 articles about bonding were published in fifty-one pediatric journals, plus six books. Of the articles, 38 were actual reports of research findings; the remaining 69 were discussions of applications of bonding and evaluative commentaries. In the allied health sciences literature between 1974 and 1986, 43 articles in twenty-five journals discussed the implementation of bonding. Only three questioned the paradigm. (For a complete listing of the

journals surveyed, see Eyer 1988, chap. 2.) Additional articles suggest a link between premature and low-birthweight babies—hence babies whose mothers had no opportunity to bond—and later child abuse and failure to thrive.

7. In a personal interview, Leiderman (May 1990) explained that the study originated when Klaus, his neighbor, in a "backyard discussion over the fence," asked Leiderman, a psychiatrist, to talk to mothers of premature infants who were suffering from depression. Leiderman did so and concluded that the problem was due in part to these mothers' exclusion from the NICU. They discussed the problem of separation as evidenced in animal models, particularly studies done at Cornell (Klopfer, Adams, and Klopfer 1964), and modeled their study on the work of pediatrician Julius Richmond (1959).

8. This, of course, is an outlandish claim and by the rules of evidence described above cannot be credited. The fact that the claim was made illustrates how much some scientists were primed to find effects of bonding.

9. Kennell had long been concerned with the initial parental response to premature and sick infants. In a 1960 study, for instance, he and his co- author, Rolnick (1960), claimed that early problems have a grave impact on the parents' future handling of the child and that "letting the mother see the baby as soon and often as is possible" is helpful as it will offer her "far more reassurance than words can give." Kennell had also been concerned with the effects of parent-child separation on children (Kennell and Bergen 1966). He pursued research on predicting "mothering-disorders" with Klaus in a 1972 study of mothers of premature infants (Fanaroff, Kennell, and Klaus 1972). They found that mothers' visiting patterns were predictive of disorders of mothering, such as battering and infants who "fail to thrive" without organic cause.

10. Until the 1960s most psychologists agreed that a newborn's experience of the world was a "blooming, buzzing confusion," as psychologist William James put it at the turn of the century. In the late 1960s new research techniques were developed to measure the responses of infants to the environment, such as eye-tracking machines to record gaze and focus and pacifiers to record sucking responses. The variations of these naturally occurring responses were then observed in connection with various environmental stimuli. The researchers discovered that a newborn's sensory equipment is "wired" to facilitate social responsiveness. For instance, newborns turn their head in the direction of human voices but not in response to artificial sounds. They gaze more at a drawing of a human face than at a bull's eye pattern, etc. (See Fantz 1961; Mills and Melhuish 1974; Stern 1977.)

11. De Chateau was aided in these studies by Klaus and his colleagues. He spent several months with them in Cleveland and used some of the instruments they had developed in his own study (personal interview with Kennell, June 1990).

12. A Canadian study conducted by Kontos (1978) found that early contact and rooming-in facilitate affectionate behaviors, as measured by amount of attention, bodily contact, and stimulation of the infant. In a German study (Grossman,

Thane, and Grossman 1981), the authors varied the amount of early contact and filmed feedings during a ten-day lying-in period, which is standard in Germany. Mothers in the early-contact group showed more tender touching and cuddling during the first two observations than did mothers in the extended contact and control groups, but these differences disappeared by the third observation. (In addition, these differences were evident only among mothers who had planned the pregnancy in the first place.)

13. For example, Margaret Lynch (1976) and her colleagues conducted a retrospective study of fifty abused children. They concluded that it was possible to predict abuse by identifying problems in the early mother-infant relationship: "At least 3 percent of all mothers delivered at a large modern maternity hospital have identifiable problems likely to lead to a bonding failure or child abuse." They also found that the abused group were more likely to have been in a special care nursery (59 percent). Another team set out to check the claim that mothers prone to baby battering are those who have not been bonded to their babies soon after delivery (Cater and Easton 1980). They investigated eighty cases of child abuse with particular reference to the separation of the abusing parents from their newborn infants. They found that unstable domestic arrangements, psychiatric disturbance, and immaturity of parents were the primary contributors, although they do not rule out the possibility that the failure of early bonding had an effect. Also see Patton and Gardner (1962); Elmer and Gregg (1967); Klein and Stern (1971); Fomufod, Sinkford, and Louy (1975); and Lynch and Roberts (1977).

14. Philosopher of science Thomas Kuhn (1962) explores the ways in which researchers construct and use research models. He finds that the influence of culture and the professional politics of the researchers are important in deciding how research is conducted and evaluated. See chapter 4 for further discussion of the concept of paradigms in "normal science."

Chapter 3
Maternal Deprivation and Attachment

1. In the 1930s, Ripin (1933), and Durfee and Wolf (1933) found developmental deficits in institutionalized infants between three months of age and a year or more. In the early 1940s, Bakwin (1942, 1949) and Ribble (1943) gave detailed accounts of the adverse effects on the physical health of institutionalized infants.

2. Bowlby's influence in England was extended through a government committee set up at the end of the war. The Curtis Committee, on the care of children outside their homes, needed a theoretical background to guide its policy. Bowlby's report enhanced the case for the expansion of child therapy services (Senn 1977, 20; Riley 1983, 100).

3. In England, the popular version of Bowlby's book sold twenty thousand copies a year for twenty-five years (Senn 1977, 19–21). The 1951 report has been

translated into French, Danish, Yugoslavian, Swedish, Spanish, Finnish, Hebrew, Arabic, Italian, Japanese, and Greek (Dicks 1970, 143, 158).

4. Bowlby attended University College Medical School at Cambridge (1929–1933) and worked as a clinical assistant at the Maudsley Hospital (1933–36). During this period, he was also a student-candidate with the British Psychoanalytic Society and was analyzed by Joan Riviere and supervised by Melanie Klein. Bowlby's medical thesis, published in 1942, described the case of a patient who exhibited schizoid traits, which Bowlby felt to be the result of depression due to the patient's loss of her mother at age two (Newcombe and Lerner 1981).

5. The mental hygiene movement in the first decade of the twentieth century was inspired by the great advances made in bacteriology and hygiene at the end of the nineteenth century. These discoveries caused the public to become prevention conscious; public health agencies came into being, and mental hospitals were reformed. The development of insanity and delinquency, it was thought, might be arrested with the earliest possible signs in the formative years of childhood. In this interest, juvenile courts were given the authority to move children from their homes to foster homes as a means of prevention (Kanner 1972, 10).

6. Burt seems to have been adapting Freudian psychology to the mental hygiene approach. One must be skeptical of this research in any case, however, since Burt has been found to have fabricated the data for the research on which his reputation was based—the famous twin studies purportedly showing that IQ was hereditary (see Hearnshaw 1979; Kamin 1974; Wade 1976; Norton 1978.)

7. Sutties' work appealed to the founders of the Tavistock, J. A. Hadfield and Hugh Crichton Miller, who were, along with other members of the clinic, very religious—in fact, the "Tavi" was often referred to as the "parson's clinic." These doctors objected to Freud as being insufficiently hopeful (Newcombe and Lerner 1981).

8. The Tavi was founded in 1920 in part to treat victims of shell shock but increasingly provided psychological treatment for the problems of children. Nervous children from middle-class families, maladjusted children having troubles at school, and children referred from the juvenile courts were the population it served. The approach was interdisciplinary, guided by doctors but with psychologists used for testing and social workers for home visits (Rose 1985, 198–99).

9. This emphasis fit the tendency of psychoanalysis in America to be linked with sociology and anthropology and a concern with the psychodynamic means by which a national or cultural character could be formed through variations in feeding practices and other childrearing customs (Riley 1983, chap. 3).

10. Rutter also addresses some matters of attachment theory. For example, Bowlby's concept of monotropy—the idea that an infant can attach to only one person at a time, preferably his mother. Rutter cites research evidence to the contrary showing that infants often develop multiple attachments. Bowlby later revised this idea to allow for a hierarchy of attachments in which the mother, however, was usually the primary figure (Rutter 1974, 1979, 1981).

Chapter 4
Models and Reasoning in the Scientific Community

1. The research teams often involved psychologists, nurses, social workers, and others, as well as pediatricians. But the conceptual leader of the team was generally a physician. Exceptions were Byron Egeland, Karin Grossman, and Donna Kontos, all psychologists, and Svejda, a nurse. (The original bonding study—Klaus et al., 1972—was conducted by pediatricians Kennell and Klaus and four medical students.)
2. Lamb and other critics of the bonding research, it should be pointed out, do not fall into this category. See Natalie Angier (1990) for an update on the crisis proportions of this problem.
3. *The Diagnostic and Statistical Manual of Mental Disorders* (DSM), published by the American Psychiatric Association, is a classification system for mental illness based on the medical model of disease, which assumes that disorders defined by similar groups of symptoms have a common etiology or cause and therefore require similar treatment.

Chapter 5
Constructing Motherhood and Infancy

1. This literature was aimed at the middle and upper classes. Many advice books warned mothers against relying on servants since they, with their own bad habits, could reduce or eliminate entirely the mother's indispensable control over the child's development. Such advice may actually have been directed against the working-class women who were, after all the servants and nurses. According to Degler, about three-fifths of the population was middle class in the mid-1800s, and they set the tone for the working class as well, the majority of whom could read (Degler 1980, 81–83).
2. Physicians saw the body as a closed system possessing only a limited amount of vital force; energy expanded in one area was necessarily removed from another.
3. Although the Lanham Act provided funds for day-care centers for the children of war workers, the number of centers remained very low. As of 1944, only 66,000 children were enrolled in federally supported facilities; in 1945, the number was 100,000. The centers met less than 10 percent of the need. (Rothman 1978, 223). That the centers were so scarce (and so poorly run) reflected their temporary character.

Chapter 6
Medicine Frames Motherhood and Infancy

1. Eclampsia, convulsions and coma, can occur in the last trimester of pregnancy. The primary contributing factor is malnutrition, which causes metabolic toxemia, of which eclampsia is the final stage. Preeclampsia is characterized by edema (swelling due to water retention). Toward the third trimester, severe preeclampsia

is indicated by high blood pressure, a large amount of protein in the urine with a decrease in the amount of urine, blurred vision, severe and continuous headache, or swelling of the face and fingers. Severe preeclampsia can develop in a few hours (Boston Women's Health Collective 1976, 255, 261).

2. Dick-Read's book was published in London under the title *Natural Childbirth* in 1933 but did not reach the United States until 1944 (Sullivan and Weitz 1988, 28).

3. Developing family-centered maternity and newborn care held three distinct advantages for the profession. First, responsibility for birth became diffused. The Interprofessional Task Force on Health Care of Women and Children, in 1978, put it simply: "While physicians are responsible for providing direction for medical management, other team members share appropriately in managing the health care of the family, and each team member must be individually accountable for the performance of his/her facet of care." According to Arney, although the team approach did not absolve the physician from his legal responsibility for birth, it made women partially accountable for the quality of the birth experience. As the relationship between doctor and patient grew increasingly adversarial in the 1970s, the diffusion was welcome (Arney 1982, 223).

Chapter 7
The Reform Movement

1. The study of this hospital (the names of the hospital and of all subjects have been changed) was conducted over a six-month period in 1987. All staff was interviewed as well as a sample of parents. Their descriptions of bonding differed consistently from group to group (nurses, parents, doctors, and so on).

2. The Maternity Center Association was founded in 1917 to demonstrate prenatal care, which included parent education. In 1931 it introduced nurse midwifery education into the United States. In the 1940s it became involved in promoting natural childbirth (Sumner 1981, 168–69).

3. The Women's Health Movement has significantly changed the way many women look at medical care and is successfully fighting in legislatures, hospital administrations, and law courts for improvements. Yet the abuses continue. The medical care system remains basically unresponsive, deeply entrenched as it is in American economic, political, and social structures, and the influence of medicine in people's lives continues to grow. The critique of medicine has taken on a new dimension. It sees basic errors in medicine's fundamental assumptions about health and healing. In many situations it may be bad for women's health because it emphasizes drugs, surgery, psychotherapy (especially for women) and crisis action rather than prevention (Rothman, 1982, 556–57).

4. In 1973 the number of nurse midwives in the United States was estimated at 1,300, mostly in the eastern half of the country. There were also 2,900 licensed lay midwives, clustered in the South (Wertz and Wertz 1989, 218). This is compared to 20,500 obstetricians and 366,400 physicians as a whole. Midwives are still less likely to have access to specialized equipment.

References

Ainsworth, M. 1967. *Infancy in Uganda: Infant Care and the Growth of Attachment*. Baltimore, Md.: Johns Hopkins University Press.

Ainsworth, M., M. Blehar, E. Waters, and S. Wall. 1978. *Patterns of Attachment*. Hillsdale, N.J.: Erlbaum.

Ainsworth, M., R. Andry, H. Harlow, S. Lebovici, M. Mead, D. Prugh, B. Wootton. 1962. Deprivation of maternal care: A reassessment of its effects. *Public Health Papers,* no. 14. Geneva: World Health Organization.

Albert, D., R. Munson, and M. Resnik. 1988. *Reasoning in Medicine: An Introduction to Clinical Inference*. Baltimore, Md.: Johns Hopkins University Press.

Anderson, M. 1988. *Thinking about Women: Sociological Perspectives on Sex and Gender*. 2d ed. N.Y.: Macmillan.

Angier, N. 1990. Cultures in conflict: M.D.s and Ph.D.s. *New York Times,* 24 April, sec. C, pp. 8–9.

Anisfeld, E., M. Curry, D. Hales, J. Kennell, M. Klaus, M. Lipper, S. O'Connor, E. Siegel, and R. Sosa. 1983. Maternal-infant bonding: A joint rebuttal. *Pediatrics* 72(4) (Oct.): 569–72.

Anisfeld, E., and E. Lipper. 1983. Early contact, social support, and mother-infant bonding. *Pediatrics* 72:79–83.

Annexton, M. 1978. Parent-infant bonding sought in birthing centers. *JAMA* 240(9) (Sept.): 823.

Argles, P. 1980. Attachment and child abuse. *Brit. J. Social Work* 10:33–42.

Ariès, P. 1962. *Centuries of Childhood: Social History of Family Life*. N.Y.: Vintage.

Arms, S. 1975. *Immaculate Deception*. N.Y.: Bantam.

Arney, W. 1982. *Power and the Profession of Obstetrics*. Chicago, Ill.: University of Chicago Press.

Avant, K. 1981. Anxiety as a potential factor affecting maternal attachment. *JOGN Nursing* 10(6) (Nov./Dec.): 416–19.

Bakwin, H. 1942. Loneliness in infants. *Amer. J. Dis. Child.*. 63:30.

———. 1949. Emotional deprivation in infants. *J. Pediatrics* 35:512.

Banner, L. 1974. *Women in Modern America: A Brief History.* N.Y.: Harcourt Brace Jovanovich.

Barash, D. 1977. *Sociobiology and Behavior.* N.Y.: Elsevier.

———. 1979. *The Whisperings Within.* N.Y.: Harper and Row.

Barber, E. 1943. Marriage and the family after the war. *Annals of the American Academy of Political and Social Science* 229.

Barnett, C. R., P. H. Leiderman, R. Grobstein, and M. Klaus. 1970. Neonatal separation: The maternal side of interactional deprivation. *Pediatrics* 45:2 (Feb.).

Barrie, H. 1976. Personal opinion: Of human bondage. *Midwife, Health Visitor and Community Nurse* 12 (June): 82–86.

Beach, F. 1948. *Hormones and Behavior.* N.Y.: Hoeber.

———. 1960. Experimental investigations of species-specific behavior. *Amer. Psychologist* 15:325–76.

———. 1975. Behavioral endocrinology: An emerging discipline. *American Scientist* 63:178–87.

———. 1981. Historical origins of modern research on hormones and behavior. *Hormones and Behavior* 15:325–76.

Beck, N., and D. Hall. 1978. Natural childbirth: A review and analysis. *Obstet. Gynec.* 52(3): 371–79.

Bernard, L. 1924. *Instinct: A Study in Social Psychology.* London: Allen and Unwin.

Bing, E. 1969. *Six Practical Lessons for Easier Childbirth.* N.Y.: Norton.

Birns, B., and D. Hay. 1988. *The Different Faces of Motherhood.* N.Y.: Plenum.

Bleier, R. 1984. *Science and Gender: A Critique of Biology and Its Theories on Women.* N.Y.: Pergamon.

Boakes, R. 1984. *From Darwin to Behaviorism: Psychology and the Minds of Animals.* Cambridge: Cambridge University Press.

Boll, E. 1943. The child. *Annals of the American Academy of Political and Social Science* 229 (Sept.).

Bonaparte, M. 1953. *Female Sexuality.* International Universities Press.

Boston Women's Health Collective 1973, 1976, 1984. *Our Bodies, Ourselves.* N.Y.: Simon and Schuster.

Boudreaux, M. 1981. Maternal attachment of high-risk mothers with well newborns: A pilot study. *JOGN Nursing* 10(5) (Sept./Oct.): 366–69.

Bowlby, J. 1946. *Forty-four Juvenile Thieves and Their Characters and Home Life.* London: Balliere, Tyndal, and Cox.

———. 1951. *Maternal Care and Mental Health,* 2d ed. Geneva: World Health Organization. Monograph series no. 2.

———. 1958. The nature of the child's tie to his mother. *Int. J. Psycho-Analysis* 38(9): 350–72.

———. 1969. *Attachment.* N.Y.: Basic Books.

———. 1973. *Attachment and Loss.* Vol. 2. *Separation: Anxiety and Anger.* N.Y.: Basic Books.

———. 1984. Violence in the family as a disorder of the attachment and caregiving systems. *Amer. J. Psychoanalysis* 44(1) (Spring): 9–27, 29–30.

Brackbill, Y., J. Rice, and D. Young. 1984. *Birth Trap.* N.Y.: Warner.

Brannigan, A. 1981. *The Social Basis of Scientific Discoveries.* Cambridge: Cambridge University Press.

Brazelton, T. B. 1969. *Infants and Mothers: Differences in Development.* N.Y.: Delacorte.

———. 1971. What childbirth drugs can do to your child. *Redbook,* Feb., p. 65.

———. 1979. Welcoming your baby. *Redbook,* Sept., p. 35.

———. 1981. *On Becoming a Family: The Growth of Attachment,* N.Y.: Delacorte.

———. 1985. *Working and Caring.* Reading, Mass.: Addison-Wesley.

Bretherton, L., and E. Waters. 1985. Growing points of attachment theory and research. *Monographs of the Society for Research in Child Development* 209, p. 50.

Brimblecombe, F., J. Robinson, A. Edelston, and J. Jones, eds. 1978. *Separation and Special Care Baby Units.* London: Heinemann.

Brown, S. 1985. Which birth style is best for you? Within the limits of safety, you can make choices that reflect your own personality. *Parents* (Aug.): 53.

Buckle, D. 1968. Child psychiatry and the World Health Organization. In *Foundations of Child Psychiatry,* ed. E. Miller. N.Y.: Pergamon.

Bullough, V., and Bullough, B. 1984. *History, Trends, and Politics of Nursing.* Norwalk, Conn.: Appleton-Century Crofts.

Burst, H. 1983. The influence of consumers on the birthing movement. *Topics in Clinical Nursing* 55(3) (Oct.): 42–54.

Burt, C. 1925. *The Young Delinquent (The Sub-normal Child).* Vol. 1. London: University of London Press.

———. 1955. The evidence for the concept of intelligence. *Brit. J. Educational Psych.* 25:58–177.

———. 1958. The inheritance of mental ability. *Amer. Psychologist* 13:1–15.

———. 1966. The genetic determination of differences in intelligence: A study of monozygotic twins reared together and apart. *Brit. J. Psych.* 57 (1–2): 137–53.

Call, J. 1984. Child abuse and neglect in infancy: Sources of hostility within the parent-infant dyad and disorders of attachment in infancy. *Child Abuse and Neglect* 8(2): 185–202.

Campos, J., K. Barrett, M. Lamb, H. Goldsmith, and C. Stenberg. 1983. Socioemotional development. In *Carmichael's Handbook of Child Psychology,* ed. C. Mussen. N.Y.: Wiley.

Caplan, P. 1985. *The Myth of Women's Masochism.* N.Y.: Dutton.

Care by parents' ward—Hospitals have found that sick children get better faster when their parents are there with them. 1971. *Parents* (July): 34.

Cater, J., and P. Easton. 1980. Separation and other stress in child abuse. *Lancet* 2:972–74.

Chess, S. 1982. The "blame the mother" ideology. *Int. J. Mental Health* 11(1–2) (June): 95–107.

———. 1983. Mothers are always the problem—Or are they? Old wine in new bottles. *Pediatrics* 71(6) (June): 974–76.

Chess, S., and A. Thomas. 1982. Infant bonding: Mystique and reality. *Amer. J. Orthopsychiatry* 52(2) (April): 213–22.

Chodorow, N. 1978. *The Reproduction of Mothering: Psychoanalysis and the Sociology of Gender.* Berkeley: University of California Press.

———. 1989. *Feminism and Psychoanalytic Theory.* New Haven: Yale University Press.

Choice. 1984. Childbirth options: A study of consumer expectations and available resources. Unpublished report.

Chu, J., J. Clements, E. Cotton, M. Klaus, A. Sweet, W. Tooley, B. Bradley, and L. Brandoff. 1967. Neonatal pulmonary ischemia. *Pediatrics* 40(4) (Oct.): 709–66.

Clark, A. 1976. Recognizing discord between mother and child and changing it to harmony. *Amer. J. Maternal Child Nursing* (March/April): 100–106.

Clark, A., and D. Affonso. 1976. Infant behavior and maternal attachment: Two sides to the coin. *Amer. J. Maternal Child Nursing* (March/April): 94–99.

Clouston, T. 1882. *Female Education from a Medical Point of View.* Edinburgh.

Collingwood, J., and E. Alberman. 1979. Separation at birth and the mother-child relationship. *Developmental Medicine and Child Neurology* 21:608–17.

Cone, T. 1979. *History of American Pediatrics.* Boston: Little, Brown.

Cooke, W. 1944. The differential psychology of American women. [Presidential address] *Amer. J. Obstet. Gynec.* 57:466–70.

Dally, A. 1983. *Inventing Motherhood: The Consequences of an Ideal.* N.Y.: Schocken.

Darwin, C. [1859] 1929. *On the Origin of the Species.* Thinker's Library Edition. Watts.

———. [1871] 1946. *The Descent of Man.* Thinker's Library Edition. Watts.

Davis, G. 1976. *Childhood and History in America.* N.Y.: Psychohistory Press.

Davis, M. 1987. The effects of promoting intrauterine attachment in primiparas on post-delivery attachment. *J. Obstet. Gynec. Neonatal Nurs.* 16(6) (Nov.–Dec.): 430–37.

de Chateau, P. 1976. The influence of early contact on maternal and infant behavior in primiparae. *Birth and the Family J.* 3:4 (Winter): 149–55.

———. 1980. Early postpartum contact and later attitudes. *Int. J. Behavioral Dev.* 3:273–86.

———. 1981. Parent-neonate interaction and its long-term effects. In *Early Experiences and Early Behavior: Implications for Social Development,* ed. E. G. Simmel. N.Y.: Academic.

de Chateau, P., and B. Wiberg. 1977. Long-term effect on mother-infant behaviour of extra contact during the first hour postpartum: pts. 1 and 2. *Acta Paediatrica Scandinavia* 66:137–51.

Degler, C. 1967. Revolution without ideology: The changing place of women in America. In *The Woman in America,* by R. Lifton. Boston: Beacon.

———. 1968. *Affluence and Anxiety: America since 1945.* Glenview, Ill.: Scott Foresman.

———. 1980. *At Odds: Women and the Family in America from the Revolution to the Present.* London: Oxford University Press.

Deutsch, H. 1944. *The Psychology of Women: A Psychoanalytic Interpretation.* Vols. 1 and 2. N.Y.: Grune and Stratton.

———. 1945. *Female Sexuality: The Psychology of Women.* Vol. 2. N.Y.: Grune and Stratton.

Dick-Read, G. 1959. *Childbirth without Fear: The Principles and Practice of Natural Childbirth.* 2d edition. N.Y.: Harper.

Dicks, H. 1970. *Fifty Years of the Tavistock Clinic.* London: Routledge and Kegan Paul.

Dubowitz, H. 1990. Pediatrician's role in preventing child maltreatment. *Pediatric Clinics of North America* 37(4) (Aug.): 989–1002.

Dunn, J., and M. Richards. 1977. Observations on the developing relationship between mother and baby in the neonatal period. In *Studies in Mother-Infant Interaction,* ed. H. Schaffer. N.Y.: Academic.

Durfee, H., and K. Wolf. 1933. *Z. Kinderforsch* 42:273.

Dyer, R. 1983. *Her Father's Daughter: The World of Anna Freud.* N.Y.

Eckes, S. 1974. The significance of increased early contact between mother and newborn infant. *JOGN Nursing* 3(4) (July/Aug.): 42–44.

Edwards, M., and M. Waldorf. 1984. *Reclaiming Birth: History and Heroines of American Childbirth.* N.Y.: Crossing.

Egeland, B., and A. Sroufe. 1981. Attachment and early maltreatment. *Child Dev.* 51(1) (March): 44–52.

Egeland, B., and B. Vaughn. 1981. Failure of "bond formation" as a cause of abuse, neglect, and maltreatment. *Amer. J. Orthopsychiatry* 51(1) (Jan.): 78–84.

Ehrenreich, B., and D. English. 1978. *For Her Own Good: 150 Years of The Experts' Advice to Women.* N.Y.: Doubleday.

Eisenstein, H. 1983. *Contemporary Feminist Thought.* Boston: G. K. Hall.

Elliott, R. 1983. Maternal-infant bonding: Taking stock. *Canadian Nurse* 79(8) (Jan.): 28–32.

Elmer, E., and G. Gregg. 1967. Developmental characteristics of abused children. *Pediatrics* 40:596–602.

Emde, R. 1983. *René A. Spitz: Dialogues from Infancy, Selected Papers.* N.Y.: International Universities Press.

Ensher, G., and D. Clark. 1986. *Newborns at Risk: Medical Care and Psychoeducational Intervention.* Rockville, Md.: Aspen.

Eyer, D. 1988. "Maternal infant bonding: Portrait of a paradigm." Ph.D. diss. University of Pennsylvania.

Fahlberg, V. 1981. *Attachment and Separation.* Practice Series 5. London: British Agencies for Adoption and Fostering.

Fanaroff, A., J. Kennell, and M. Klaus. 1972. Follow-up of low birth weight infants: The predictive value of maternal visiting patterns. *Pediatrics* 42:287–90.

Fantz, R. 1961. The origin of form perception. *Scientific Perception* 204:66–72.

Fitzgerald, H., B. Lester, and M. Yogsman. 1982. *Theory and Research in Behavioral Pediatrics.* Vol. 1. N.Y.: Plenum.

Fletcher, R. 1968. *Instinct in Man.* N.Y.: International Universities Press.

Floyd, L. 1981. A model for assisting high-risk families in neonatal nurturing. *Child Welfare* 60:4.

Fomufod A., S. Sinkford, and V. Louy. 1975. Mother-child separation at birth. A contributing factor in child abuse. *Lancet* 2:549–50.

Fortier, J. 1988. The relationship of vaginal and cesarian births to father-infant attachment. *JOGN Nursing* 17(2) (March–April): 128–34.

Fraiberg, S. 1977. *Every Child's Birthright: In Defense of Mothering.* N.Y.: Basic Books.

———. 1971. How a baby learns to love. *Redbook* (May), p. 76.

Freud, A., and D. Burlingham. 1973. *The Writings of Anna Freud.* Vol. 3. Infants without Families: The Case for and against Residential Nurseries. N.Y.: International Universities Press.

———. 1943. *War and Children.* N.Y.: Medical War Books.

Freud, S. [1925] 1962. *Three Contributions to the Theory of Sex,* trans. A. A. Brill. N.Y.: Dutton.

Friedan, B. [1963] 1983. *The Feminine Mystique.* N.Y.: Dell.

Gaines, R., A. Sandgrund, A. Green, and E. Power. 1978. Etiological factors in child maltreatment: A multivariate study of abusing, neglecting, and normal mothers. *J. Abnormal Psych.* 87:531–40.

Gathorne-Hardy, J. 1972. *The Rise and Fall of the British Nanny.* London: Hodder and Stoughton.

Giles, C. 1973. It takes two to have a baby—And those two should share the whole experience . . . *Parents* (March), p. 42.

Goldberg S. 1983. Parent-to-infant bonding: Another look. *Child Dev.* 54:1355–82.

A good start for premature babies . . . 1970. *Parents* (June), p. 44.

Gordon, I. 1978. As they grow—Birth through one year . . . *Parents* (Nov.), p. 89.

Gould, S. 1978. Morton's ranking of races by criminal capacity. *Science* 200 (May 5): 503–9.

———. 1981. *The Mismeasure of Man,* N.Y.: Norton.

Greer, G. 1971. *The Female Eunuch.* N.Y.: McGraw-Hill.

Grosskurth, P. 1986. *Melanie Klein: Her World and Her Work.* N.Y.: Knopf.

Grossman, K., K. Thane, and K. E. Grossman. 1981. Maternal tactual contact of the newborn after various postpartum conditions of mother-infant contact. *Dev. Psych.* 17:159–69.

Hales, D., B. Lozoff, R. Sosa, and J. Kennell. 1977. Defining the limits of the maternal sensitive period. *Dev. Med. Child Neurology* 4 (Aug.): 454–61.

Hall, C., and G. Lindzey. 1985. *Introduction to Theories of Personality.* N.Y.: Wiley.

Halpern, S. 1988. *American Pediatrics: The Social Dynamics of Professionalism: 1880–1980.* Berkeley: University of California Press.

Harlow, H. 1958. The nature of love. *American Psychologist* 15:673–85.

Hearnshaw, L. 1979. *Cyril Burt Psychologist.* London: Hodder and Stoughton.

Heiman, M. 1965. A Psychoanalytic View of Pregnancy. In *Medical, Surgical, and Gynecological Complications of Pregnancy,* ed. J. Rovinsky and A. Guttmacher. White Williams and Wilkins.

Helfer, R., and C. Kempe. 1976. *Child Abuse and Neglect.* Cambridge, Mass.: Ballinger.

Herbert. M. 1983. *Maternal Bonding.* Oxford: Basil Blackwell.

Herbert, M., W. Sluckin, and A. Sluckin. 1982. Mother-to-infant bonding. *J. Child Psych. Psychiatry* 23(3): 205–22.

Hesse, M. 1963. *Models and Analogies in Science.* N.Y.: Sheed and Ward.

Hilgard, E. 1987. *Psychology in America: A Historical Survey.* N.Y.: Harcourt Brace Jovanovich.

Hinds, L. 1989. Editorial. *New York Times,* 20 Feb., A 18.

Ho, E. 1984. Mother and child bonding. *Nursing Mirror* 158(2) (11 Jan.): i–iv.

Hofstadter, R. 1959. *Social Darwinism in American Thought.* Boston: Beacon.

Holt, E. 1896. *The Care and Feeding of Infants.* N.Y.: Holt.

Honey, M. 1984. *Creating Rosie the Riveter: Class, Gender, and Propaganda during World War II.* Amherst: University of Massachusetts Press.

Horn, M. 1989. *Before It's Too Late: The Child Guidance Movement in the United States 1922–1945.* Philadelphia: Temple University Press.

Hunter, R., N. Kilstrom, E. Kraybill, and F. Loda. 1978. Antecedents of child abuse and neglect in premature infants: A prospective study in a newborn intensive care unit. *Paediatrics* 61:629–35.

A husband and wife share the deeply satisfying experience of natural childbirth. *Parents* (March 1971): 56.

Hwang, C. 1981. Aspects of the mother-infant relationship during nursing, one and six weeks after early extended postpartum contact. *Early Human Dev.* 5(1): 1–9.

Janeway, E. 1971. *Man's World, Woman's Place: A Study in Social Mythology.* N.Y.: Dell.

Jenkins, R., and N. Westhus. 1981. The nurse role in parent-infant bonding. *JOGN Nursing,* March/April.

Jensen, A. 1969. How much can we boost IQ and scholarship achievement? *Harvard Educational Review* 39:1–123.

Jolly, H. 1978. The Importance of "bonding" for newborn baby, mother and father. *Nursing Mirror* 147(9) (31 Aug.): 19–21.

Kagan, J. 1965. The new marriage: Pediatrics and psychology. *Amer. J. Dis. Child.* 110:272–78.

Kagan, J., R. Kearsley, and P. Zelazo. 1978. *Infancy: Its Place in Human Development.* Cambridge: Harvard University Press.

Kamin, L. J. 1974. *The Science and Politics of I.Q.* Potomac, Md.: Erlbaum.

Kanner, L. 1972. *Child Psychiatry.* 4th ed. Charles Thomas.

Karen, R. 1990. Becoming attached. *Atlantic Monthly* (Feb.): 46–47.

Karmel, M. 1959. *Thank You Dr. Lamaze: A Mother's Experiences in Painless Childbirth.* Philadelphia: Lippincott.

Kawin, E. 1967. *Parenthood in a Free Nation.* Vol. 1. Basic Concepts for Parents. N.Y.: Macmillan.

Kempe, C. H., and R. Kempe. 1978. *Child Abuse.* Cambridge: Harvard University Press.

Kennell, J. 1980. Are we in the midst of a revolution? *Amer. J. Dis. Child.* 134:303–10.

Kennell, J., and M. Bergen. 1966. Early childhood separations. *Pediatrics* 37(2) (Feb.): 291–98.

Kennell, J., P. Jerauld, H. Wolfe, D. Chesler, N. Kreger, W. McAlpine, M. Steffa, and M. Klaus. 1974. Maternal behavior one year after early and extended postpartum contact. *Pediatrics* 26:832–38.

Kennell, J., and M. Klaus. 1984. Mother-infant bonding: Weighing the evidence. *Dev. Rev.* 4 (Sept.): 75–82.

Kennell, J., and A. Rolnick. 1960. Discussing problems in newborn babies with their parents. *Dev. Med. Child Neurology* 2 (April 16): 172–79.

Kennell, J., M. Trause, and M. Klaus. 1975. Evidence for a sensitive period in the human mother. *Ciba Foundation Symposium* 33:87–101.

Key, E. 1909. *The Century of the Child.* New York: G. P. Putnam.

Kitzinger, S. 1987. *Your Baby, Your Way: Making Pregnancy Decisions and Birth Plans.* N.Y.: Pantheon.

Klaus, M., J. Clements, and R. Havel. 1961. Composition of surface-active material isolated from beef-lung. *Proceedings of the National Academy of Sciences* 47:1858.

Klaus, M., P. Jerauld, N. Kreger, W. McAlpine, M. Steffa, and J. Kennell. 1972. Maternal attachment: Importance of the first postpartum days. *N.E. J. Med.* 286(9) (March): 460–63.

Klaus, M., and J. Kennell. 1976. *Maternal-Infant Bonding: The Impact of Early Separation or Loss on Family Development.* St. Louis: Mosby.

———. 1982. *Parent-Infant Bonding.* St. Louis: Mosby.

———. 1983. Parent-to-infant bonding: Setting the record straight. *J. Pediatrics* 102(4) (April): 575–76.

Klaus, M., J. Kennell, N. Plumb, and S. Zuehlke. 1970. Human maternal behavior at the first contact with her young. *Pediatrics* 46(2) (Aug.): 187–92.

Klaus, M., J. Kennell, and M. Trause. 1975. Does human maternal behavior after delivery show a characteristic pattern? *Ciba Foundation Symposium* 33:69–85.

Klein, M., and L. Stern. 1971. Low birth weight and the battered child syndrome. *Amer. J. Dis. Child.* 122:15.

Klopfer, P. 1971. Mother love: What turns it on? Studies of maternal arousal and attachment in ungulates may have implications for man. *American Scientist* 59 (July–Aug.): 404–7.

Klopfer, P., D. Adams, and M. Klopfer. 1964. Maternal "imprinting" in goats. *Proceedings of the National Academy of Sciences* 52:911.

Kontos, D. 1978. A study of the effects of extended maternal-infant contact on maternal behavior at one and three months. *Birth Family J.* 5(3) (Fall): 133–40.

Korsch, B. 1983. More on parent-infant bonding. Editorial. *J. Pediatrics* 102 (Feb.): 249–50.

Kosmak, G. 1944. Women in this changing world. Presidential address. *Amer. J. Obstet. Gynec.* 48:749–59.

Kuhn, T. 1962. *The Structure of Scientific Revolutions*. Chicago: University of Chicago Press.

Lamb, M. E. 1982a. The Bonding phenomenon: Misinterpretations and their implications. *J. Pediatrics* 101(4) (Feb.): 555–57.

———. 1982b. Second thoughts on first touch. *Psychology Today* (April): 9–11.

———. 1982c. Early contact and maternal-infant bonding: One decade later. *Pediatrics* 70(5) (Nov.): 763–68.

———. 1983. Early mother-neonate contact and the mother-child relationship. *J. Child Psych. Psychiatry Allied Disciplines* 24(3) (July): 487–94.

Lamb, M., and C. Hwang. 1982. Maternal attachment and mother-neonate bonding: A critical review. In *Advances in Developmental Psychology*. Vol. 2, ed. M. E. Lamb and A. L. Brown. Hillsdale, N.J.: Erlbaum.

Lamb, M. E., J. Campos, C. Hwang, P. Leiderman, A. Sagi, and M. Svejda. 1983. Joint reply to "Maternal-infant bonding: A joint rebuttal." *Pediatrics* 72(4) (Oct.): 574–76.

Landers, Ann. 1987. Los Angeles Times Syndicate.

Lang, D. 1972. The midwife returns modern style . . . *Parents* (Oct.): 28.

Lang, R. 1972. *Birth Book.* Ben Lomond, Calif.: Genesis.

Lasch, C. 1977. *Haven in a Heartless World: The Family Besieged.* N.Y.: Basic Books.

Lea, S. 1984. *Instinct, Environment and Behavior.* London: Methuen.

Leatherdale, W. 1974. *The Role of Analogy, Model, and Metaphor in Science.* Oxford: North-Holland.

Leavitt, J. W. 1985. Science enters the birthing room: Obstetrics in America since the eighteenth century. In *Sickness and Health in America,* by J. Leavitt and R. Numbers. Madison: University of Wisconsin Press.

Leiderman, P., and M. Seashore. 1975. Mother-infant neonatal separation: Some delayed consequences. *Ciba Foundation Symposium* 33:213–39.

Leiderman, P. 1981. Human mother-infant social bonding: Is there a sensitive phase? In *Behavioral Development,* ed. K. Immelmann, G. W. Barlow, L. Petrinovich, and M. Main. Cambridge: Cambridge University Press.

Leifer, A., P. Leiderman, C. Barnett, and J. Williams. 1972. Effects of mother-infant separation on maternal attachment behavior. In *Child Development and Behavior,* ed. F. Rebelsky and L. Dorman. 2d ed. N.Y.: Knopf.

Levy, D. 1931. Maternal overprotection and rejection. *Archives of Neurology and Psychiatry* 25:886–89.

———. 1944. *Maternal Overprotection.* N.Y.: Norton.

Loehlin, J., G. Lindzey, and J. Spuhler. 1975. *Race Differences in Intelligence.* San Francisco: Freeman.

Lorenz, K. 1950. The comparative method in studying innate behavior patterns. In *Physiological Mechanisms of Animal Behavior, Symposia of the Society of Experimental Biology in Great Britain.* No. 4. Cambridge: Cambridge University Press.

———. 1952. *King Solomon's Ring.* London: Methuen.

Lublin, J. 1979. The birthing room: More hospitals offer maternity facilities that feel like home. *Wall Street Journal* (15 Feb.), p. 1.

Lundberg, F., and M. Farnham. 1947. *Modern Women: The Lost Sex.* N.Y.: Harper.

Lynch, M., J. Roberts, and M. Gordon. 1976. Child abuse: Early warning in the maternity hospital. *Dev. Med. Child Neurology* 18(6): 759–66.

Lynch M., and J. Roberts. 1977. Predicting child abuse: Signs of bonding failure in the maternity hospital. *Brit. Medical J.* 1:624–36.

Lynch, M., and J. Golding. 1980. Postneonatal mortality in children from abusing families. *Brit. Medical J.* 281(6233) (12 July): 102–4.

McCall, R. 1980. As they grow, birth through one year: Parent-infant bonding. *Parents* (Sept.): 92.

MacCormac, E. 1976. *Metaphor and Myth in Science and Religion.* Durham, N.C.: Duke University Press.

MacDonald, P., A. Grant, M. Sheridan-Pereira, P. Boylan, and I. Chalmers. 1985. The Dublin randomized controlled clinical trial of intrapartum fetal heart-rate monitoring. *Amer. J. Obstet. Gynec.* 152:524–39.

MacFarlane, J. 1978. What a baby knows. *Human Nature,* 74–81.

Matthaei, J. 1982. *An Economic History of Women in America.* N.Y.: Schocken.

Mead, M. 1949. *Male and Female.* N.Y.: Morrow.

———. 1970. Instinct and the origins of love. *Redbook* (Dec.), p. 39.

Mead, M., and M. Wolfenstein. 1955. *Childhood in Contemporary Cultures.* Chicago: University of Chicago Press.

Miller, J. 1976. *Toward a New Psychology of Women.* Boston: Beacon.

Millet, K. 1970. *Sexual Politics.* London: Penguin.

Mills, M., and E. Melhuish. 1974. Recognition of mother's voice in early infancy. *Nature* 252(8) (Nov.): 123.

Minde, K. 1986. Bonding and attachment: Its relevance for the present-day clinician. *Dev. Med. Child Neurology* 28(6) (Dec.): 803–6.

Minde, K., S. Trehub, C. Corter, C. Boukydis, L. Celhoffer, and P. Marton. 1978. Mother-child relationships in the premature nursery: An observational study. *Pediatrics* 61(3) (March): 373–77.

Mitchell, K., and N. Mills. 1983. Is the sensitive period in parent-infant bonding overrated? *Pediatric Nursing* (March/April): 94–99.

Montgomery, S. 1982. Problems in the perinatal prediction of child abuse. *British J. Social Work* 12:189–96.

Moore, M. 1971. *The Newborn and the Nurse.* Philadelphia: Saunders.

More on infant-maternal bonding (letter). *J. Pediatrics* 103(5) (Nov.): 829–30.

Morgan, L. 1981. Methodological review of research on mother-infant bonding. In *Advances in Behavioral Pediatrics*, vol. 2, ed. B. W. Camp. Greenwich, Conn.: JAI.

Moyers, B. 1988. *The World of Ideas: Dr. Berry Brazelton on Bonding.* Produced for National Public Broadcasting.

Myers, B. 1984a. Mother-infant bonding: The status of the critical period hypothesis. *Dev. Rev.* 4 (Sept.): 240–74.

———. 1984b. Mother-infant bonding: Rejoinder to Kennell and Klaus. *Dev. Rev.* 4(3) (Sept.): 283–88.

"The new science of birth." 1976. Editorial. *Newsweek,* 15 Nov.

Newcombe, N., and J. Lerner. 1981. Britain between the wars: The historical context of Bowlby's theory of attachment. *Psychiatry* 44(1) (Feb.): 1–12.

Norton, B. 1978. A "fashionable fallacy" defended. *New Scientist* 78 (27 April): 223–25.

O'Connor, S., K. Sherrod, and H. Sandler. 1978. The effects of extended postpartum contact on problems with parenting: A controlled study of 301 families. *Birth and the Family J.* 5(4) (Winter): 5–231.

———. 1980. Reduced incidence of parenting inadequacy following rooming-in. *Pediatrics* 66:176–82.

Oakley, A. 1985. *The Captured Womb: A History of the Medical Care of Pregnant Women.* Oxford: Basil Blackwell.

Parker, S., S. Greer, and B. Zuckerman. 1988. Double jeopardy: The impact of poverty on early development. *The Pediatric Clinics of North America* 35(6) (Dec.): 1227.

Patton, R., and L. Gardner. 1962. Influence of family environment on growth: The syndrome of maternal deprivation. *Pediatrics* 30:957.

Pearse, W. 1987. Parturition: Places and Priorities. *Amer. J. Public Health* 177(8): 635–37.

Peckham, G., and E. Peckham. 1905. *Wasps, Social and Solitary.* Boston: Houghton Mifflin.

Peters, P. 1985. *Anna Freud: A Life Dedicated to Children.* N.Y.: Schocken.

Peterson, L., and C. Harbeck. 1988. *The Pediatric Psychologist: Issues in Professional Development and Practice.* Health Psychology Series, ed. G. Leon. Champaign, Ill.: Research Press.

Pillitteri, A. 1976. *Nursing Care of the Growing Family.* Boston: Little, Brown.

Pinneau, S. 1955a. The infantile disorders of hospitalism and anaclitic depression. *Psychol. Bull.* 52(5): 429–52.

———. 1955b. Reply to Dr. Spitz. *Psychol. Bull.* 52(5): 459–562.

Pollitt, E., A. Eichler, and C. Chan. 1975. Psychosocial development and behavior of mothers of failure-to-thrive children. *Amer. J. Orthopsychiatry* 45:526–36.

Potter, W. 1891. *How Should Girls be Educated? A Public Health Problem for Mothers, Educators and Physicians.* Philadelphia.

Rajecki, D., and M. Lamb. 1978. Toward a general theory of infantile attachment: A comparative review of aspects of the social bond. *Behavioral and Brain Sciences* 3:417–64.

Reed, G., and P. Leiderman. 1983. Is imprinting an appropriate model for human infant attachment? *Int. J. Behavioral Dev.* 6(1) (March): 51–69.

Reid, D., and M. Cohen. 1950. Evaluation of present-day trends in obstetrics. *JAMA* 142:615–22.

Research Issues in the Assessment of Birth Settings. 1982. Institute of Medicine, Division of Health Sciences Policy and National Research Council, Commission on Life Sciences. Washington, D.C.: National Academy Press.

Rheingold, J. 1964. *The Fear of Being a Woman: A Theory of Maternal Destructiveness.* N.Y.: Grune and Stratton.

Rhodes, P. 1982. Human relations in obstetrics. Quoted in *AIMS Quar. J.* (U.K.) (Spring), p. 1.

Rhone, M. 1980. Six steps to better bonding. *Canadian Nurse* 76 (Oct.): 38–41.

Ribble, M. 1943. *The Rights of Infants.* N.Y.: Columbia University Press.

Rich, A. 1976. *Of Woman Born: Motherhood as Experience and Institution.* N.Y.: Norton.

Richmond, J. B. 1959. The role of the pediatrician in early mother-child relationships. *Proceedings of the Children's Hospital* [Washington, D.C.] 5(5): (May): 101–17.

Riesman, D. 1950. *The Lonely Crowd.* New Haven: Yale University Press.

Riley, D. 1983. *War In the Nursery.* London: Virago.

Ringler, N., J. Kennell, R. Jarvella, B. Navajosky, and M. Klaus. 1975. Mother-to-child speech at two years: Effects of early postnatal contact. *J. Pediatrics* 86(1) (Jan.): 141–44.

Ringler, N., M. Trause, and M. Klaus. 1976. Mother's speech to her two-year old: Its effect on speech and language comprehension at five years. *Pediatric Res.* 10:307.

Ringler, N., M. Trause, M. Klaus, and J. Kennell. 1978. The effects of extra postpartum contact and maternal speech patterns on children's IQ's, speech, and language comprehension at five. *Child Dev.* 49:862–65.

Ripin, R. 1933. A comparative study of the development of infants in an institution with those in homes of low socio-economic status. *Psych. Bull.* 30(9) (Nov.): 680.

Ritvo, L. 1990. *Darwin's Influence on Freud.* New Haven: Yale University Press.

Rose, N. 1985. *The Psychological Complex: Psychology, Politics, and Society in England, 1869–1939.* N.Y.: Routledge and Kegan Paul.

Rosenberg, C. E. 1987. *The Care of Strangers: The Rise of America's Hospital System.* New York: Basic Books.

Rosenberg, C. E., and C. S. Rosenberg. 1984. The female animal: Medical and biological views of woman and her role in nineteenth-century America. In *Women and Health in America,* ed. J. W. Leavitt, pp. 12–27. Madison: University of Wisconsin.

Ross, G. 1980. Parental responses to infants in intensive care: The separation issue reevaluated. *Clinical Perinatology* 7(1) (March): 47–60.

Rossi, A. 1977. A biosocial perspective on parenting. *Daedalus* 106(2) (Spring): 1–31.

Rothman, B. K. 1982. *In Labor: Women and Power in the Birthplace.* N.Y.: Norton.

———. 1989. *Recreating Motherhood: Ideology and Technology in a Patriarchal Society.* N.Y.: Norton.

Rothman, S. 1978. *Woman's Proper Place.* N.Y.: Basic Books.

Rubin, R. 1963. Maternal touch. *Nursing Outlook* 11 (Nov.): 828–31.

Rutter, M. [1972, U.K.] 1974. *The Qualities of Mothering: Maternal Deprivation Reassessed.* N.Y.: Jason Aronson.

———. 1979. "Maternal deprivation," 1972–1978: New findings, new concepts, new approaches. *Child Dev.* 50:283–305.

———. 1981. *Maternal Deprivation Reassessed.* Middlesex, England: Penguin.

Sawyer, B., and T. River. 1946. Experience with the labor procedure of Grantly Dick Read. *Amer. J. Obstet. Gynec.* 51:852–58.

Schaffer, H., and P. Emerson. 1964. The development of social attachments in infancy. *Monographs of the Society for Research in Child Development* 29(3): 1–77.

Schultz, G. 1958. Cruelty in the maternity wards. *Ladies' Home Journal.* May, pp. 51–55.

Sears, R. 1975. Your ancients revisited: A history of child development. In *Review of Child Development Research.* Vol. 5. Chicago: University of Chicago Press.

Seigel, E. 1982. Early and extended maternal-infant contact: A critical review. *Amer. J. Dis. Child.* 136(3) (March): 251–57.

Seigel, E., K. Bauman, E. Schaefer, M. Saunders, and D. Ingram. 1980. Hospital and home support during infancy: Impact on child abuse and neglect, and health care utilization. *Pediatrics* 66(2) (Aug.): 183–90.

Senn, M. 1977. Interview with John Bowlby in London, 19 Oct. National Library of Medicine.

Sluckin, W., M. Herbert, and A. Sluckin. 1983. *Maternal Bonding.* Oxford: Basil Blackwell.

Sluckin, W., A. Sluckin, and M. Herbert. 1984. On mother to infant bonding. *Midwife Health Visitor Community Nurse* 20(11) (Nov.): 404–07.

Smith, S. 1975. *The Battered Child Syndrome.* London: Butterworth.

Speert, H. 1980. *Obstetrics and Gynecology in America.* American College of Obstetricians and Gynecologists. Baltimore, Md.: Waverly.

Spilker, B. 1986. *Guide to Clinical Interpretation of Data.* N.Y.: Raven.

Spitz, R. 1945. Hospitalism: An inquiry into the genesis of psychiatric conditions in early childhood. *Psychoanalytic Study of the Child* 1:53–75.

———. 1955. Reply to Dr. Pinneau. *Psych. Bull.* 52(5): 452–59.

———. 1965. *The First Year of Life: A Psychoanalytic Study of Normal and Deviant Development of Object Relations.* N.Y.: International Universities Press.

Spitz, R., and K. Wolf. 1946. Anaclytic depression. *Psychoanalytic Study of the Child* 2:313–42.

Spock, B. 1964, 1976, 1985. *Baby and Child Care.* N.Y.: Pocket Books.

Stainton, M. 1986. Parent-infant bonding: A process, not an event. *Dimensions in Health Services* 63(3) (April): 19–20.

Stendler, C. 1950. Psychological aspects of pediatrics: Sixty years of child training practices, revolution in the nursery. *J. Pediatrics* 36:122–34.

Stern, D. 1977. *The First Relationship.* Cambridge: Harvard University Press.

Stone, L. 1977. *The Family, Sex, and Marriage, 1500–1800.* N.Y.: Harper and Row.

Sullivan, D., and R. Weitz. 1988. *Labor Pains: Modern Midwives and Home Births.* New Haven: Yale University Press.

Sumner, P., and C. Phillips. 1981. *Birthing Rooms: Concept and Reality.* St. Louis: Mosby.

Sumney, P., and M. Hurst. 1986a. Ob/Gyn on the rise: The evolution of professional ideology in the twentieth century—part 1. *Women and Health* 11(1) (Spring): 133–45.

———. 1986b. Ob/Gyn on the rise: The revolution of professional ideology in the twentieth century. Part 2. *Women and Health* 11(2) (Summer): 103–22.

Susser, M. 1988. Falsification, verification, and causal inference. In *Causal Inference,* ed. K. Rothman, pp. 33, 34. Chestnut Hill, Mass.: Epidemiology Resources.

Suttie, I. 1935. *The Origins of Love and Hate.* London: Kegan Paul, Trench, Trubner.

Svejda, M., J. Campos, and R. Emde. 1980. Mother-infant "bonding": Failure to generalize. *Child Dev.* 51:775–79.

Svejda, M., B. Pannabecker, and R. Emde. 1982. Parent-to-infant attachment: A critique of the early "bonding" model. In *The Development of Attachment and Affiliative Systems,* ed. R. Emde and R. Harmon. N.Y.: Plenum.

Swanson, J. 1978. Nursing intervention to facilitate maternal-Infant attachment. *JOGN Nursing* (March/April): 35–38.

Tavris, C. 1992. *The Mismeasure of Woman.* New York: Simon and Schuster.

Taylor, H. 1958. Competition and cooperation. Presidential address. *Amer. J. Obstet. Gynec.* 76:931–38.

Taylor, L. 1981. Newborn feeding behaviors and attaching. *Amer. J. Maternal Child Nursing* 6(3) (May/June): 201–2.

Taylor, P., F. Taylor, S. Campbell, J. Maloni, and D. Dicky. 1979. Effects of extra-contact on early maternal attitudes, perceptions, and behaviors. In *Early Contact and Rooming-in: Effects on Bonding and Attachment,* by P. Taylor. Paper presented at the March meeting for the Society for Research in Child Development, San Francisco.

ten Bensel, R., and C. Paxson. 1977. Clinical notes: Child abuse following postpartum separation. *J. Pediatrics* 90. p. 490.

Terkel, J., and J. Rosenblatt. 1972. Humoral factors underlying maternal behavior at parturition: Cross transfusion between freely moving rats. *J. Comp. Physiol. Psych.* 80:365–71.

Thompson, R., M. Lamb, and D. Estes. 1893. Harmonizing discordant notes: A reply to Waters. *Child Dev.* 54(2) (April): 521–24.

Thomson, J., and J. Kramer. 1984. Methodologic standards for controlled clinical trials of early contact and maternal-infant behavior. *Pediatrics* 73(3) (March): 294–300.

Tulman, L. 1981. Theories of maternal attachment. *Advances in Nursing Science* 3(4) (July): 7–14.

———. 1985. Mothers' and unrelated persons' initial handling of newborn infants. *Nursing Research* 34(4) (July/Aug.): 205–10.

Valman, H. 1980. The first year of life: Mother-infant bonding. *British Medical J.* 280 (6210) (Feb.): 308–10.

van den Berg, J. 1972. *Dubious Maternal Affection.* Pittsburgh: Duquesne University Press.

Vander Zanden, J. 1978. *Human Development.* N.Y.: Knopf.

Vietze, P. 1980. Newborn behavioral and interactional characteristics of nonorganic failure-to-thrive infants. In *High-Risk Infants and Children: Adult and Peer Interactions,* ed. J. M. Field. London: Academic.

Vines, D. 1979. Bonding, grief, and working through in relationship to the congenitally anomalous child and his family. *ANA* 1979 (NP-59): 185–92.

Wade, N. 1976. I.Q. and heredity: Suspicion of fraud beclouds classic experiment. *Science* 194 (20 Nov.): 916–19.

Waechter, E. 1977. Bonding problems of infants with congenital anomalies. *Nursing Forum* 16(3–4): 298–318.

Wallick, M. 1985. The effects of maternal infant bonding. *J. Louisiana State Med. Soc.* 137(1) (Jan.): 40–42, 45–47.

Warshaw, R. 1984. The American way of birth: High-tech hospitals, birthing centers, or no options at all. *Ms. Magazine* (Sept.): 45–50.

Waters, E. 1983. The stability of individual differences in infant attachment: Comments on the Thompson, Lamb, and Estes contribution. *Child Dev.* 54(2) (April): 516–20.

Welter, B. 1979. The cult of true womanhood: 1820–1860. In *American Vistas (1607–1877),* ed. L. Dinnerstein and K. Jackson. 3d ed. N.Y.: Oxford University Press.

Wertz, R., and D. Wertz. 1989. *Lying In: A History of Childbirth in America.* Expanded ed. New Haven: Yale University Press.

Whyte, W. 1956. *The Organization Man.* N.Y.: Simon and Schuster.

Williams, E. 1983. Development potential of the child in relation to parent-child bonding. *Curatonis* 6(4) (Dec.): 25–26, 29.

Williams, G., and J. Money, eds., 1980. *Traumatic Abuse and Neglect of Children at Home.* Baltimore, Md.: John Hopkins University Press.

Winnicott, D. 1957. *Mother and Child: A Primer of First Relationships.* N.Y.: Basic Books.

Wishy, B. 1972. *The Child and the Republic: The Dawn of Modern American Child Nurture.* Philadelphia: University of Pennsylvania Press.

Wolfenstein, M. 1953. Trends in infant care. *Amer. J. Orthopsychiatry* 23:120–30.

Wright, L. 1967. The pediatric psychologist: A role model. *American Psychologist* 22:323–25.

Yarrow, L. 1961. Maternal deprivation: Toward an empirical and conceptual re-evaluation. *Psychol. Bull.* 58:459–90.

Young, D. 1982. *Changing Childbirth: Family Birth in the Hospital.* Rochester, N.Y.: Childbirth Graphics.

Young-Bruehl, E. 1988. *Anna Freud: A Biography.* N.Y.: Summit.

Zeskind, P., and R. Iacino. 1984. Effects of maternal visitation to preterm infants in the neonatal intensive care unit. *Child Dev.* 55(5) (Oct.): 1887–93.

Zilboorg, G. 1957. The clinical issues of postpartum psychopathological reactions. *Amer. J. Obstet. Gynec.* 73:305–12.

Zinsser, C. 1986. Dr. Spock's Book.

Zuspan, F. 1978. Discussion of T. Dillon, B. Brennan, J. Dwyer, A. Risk, A. Sear, L. Dawson, R. Wiele. Midwifery 1977. *Amer. J. Obstet. Gynec.* 130:918–25.

Index

AIDS, 194

"A Two-Year-Old Goes to Hospital" (film), 57–58

Abbott, John S., 104

Abortion, 125

Abuse. *See* Child abuse

"Accoucheur," 132, 134

Adoption procedures, 52, 59

"Affectionless psychopathy," 49, 53

Ainsworth, Mary, 61, 62, 65–66, 68

American Academy of Pediatrics, 148, 153

American Board of Obstetrics and Gynecology, 136

American Board of Pediatrics, 154

American College of Obstetricians and Gynecologists, 185

American Journal of Maternal Child Nursing, 41

American Journal of Obstetrics and Gynecology, 136, 139, 185

American Medical Association, 185, 187

American Scientist (journal), 82

American Society for Psychoprophylaxis in Obstetrics, 175

American War Advertising Council, 117

Anaclitic depression, 51–53, 60

Analogy, 8–9, 92–94; positive and negative, 81, 82–83

Animal research, 2, 8, 25, 50; as model for bonding, 21–22, 29–30;

Harlow's monkeys, 58–59; in attachment theory, 62–63, 67, 68, 70; method in, 80–83; problems with, 93–94

Anisfeld, Elizabeth, 37

Annals, The (social science publication), 118

Annexton, M., 187

Anthropology, 93, 94

Antibiotics, 150

Antisocial disorders, 67

Arms, Suzanne, 147

"At-risk" concept, 144, 156–57

Attachment theory, 7, 9, 27, 30, 43, 46; Bowlby's research in, 61–63; Freudian response to, 63–65; methods for research in, 65–69; bonding research and, 69–70

Baby and Child Care (Spock), 150

Barash, David, 73–74

Barnett, Clifford, 81, 93

Barrie, Herbert, 42

Behavioral endocrinology, 25

Behavioral pediatrics, 151

Belsky, J., 193

Benedek, Therese, 115

Bing, Elisabeth, 175

Birth and the Family (journal), 187

Birth Book (Lang), 184–85

Birthtrap, The (Brackbill), 190

"'Blame the Mother' Ideology" (Chess and Thomas), 39

Bonaparte, Marie, 114

Bonding research: Kennell and Klaus begin, 1–4, 15–18; as scientific fiction, 5–6; reasons for acceptance of, 8–14; flaws in methodology in, 18–21; instinct problem in, 21–26; parent-infant management in, 26–28; expansion of, 28–35; criticism of, 35–41; nursing applications of, 41–44; use of in social work, 44–45

—response of scientific community to, 71; data manipulation and, 72–76; conflicting response, 76–79; medical paradigm, 79–85; case studies, 85–89; psychology paradigm, 89–90; role of analogies and, 92–94, 98; as didactic metaphor, 95–98; political timeliness of, 163–65; case study, 165–69; current awareness regarding, 193–96; need for new definitions regarding, 198–99

Boston Women's Health Collective, 178–81

Bowlby, John, 6–7, 30, 47, 53, 120, 121; view of motherhood, 57, 58; criticism of, 61, 63, 64. *See also* Attachment theory; Maternal deprivation

"Bowlbyism," 50

Brackbill, Yvonne, 190

Brazelton, T. Berry, 4, 5, 28, 155, 187; on the natural, 181, 182; on control issue, 183–84; on working mothers, 192–93

Breastfeeding, 21, 41, 172–73, 174–75

British Medical Journal, 147

Burlingham, Dorothy, 64, 65

Burt, Cyril, 54, 74

Cachexia, 52

Campos, Joseph, 34, 37, 76

Case Western Reserve University, 69, 150, 187

Century of the Child, The (Key), 107

Cesarean section, 12, 145, 191, 194, 195

Chamberlen, Peter, 131

Channing, Walter, 133

Chess, Stella, 39, 76

Child abuse, 3, 29, 158, 224n13; bonding as panacea for, 4, 5, 13, 14, 32, 34–35; mothers as abusers, 42, 43, 159–62; social work and, 44–45

Child as redeemer, 106–7

Childbirth: Freudian view of, 112–16

Childbirth practices, 11, 41, 76. *See also* Hospital practices; Natural childbirth movement; Obstetrics

Childbirth without Fear (Dick-Read), 169

Child Care and the Growth of Love (Bowlby), 50

Child Development (journal), 76, 77

Child guidance movement, 53–54, 56–58, 69

Children's Bureau. *See* U.S. Children's Bureau

Child Study (journal), 122

Clark, Ann, 41–42

Clarke, Edward, 109

Clergy: authority of, 103, 104–5; replaced by science, 197–98

Collier's magazine, 171

Commonwealth Fund, 54

Communism, 123

Consumerism, 123

Consumer rights activism, 164

Contraception, 125

Control, issue of, 182–84

Cooke, W.R., 139

Couney, Martin, 152

Counterculture, 11, 164, 196

Coventry, Charles, 134

Craniometry, 5, 74
Criminality, 186–87. *See also* Juvenile delinquency
Critical period concept, 16–18
Cult of true womanhood, 9, 100–106, 110. *See also* Motherhood
Curry, Mary Ann, 37

Danforth, T. N., 103
Darwin, Charles, 22
Darwinism, 73, 74, 107. *See also* Social Darwinism
Davis, Glenn, 106
Dawkins, Richard, 73
Day care, 7, 67, 69, 118
Death instinct, 24
De Chateau, Peter, 31–32, 76
Defense mechanisms, 64
DeLee, Joseph, 136
Depression, 6, 53. *See also* Anaclitic depression
Deprivation. *See* Maternal deprivation
Descent of Man, The (Darwin), 22
Deutsch, Helene, 114–15, 170
Developmental Medicine and Child Neurology (journal), 41
Developmental Review, 39, 40
Dick-Read, Grantly, 141, 169, 170–73, 174. *See also* Natural childbirth movement
Division of Maternal Child Health (federal), 151
Divorce, 125
Drive concept, 24, 56
Drive reduction theory, 59
Drugs in childbirth, 135, 137, 144–45, 164, 170, 182, 189–90
Dubowitz, H., 160
Dystocia, 195

Eckes, Sandra, 41
Eclampsia, 138, 226n1
Education: effects on women, 109–10, 127

Edwards, Jonathan, 104
Ego, 24, 55
Ego failure, 56
Ego psychology, 56
Emde, Robert, 34
Emerson, P., 62
"En face looking," 18, 44
Episiotomies, 135, 164, 190, 194
Equipment industries, 147
Eros, 24
Ether, 132
Ethology, 25
Eugenicists, 107

Failure-to-thrive syndrome, 28, 32, 33–34
Family, 10, 33, 69; professional views of, 56–58; postwar, 121–22
Family-centered care, 143, 144, 150, 183, 189, 194, 227n3; in natural childbirth, 174, 176
Family failure, 35
Farley, S. E., Mrs., 102
Farnham, Marynia, 124
Father, role of, 33, 35
Fear of Being a Woman, The (Rheingold), 127
Female Eunuch, The (Greer), 128
Feminine Mystique, The (Friedan), 9, 110–12, 116, 177
Femininity. *See* Motherhood, ideology of; Womanhood
Feminist movement, 9, 10, 11, 73, 125, 127, 128; response of to bonding, 164, 177–81, 196
Fetal monitoring, 12, 145, 147, 163, 164; problems with, 190–91, 195–96
Fetal rights, 196, 198–99
"Fixed action pattern," 25
Forceps, 130–31, 132–33, 136, 163, 191, 194
"Forty-Four Juvenile Thieves" (study), 53

Foster care, 32, 52, 53, 59
Freud, Anna, 56, 63, 64–65, 69, 150
Freud, Sigmund, 24, 56; view of
   women, 112–16. *See also*
   Attachment theory
Freudian psychology, 6, 9, 10, 47,
   54–56
Friedan, Betty, 110, 128, 177

Galton, Francis, 107
Gamper, Margaret, 171
Gender differences, 103
Gender identity, 101–2
Generation of Vipers (Wylie), 111
Gesell, Arnold, 90
Goats, bonding of, 2, 8, 21, 81–82.
   See also Animal research
Goldberg, Susan, 76
Gordon, Ira J., 188
Gould, S., 74
Grace-New Haven Hospital, 174
Greer, Germaine, 128
Grobstein, Rose, 81
Gynecology, 139

Haire, Doris, 190
Hales, Deborah, 37, 76
Hampstead Child Therapy Clinic,
   64–65
Harlow, Harry, 58–59, 66, 67, 186
Harper's Bazaar, 175
Harrington, the Reverend Mr., 103
Harvard Educational Review, 73
Healy, William, 54
"Hearth angel" concept, 9, 100–106
Helfer, Ray, 45, 159
Herbert, Martin, 38, 76, 77
Heredity, 73
Hess, Julius, 152
Hodge, Hugh, 134
Home-birth movement, 28, 184–85
Hormones in bonding, 2–3, 21, 25,
   30, 112

Horney, Karen, 112
Hospitalism, 49, 51, 52, 53
Hospital practices, 8, 9, 11–12;
   response of to bonding, 34–35, 50;
   in childbirth, 41, 133–34, 135,
   137–38, 147, 163; changing
   attitudes toward parents, 57–58;
   reform in birth practices, 59, 186–
   92; in nurseries, 152–56; response
   to natural childbirth, 174–76
Husband. *See* Family-centered care
Hwang, Carl-Phillip, 35, 37, 76, 78,
   79

IQ studies, 5, 73, 74
Id, 24, 55
Imprinting, 47–48, 62–63
Induced labor, 190, 194
Industrialization, 101
Infancy, concept of, 9–10, 96, 99,
   105, 106–7
Infant mortality, 145, 148
Infants and Mothers (Brazelton), 181
*Infants without Families: The Case for
   Residential Nurseries* (Freud and
   Burlingham), 65
Infections in hospitals, 26, 150, 152,
   153, 156
Instinct, 5–6, 55, 62. *See also*
   Bonding research
"Instinct and the Origins of Love"
   (journal article), 181–82
Institutionalized infants, 6, 7, 48,
   49–50, 51–53, 67
Insurance companies, 146, 195
Intensive care units, 154–55, 156
International Childbirth Education
   Association, 176, 182
Isolation, 59, 60

JOGN Nursing (journal), 41
James, William, 23, 223n10
Janeway, Elizabeth, 128

Jenkins, R., 43
Jensen, Arthur, 73
Jolly, Hugh, 42
Journal of Child Psychology and Psychiatry, 38
Journal of Obstetrics and Gynecology, 142
Journal of Pediatrics, 36, 79
Journal of the American Medical Association, 142, 187
Juvenile delinquency, 49, 53–54, 120

Kagan, Jerome, 68
Karmel, Marjorie, 175
Kempe, Henry, 45, 159
Kennell, John, 2, 3, 4, 5, 37, 77, 78; doctor-patient study, 85–86, 91–92; separation studies, 87–89
Kennell-Klaus research. *See* Bonding research
Key, Ellen, 107, 108
Kitzinger, Sheila, 193–94
Klaus, Marshall, 2, 3, 4, 5, 37, 77, 94, 156; early research of, 79–80
Klein, Melanie, 63, 65, 120
Klopfer, P., 8, 82
Koch, Robert, 71–72
Korsch, Barbara, 36, 76, 79
Kuhn, Thomas, 7, 71

Ladies' Home Journal, 127, 173, 174
"Ladies'" magazines, 102, 103
La Leche League, 174–75
Lamaze, Fernand, 175
Lamaze method, 142, 175, 176
Lamb, Michael, 35–37, 65, 68, 76, 77, 78, 79
Lang, Pat "Raven," 184–85
Lanham Act, of 1943, 118, 226n3
Lawsuits, 13, 195
Leiderman, P. Herbert, 37, 38, 68, 76, 77–78, 81, 93, 156
Leifer, A. D., 76

Levy, David, 57, 111–12
Libido, 24, 55
Life magazine, 127
Lipper, Evelyn, 37, 76
Lithotomy position, 136, 137–38
London Child Guidance Clinic, 53, 54
Look magazine, 127
Lorenz, Konrad, 24–25, 62
Lozoff, Betsy, 76
Lundberg, Ferdinand, 124
"Lying-in," 133
Lynch, Margaret, 224n13

McCall, Robert B., 188, 189
Malpractice suits, 145
Man's World, Woman's Place (Janeway), 128
Masochism of women, 113
"Maternal attachment: Importance of the first postpartum days" (Klaus et al.), 16
Maternal Care and Mental Health (Bowlby), 48
Maternal deprivation, 6–7, 9, 46, 61; Bowlby's research in, 48–50; Spitz's research in, 51–53; juvenile delinquency and, 53–54; Freudian response to, 54–56; guidance clinic policy and, 56–58; Harlow's monkeys and, 58–59; critiques of research, 59–61; bonding and, 69–70; as conservative fiction, 76. *See also* Attachment theory
Maternal Infant Bonding: The Impact of Early Separation or Loss on Family Development (Kennell and Klaus), 3, 28
Maternal Overprotection (Levy), 111–12
"Maternal sensitive" period, 30–31
Maternity Center Association of New York, 171

Mead, Margaret, 115–16, 176, 181
Medical schools, 131–32
Medicine, authority of, 8, 10–11, 12, 129–30, 164; specialization and, 141–42; natural childbirth and, 142–43; in premature births, 153–56; intensive care and, 156–58; child abuse and, 159–62; women's protest against, 173–76, 182–84; return of midwife and, 184–85; current status of, 193–96. *See also* Obstetrics
Mental hygiene movement, 53, 54, 225n5
"Midwife Returns Modern Style" (journal article), 184
Midwifery, 131, 132
Midwives, 130–31, 133, 141; movement against, 134, 135, 136; return of, 184–85, 227n4
Millett, Kate, 128
Minde, K., 41, 76
Misogyny, 110, 112, 124
Modern Woman: The Lost Sex (Farnham), 124, 125
Monkeys, 29, 58–59, 67. *See also* Animal research
Monotropy, 29
Montagu, Ashley, 176
Montgomery, Stuart, 45, 159–60
Morton, Samuel George, 74
Mother at Home, The (journal), 104–5
Motherhood, ideology of, 9, 99–100; defined by religion, 101–6; defined by science, 107–10; feminine mystique and, 110–12, 123–28; Freudian psychology and, 112–16; effects of World War II on, 116–22; woman as receptacle, 146; women as scapegoats, 198–99. *See also* Working mothers
"Motherhood without Misery" (Sawyer), 171

Mother-infant bonding. *See* Bonding research
Mother's Assistant (journal), 105
Mothers' Magazine, 105
Moyers, Bill, 4
Myers, Barbara, 39, 40–41, 76

Narcissism of women, 113
National Research Council on Birth Settings, 188
Natural childbirth movement, 11, 76, 141, 163, 164, 196; doctors' response to, 142–43; women's demand for, 169–73; ideology of the natural in, 181–82
"Nature of the Child's Tie to the Mother" (Bowlby), 63
Neonatal intensive care units, 26, 32
Neonatology, 27, 152–53
New England Journal of Medicine, 16, 180
New Our Bodies, Ourselves, The (Boston Women's Health Collective), 180
Nurseries. *See* Hospital practices
Nurses, 41–44, 163; response of to bonding, 168–69

Object relations, 56
Obstetrics, 13; pathology of childbirth and, 130–36; maternal mortality rate and, 136–38; high and low risk women, 143–44; role of technology in, 144–46
Obstetrics-gynecology, 141–42
O'Connor, Susan, 32, 37, 76
Office of War Information, 116, 117
Of Human Bondage (Barrie), 42
Origin of Species, The (Darwin), 22
Origins of Love and Hate, The (Suttie), 55–56
Our Bodies, Ourselves (Boston

Women's Health Collective), 179–81

Overprotection, 57, 60, 111–12, 193

Pain in childbirth, 170
Paradigm shifts, 7, 71, 72–76
Parent-Infant Bonding (Kennell and Klaus), 3, 35
Parent-infant management, 26–28
Parents (journal), 182, 184, 189, 191
Parents' Magazine, 105, 188–89
"Parent to Infant Attachment Conference," 187
Passivity of women, 113, 114–15
"Pathogen," 85, 88
Pathology of childbirth. *See* Obstetrics
Patriarchy, 177
Pediatric Clinics of North America (journal), 160
Pediatrics, 7–8, 69, 148–51
Pediatrics (journal), 37, 86, 87
Penis envy, 113, 114, 140
Perinatal concept, 146
Personality, 47, 55, 70
Pharmaceutical industry, 147
Piaget, Jean, 90
Pinneau, S., 60
Pitocin, 190
Pleasure principle, 24, 55
Postpartum depression, 140
Poverty factor, 19, 34
Premature and sick infants, 8, 15, 28; challenge of prematurity, 153–56. *See also* Technology
Premium pregnancy, 146–48, 196
Prenatal care, 136
Propaganda, 117, 118–19, 120
Psychoanalysis: theories of, 24
Psychological Bulletin, 60
Psychological pathology of women, 139–41
Psychology: in childbearing, 150–51.

See also Bonding research; Freudian psychology
Psychology Today (journal), 35
Psychosis, 56
Psychotherapeutic approach, 53, 54
Public health, 148–51
Puerperal fever, 133–34

Rainbow Babies' and Children's Hospital, 187
Rats, studies of, 2, 25, 80, 93. *See also* Animal research
Redbook magazine, 127, 181, 182, 183, 186
Reed, G., 68
Rejection, 57, 60, 112, 193
Reliability in research, 19–20
Religion: childbirth and, 171–73
Repression, 55
Retardation, developmental, 48, 52
Rheingold, Joseph, 127
Rhone, Margaret, 43
Ribble, Margaret, 111
Rich, Adrienne, 177
Risk, at risk mothers, 143–44
Robertson, James, 57, 58
Rolnick, A., 86
"Rooming in," 153, 174
Rosenblatt, J. S., 25, 28, 93
Ross, Gail, 76, 78
Rossi, Alice, 177–78
Rubin, Reva, 28, 41
Rutter, Michael, 66–67

Sagi, Abraham, 37
Sanford, Mrs., 102
Saturday Evening Post, 118, 119
Sawyer, Blackwell, 143, 171
Schaffer, H., 62
Schlossman, Arthur, 49
Schuman, Edward, 137–38
Scientific community, 71–72. *See also* Bonding research

Scientific motherhood, 108
Seigel, Earl, 33, 37, 76
Self-fulfillment issue, 182–84
Sensitive periods, 40–41, 67, 93
Separation, 3, 61, 85, 87–89. *See also* Maternal deprivation
Sex differences, 5
Sexual impulse, 54, 55
Sexual Politics (Millett), 128
Siblings, 35. *See also* Family-centered care
Sigourney, Mrs., 103
Simpson, James, 170
Single parents, 193
Sluckin, Alice, 38
Sluckin, Wladyslaw, 38, 76, 77
Smellie, William, 131
Social Darwinism, 5, 22, 23
Social health movements, 152
Social isolation, 34
Social support factor, 19
Social work, 44–45, 56; theory of, 50. *See also* Maternal deprivation
Society for Behavioral Pediatrics, 151
Society for Developmental Pediatrics, 151
Society for Research in Child Development, 149
Sociobiology, 5, 73–74
Son Unguided: His Mother's Shame (Davis), 106
Sosa, Robert, 37, 76
"Species specific" behaviors, 25, 29
"Specific action potential," 25–26
Speech, 25, 222n3
Spencer, Herbert, 22, 23
Spitz, René, 6, 7, 47, 60, 61, 63, 66. *See also* Maternal deprivation
Spock, Benjamin, 69, 86, 89, 126, 140, 150, 155; on need for hospital reform, 186, 192
Spoiling children, 100
Stafford, Henry B., 173

Stanford Premature Research Center Nursery, 156
Statistics, 20, 222n5
Stevenson, Adlai, 127
Stimulus deprivation, 67
"Strange situation," 65–66, 68
Strecker, Edward, 125–26
Stroufe, Alan, 66
Structure of Scientific Revolutions, The (Kuhn), 71
Sumner, William Graham, 22–23
Superego, 55
Survival instinct, 63
"Survival of the fittest," 22
Suttie, Ian, 55–56
Svejda, Marilyn, 34, 37, 76

Tavistock Clinic, 55, 56, 57, 225n8
Taylor, Howard, 141
Technology, 26, 144–46, 147, 163, 190; unnecessary use of, 194, 195–96
"Tell Me Doctor" (journal article), 173
Thanatos, 24
Thank You Dr. Lamaze (Karmel), 175
Thomas, Alexander, 39, 76
Thoms, Herbert, 174
Tinbergen, Nicholas, 25
"Twilight sleep," 137

U.S. Children's Bureau, 136, 148, 149–50
Ultrasound, 194
Unconscious, the, 55

Validity in research, 19
Victorian prudery, 134

Watson, J. B., 90
Well-baby clinics, 149
Welter, Barbara, 102
Wertz, Dorothy, 138

Wertz, Richard, 138
Wessel, Helen, 115
"What Childbirth Drugs Can Do to
    Your Child" (journal article), 182
"Which Birth Style Is Best for You?"
    (journal article), 191–92
Wilson, Edmund O., 73–74
Winnicott, D. W., 64, 120, 141
Wolf, K., 60
Wollstonecraft, Mary, 125
Womanhood, 9, 58; cult of true
    womanhood, 101–6, 110–12
Women and men: redefining
    responsibility of, 198–200
Women's Bureau, 116
Women's health movement, 179–81,
    227n3
Women's magazines, 102–3
Women's movement. *See* Feminist
    movement
Working and Caring (Brazelton), 192–
    93
Working mothers, 9, 10; effects of
    bonding theory on, 192–93. *See
    also* World War II
World Health Organization, 48, 50,
    195
"World of Ideas, The" (TV series), 4
World War II, 52–53, 57; effects of
    on women, 116–22
Wylie, Philip, 111

Yarrow, Leon, 61
Young Delinquents, The (Burt), 54
Young Ladies Class Book, 102